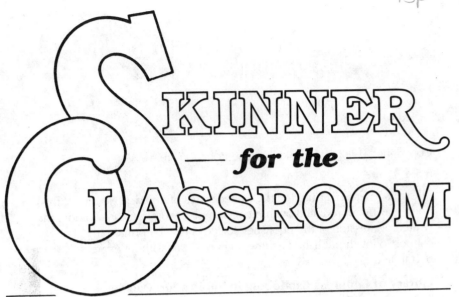

SELECTED PAPERS

*Edited
and with an introduction by*

ROBERT EPSTEIN

*with commentaries and
an updated autobiography by*

B. F. SKINNER

Research Press
2612 North Mattis Avenue
Champaign, Illinois 61820

Library of Congress Cataloging in Publication Data

Skinner, B.F. (Burrhus Frederick), 1904–
   Skinner for the classroom.

   Bibliography: p.
   Includes index.
   1. Behaviorism (Psychology)—Addresses,
essays, lectures. 2. Operant conditioning—
Addresses, essays, lectures. 3. Psychological
research—Addresses, essays, lectures.
I. Epstein, Robert.   II. Title.
BF199.S56   1982   150.19'434   82-80868
ISBN 0-87822-261-8 (pbk.)

Copies of this book may be ordered from the publisher at the address given on the title page.

Cover design by John Reinhardt

Composition by Publication Services

To Julie and Ernie,
classroom managers.
B.F.S.

To Ken Keller, for keeping me there.
R.E.

Contents

Introduction

Presumably your instructor has told you or will soon tell you some things about B.F. Skinner—what he advocates, what he believes, what kind of research he has done, and so on. For some reason, it occasionally happens that students who have just been introduced to Skinner come away with some mistaken notions, though they have been given accurate information. Here, then, are a few disclaimers.

Stimulus-Response. Skinner, first of all, is *not* a stimulus-response psychologist, no matter what you might have heard. The founder of behaviorism, John B. Watson, and some of the early reflexologists, such as Pavlov and Sechenov, did believe that all behavior was reflexive, but Skinner moved in a different direction. As a graduate student, he was taken with the fact that many responses didn't seem to have any eliciting stimuli. He gradually developed the concept of the "operant," a kind of behavior which, by definition, has no eliciting stimulus. It isn't "drawn out," like the knee jerk; it is just "emitted" by the organism. Its occurrence in the future is determined by the effect it produces. It is, like a member of a species in Darwin's scheme, selected by its consequences (Skinner, 1981). With the concept of the operant, Skinner moved psychology a giant step away from the old reflex (S-R) psychologies. He brought science into meaningful contact with what is commonly called "voluntary" behavior, thought by many to be beyond the scope of an objective analysis.

The terms "stimulus" and "response" are still used in the analysis of operant behavior, but by no means as Watson used them. Skinner recognized the stimulus, for example, as only one of a large number of variables that affect behavior, and his interest has been in all such variables. Deprivation, for example, is an important determinant of behavior that cannot easily be characterized as a stimulus.

He has been critical even of the very concepts "stimulus" and "response." There really aren't, he has noted, any *things* one can call a "stimulus" or a "response." Both are names for events. The names are applied as though such events are distinct and separate, but that usually isn't the case. In fact, both behavior and the environment are continuous over time and almost always changing. A stimulus or response, therefore, is at best a tiny sample—a slice—of something much more complicated. Since behavior and the environment constantly vary, the notion that stimuli and responses "recur" is also a simplification.

Skinner recognized the problem early in his career and in a paper called "The Generic Nature of the Concepts of Stimulus and Response" described what he believed to be the relevant properties of behavior and the environment that give rise to the terms "stimulus" and "response." He also proposed criteria for applying these terms so as to more closely approximate "the natural lines of fracture along which behavior and environment actually break." Traditionally, a response was defined in terms of its physical characteristics. Skinner abandoned this in favor of a "functional" definition: A response was defined by its function, by its effect on the world.

That Skinner is not an S-R psychologist is also clear from the way he views causal relations between environmental and behavioral events. Behavior, as I noted, is not just drawn out by antecedent events; one might say, rather, that it is *embedded* in the environment. If anything, one might call Skinner an "S-R-S" psychologist, since he is concerned with (1) the circumstances under which behavior occurs (the first "S"), (2) the behavior itself (the "R"), and (3) the consequences that the behavior produces (the second "S"). The subtle and complex relations that may exist among these three things is what is meant by Skinner's term "contingencies of reinforcement."

Black Box. Skinner does not see people as "black boxes"—organisms with empty or unimportant insides. Though he has been interested primarily in observable behavior, and though he avoids the "intervening variables" that beclouded the systems of Tolman and Hull, he does not *deny* that there are "thoughts," "feelings," and so on. He simply regards them as physical states of the body, as opposed to metaphysical or psychical entities. He also questions their causal status. Just because you felt afraid and thought to yourself, "I'm getting out of here!" at the approach of a tiger doesn't mean that either the thought or the feeling *caused* you to run away. Rather, says Skinner, the thought, the running, and the feeling that you would report as fear are *all* caused by the approach of the tiger. It's not that the inner events don't exist; it's just that they aren't necessarily the causes of your behavior, though it often seems that way. Activity inside your body is as strictly determined by your genes and the environment as is the behavior others can see.

Watson insisted that private events were out of bounds for psychology on the grounds that science can study only observables. Unlike Watson, Skinner sees private events as an important domain of study. He has written extensively about them since the 1940s (see Chapter 5 in this text, for example, and the accompanying Editor's Note).

Environmentalism. A third disclaimer: Skinner is not an "extreme environmentalist," as Watson certainly was. (It may have occurred to you by now that many misconceptions about Skinner are probably based on the persistent reverberations of Watson's work.) Behavior, for Skinner, is not merely the product of the environment, but also of an organism's "genetic endowment." Though he has not emphasized the study of innate behavior or of genetic constraints on learning in his research, he does not deny their existence, and in fact he has written several essays about the genetic bases of behavior. (See the Editor's Note at the beginning of Chapter 7 for an elaboration of this point.)

Theory. Fourth, an essay Skinner published in 1950 called "Are Theories of Learning Necessary?" (Chapter 1 in this text) led many to believe that he was opposed to theorizing, but his system of study is *not* without theory; nor did he ever suggest it should be. Skinner simply rejects a certain type of theory—in particular, the hypothetico-deductive theories of Hull and other learning theorists active in the 1940s and 50s. One of his recent books is entitled *Contingencies of Reinforcement: A **Theoretical** Analysis.*

Animals. Fifth, Skinner is not just an "animal psychologist." Though most of his research was done with rats and pigeons, this was mainly for the sake of expediency. His concern with humans has been apparent through most of his career, and even his animal research has been characterized by a concern with practical human problems which is unusual among basic researchers. He has long encouraged the application of a science of behavior to human affairs; his research with animals has led to the development of hundreds of techniques that are now used routinely in business and industry, therapy, education, and institutional management—even in energy conservation efforts sponsored by the federal government. He has also made a number of direct contributions: He developed the programmed textbook, now used widely in such diverse areas as music and chemistry. He devised a variety of machines to aid in instruction; some of the principles of programmed teaching which he devised in the 1950s are now applied in programs for "computer-aided instruction." And, of course, in his novel, *Walden Two,* he offered a blueprint for a utopian community. Twin Oaks in Virginia, Los Horcones in Mexico, and at least four other small communities have been inspired by this blueprint.

Reinforcement. Several disclaimers can be made about Skinner's concept of reinforcement. First of all, though it is an important determinant of behavior and the one to which Skinner devoted most of his research, Skinner readily acknowledges that it is not the *only* determinant of behavior. For reasons that have more to do with sociology than science, demonstrations of so-called "observational learning" and other phenomena have often been presented as refutations of Skinner's views. They most certainly are not. They are simply other mechanisms of behavior change.

Second—and this point is critical to understanding what Skinner is all about—reinforcement is *not* a circular concept. Here is a quick and simplified definition of *reinforcement,* as elaborated years ago by one of

Skinner's students: If we can show that a response increases in frequency because (and only because) it is followed by a particular stimulus, we call that stimulus a *reinforcer* and its presentation, *reinforcement*. Note the lack of circularity. *Reinforcement* is a term we invoke when we observe certain relations between events in the world. We speak of reinforcement when we observe that a stimulus has a strengthening effect on the behavior it follows.

Unfortunately, the term has often been used incorrectly, and this has taken a toll on the credibility of the concept. If we say, for example, that a particular stimulus strengthens a response *because* it is a reinforcer, we are using the term *reinforcer* in a circular fashion. It is *because* it strengthens behavior that we call the stimulus a *reinforcer*. The concept does not tell us *why* the stimulus has a strengthening effect; it only describes that fact. Skinner occasionally speculates about why certain stimuli work in this fashion (for example, in Chapter 7); the whole story must wait for advances in physiology and evolutionary biology.

In some of his writings, Skinner speculates that certain behavior (for example, verbal behavior) has come about through reinforcement. He may suggest, for example, that certain behavior is strong *because* it was reinforced. This use of the concept is not circular, only speculative or interpretive. Using the language of reinforcement in this way is reasonable when you have accumulated a large data base. Fifty years of laboratory research and field work has provided a good idea of (a) the types of stimuli that function as reinforcers, (b) the situations in which they function as reinforcers, (c) susceptible organisms, and (d) susceptible behaviors. When Skinner attributes some everyday behavior to past reinforcers, he is making a plausible guess based on a large data base and principles of behavior established under controlled conditions.

Third, Skinner does not believe that food and sex are the only reinforcers. Remember the definition I gave above: Any consequence of behavior that can be shown to strengthen that behavior is a reinforcer. It turns out that almost any stimulus—even one that you might think of as "unpleasant," such as electric shock—can function as a reinforcer under appropriate circumstances, and that reinforcers vary in effectiveness from species to species, individual to individual, and time to time. Food, for example, is not a very effective reinforcer for an organism that has eaten too much. In short, Skinner's concept of reinforcement does not correspond very well to the lay notion of "reward."

Punishment. Skinner does not advocate the use of punishment in the control of behavior. Quite the contrary; his own laboratory work convinced him early in his career that, in the long run, positive reinforcement is the most effective means of control. He has tried for decades to further the use of positive reinforcement in every domain of human activity. Because people equate "control" with aversive means of control and because they know, however vaguely, that Skinner recommends some sort of "control," they incorrectly assume that Skinner advocates punishment. *Totalitarianism.* He does not advocate this either. After the publication of his best seller *Beyond Freedom and Dignity* in 1971, Skinner was deluged with unkind criticism, largely based on misunderstanding. He was labeled, in distinguished journals and magazines, such things as: "the new Machiavelli," "a Nazi," "a high priest," "a parochialist," and so on. Somehow, at least for some readers, some of the basic points were lost.

Skinner does not advocate the control of human behavior. He believes, as did Freud and William James and as does any good determinist, that human behavior is *always* controlled. He advocates the application of the science of behavior to human affairs—if anything, humane *improvement* in existing forms of control: Where punishment or the threat of punishment has been used in education, powerful reinforcement techniques are now available. Incentive systems in industry are now more widely used, in part because of the work of some of Skinner's adherents. Back-ward patients in mental hospitals who were little more than tended for many decades can now be taught basic skills of grooming and communication. Autistic and retarded children can now be taught many things that allow them to lead more dignified lives.

Skinner has gone so far as to advocate the use of the science of behavior in the planning and running of communities. This has raised in countless classrooms the almost proverbial question: "But *who* is to control?" The assumption is often made that a clique of power-hungry behavioral psychologists—or perhaps Skinner himself—has designs on the job, and hence the "totalitarian" label. But the assumption is, once again, based on a misunderstanding. A cultural design that allows for the emergence of despotic rulers (whom, presumably, the people don't like) is a faulty design. A good design should, by definition, provide a community with leaders who are appropriate to and supported by the members of the community they serve. A science of behavior is only a means for facilitating the process. It is impossible to say who the correct leaders are and what the best design is, since these things will depend on the people involved and will change from time to time. A good design is, for Skinner, one that produces a culture that flourishes and survives. Survival is the ultimate judge. (I'd be amazed if behavioral psychologists emerged as the most effective leaders.)

ABOUT THE BOOK

As of December, 1981, Skinner has published 173 papers and books (see Figure 1). Fifteen of the papers are included in this collection. Why these?

The short autobiography that begins the book needs no justification, I suspect. Each of the other papers tends to be widely cited and is

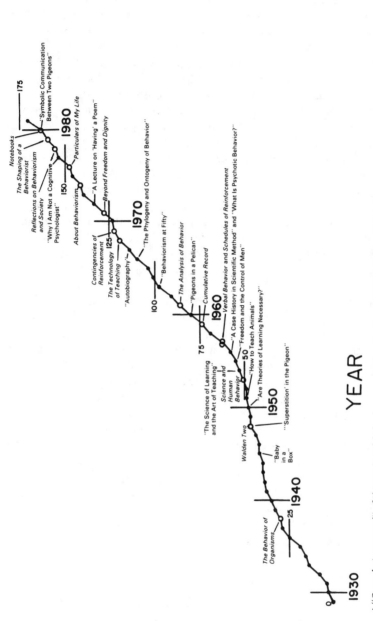

PUBLICATIONS

YEAR

Figure 1 A "Cumulative record" of Skinner's published papers and books, through 1981. Each solid circle represents 1 year. An open circle indicates the publication of a book. The titles of Skinner's books and the papers included in this text are shown. The record shows a high, steady, stable rate of publishing over most of Skinner's 50-year career in psychology, with some decrement in productivity during World War II and shortly thereafter.

6

representative of some important aspect of Skinner's work. The first section of the book includes four papers that should give you some idea of the range of Skinner's laboratory work. The second paper, "A Case History in Scientific Method," includes a fairly remarkable record of some of Skinner's early discoveries.

The second section includes five papers that will introduce you to Skinner's theories in several domains: behaviorism, freedom and control, phylogeny and ontogeny, cognition, and creativity, respectively. One theoretical area in which Skinner has made important contributions was omitted from this section (and hence, from the book as a whole)—verbal behavior. Material on Skinner's analysis of verbal behavior can be found in his book by that title, published in 1957, or in *Notebooks*, published in 1980.

The last section includes a sampling of applications of Skinner's science in child rearing, animal training, education, and so on.

Each chapter begins with an Editor's Note and concludes with a postscript Skinner has written especially for this volume. Each Note refers you to related works Skinner has written or to other relevant literature and summarizes the paper before which it appears. Skinner's postscript updates the piece for you; it gives you his current perspective on a piece he may have written decades ago. A complete listing of Skinner's published works and a detailed index appear at the end of the book.

If you go to the trouble of looking up the first published versions of the papers in this volume, you may be disturbed to find that the texts don't match exactly. Language which, according to current standards, would be judged to be sexist has been eliminated for the most part. And many errors in references, quotations, figures, and, in a few rare cases, in the text itself, have been corrected.

I am grateful to Jean Kirwan Fargo, Rose Guarino, Vivina Ree, Judy Rosenthal, and William Tisherman for help in the preparation of this text. And special thanks are due to Pat Sammann, the editor at Research Press who has nursed this book along for the good part of a year. In a remarkably careful reading of the manuscript, she identified many nontrivial errors in figures and in the text itself which had gone undiscovered, in most cases, for many years. She has greatly improved the quality of this work.

Robert Epstein
Cambridge, Massachusetts
January, 1982

B.F. SKINNER...
AN AUTOBIOGRAPHY

EDITOR'S NOTE

This brief autobiography was written for E.G. Boring and G. Lindzey's *A History of Psychology in Autobiography* (Vol. 5) (New York: Appleton-Century-Crofts, 1967, pp. 387-413) and has been republished in P.B. Dews's *Festschrift for B.F. Skinner* (New York: Appleton-Century-Crofts, 1970, pp. 1-21). Since about 1973, Skinner has been at work on a more comprehensive autobiography, two volumes of which are now in print— *Particulars of My Life* (1976), which covers the period before he entered graduate school, and *The Shaping of a Behaviorist* (1979), which covers Skinner's early professional life until he became a professor at Harvard in 1948. A third volume is scheduled for the near future. There are as yet no authoritative biographies of Skinner, though there are a few book-length works that may be of interest: *B.F. Skinner: The Man and His Ideas* by Richard I. Evans (New York: Dutton, 1968), an extensive interview with Skinner; *What Is B.F. Skinner Really Saying?* by Robert D. Nye (Englewood Cliffs, N.J.: Prentice-Hall, 1979), a readable exposition of Skinner's psychology; *The Skinner Primer: Behind Freedom and Dignity* by Finley Carpenter (New York: Free Press, 1974), an unsympathetic commentary on *Beyond Freedom and Dignity;* and *B.F. Skinner* by John A. Weigel (Boston: G.K. Hall, 1977), a brief biography.

EARLY ENVIRONMENT

My Grandmother Skinner was an uneducated farmer's daughter who put on airs. She was naturally attracted to a young Englishman who came to America

This chapter originally appeared in E.G. Boring and G. Lindzey (Eds.), *A History of Psychology in Autobiography* (Vol. 5). New York: Irvington Publishers Inc., 1967, pp. 387-413. Reprinted by permission of the publisher.

in the early 1870s looking for work, and she married him. (He had not found just the work he wanted when he died at the age of 90.) My grandmother's aspirations were passed on to her son, William, who "read law" while apprenticed as a draftsman in the Erie Railroad shops in Susquehanna, a small town in northeastern Pennsylvania. He went on to a law school in New York City and passed his bar examination in Susquehanna County before getting a degree. He suffered from his mother's ambitions all his life. He was desperately hungry for praise, and many people thought him conceited; but he secretly—and bitterly—considered himself a failure, even though he eventually wrote a standard text on workmen's compensation law which was in its fourth edition when he died.

My mother, Grace Burrhus, was bright and beautiful. She had rigid standards of what was "right," and they never changed. Her loyalties were legendary. At eleven she began to correspond with a friend who had moved away, and they wrote to each other in alternate weeks, without missing a week, for 70 years. Her father was born in New York State. He lied about his age to enlist as a drummer boy in the last year of the Civil War. After the war he came to Susquehanna looking for work as a carpenter, and eventually he became foreman of the Erie carpenter shops there. My Grandmother Burrhus had the only claim to quality in the family: An ancestor, a Captain Potter, had fought under Washington.

My home environment was warm and stable. I lived in the house I was born in until I went to college. My father, mother, and I all graduated from the same high school. I saw a great deal of my grandparents. I had a brother two and a half years younger than I. As a child I was fond of him. I remember being ridiculed for calling him "honey," a term my mother used for both of us at home. As he grew older he proved to be much better at sports and more popular than I, and he teased me for my literary and artistic interests. When he died suddenly of a cerebral aneurism at the age of 16, I was not much moved. I probably felt guilty because I was not. I had once made an arrowhead from the top of a tin can, and when I made a test shot straight up into the air, the arrow fell back and struck my brother in the shoulder, drawing blood. I recalled the event with a shock many years later when I heard Laurence Olivier speaking Hamlet's lines:

> Let my disclaiming from a purpos'd evil
> Free me so far in your most generous thought,
> That I have shot mine arrow o'er the house,
> And hurt my brother.

Susquehanna is now half deserted, and it was even then a rather dirty railroad town, but it is situated in a beautiful river valley. I roamed the hills for miles around. I picked arbutus and dogwood in early spring, chewed sassafras root and wintergreen berries and the underbark of slippery elm, killed rattlesnakes, and found flint arrowheads. With another boy I built a shack in the hills alongside a creek, and I learned to swim in the pool we made by blocking the creek with a sod-and-stone dam, sharing the pool with a poisonous watersnake. Four other boys and I once went 300 miles down the Susquehanna River in a fleet of three canoes. I was 15 at the time and the oldest in the party.

I was always building things. I built roller-skate scooters, steerable wagons, sleds, and rafts to be poled about on shallow ponds. I made seesaws, merry-go-rounds, and slides. I made slingshots, bows and arrows, blow guns and water pistols from lengths of bamboo, and from a discarded water boiler a steam cannon with which I could shoot plugs of potato and carrot over the houses of our neighbors. I made tops, diabolos, model airplanes driven by twisted rubber bands, box kites, and tin propellers which could be sent high into the air with a spool-and-string spinner. I tried again and again to make a glider in which I myself might fly.

I invented things, some of them in the spirit of the outrageous contraptions in the cartoons which Rube Goldberg was publishing in the *Philadelphia Inquirer* (to which, as a good Republican, my father subscribed). For example, a friend and I used to gather elderberries and sell them from door to door, and I built a flotation system which separated ripe from green berries. I worked for years on the design of a perpetual motion machine. (It did not work.)

I went through all 12 grades of school in a single building, and there were only eight students in my class when I graduated. I *liked* school. It was the custom for students to congregate outside the building until a bell rang and the doors were opened. I was a constant problem for the janitor, because I would arrive early and ask to be let in. He had been told to keep me out, but he would shrug, open the door just enough to let me through, and lock it after me. As I see it now, the school was good. I had 4 strong years of high school mathematics using no-nonsense texts by Wentworth. In my senior year I could read a bit of Virgil well enough to feel that I was getting the meaning in Latin. Science was weak, but I was always doing physical and chemical experiments at home.

My father was a sucker for book salesmen ("We are contacting a few of the town's more substantial citizens"), and as a result we had a fairly large library consisting mostly of sets—*The World's Great Literature, Masterpieces of World History, Gems of Humor,* and so on. Half a dozen small volumes on applied psychology, published by an "institute," were beautifully bound, with white spines and embossed seals on blue covers. I remember only one sample: It was said that an advertisement for chocolates showing a man shoveling cocoa beans into a large roasting oven was bad psychology.

A schoolteacher named Mary Graves was an important figure in my life. Her father was the village atheist and an amateur botanist who believed in evolution. Miss Graves once showed me a letter he had received from the

Prince of Monaco offering to exchange specimens of pressed plants. Miss Graves was a dedicated person with cultural interests far beyond the level of the town. She organized the Monday Club, a literary society to which my mother belonged. The club would spend a winter reading Ibsen's *Doll's House*. Miss Graves did her best to bring the little town library up to date. When I was in high school, she once whispered to me in a conspiratorial tone, "I have just been reading the strangest book. It is called *Lord Jim*."

Miss Graves was my teacher in many fields for many years. She taught a Presbyterian Sunday School class, taking six or eight of us boys through most of the Old Testament. She taught me drawing in the lower grades, and she was later promoted to teaching English, both reading and composition. I think it was in the eighth grade that we were reading *As You Like It*. One evening my father happened to say that some people believed that the plays were not written by Shakespeare but by a man named Bacon. The next day I announced to the class that Shakespeare had not actually written the play we were reading. "You don't know what you are talking about," said Miss Graves. That afternoon I went down to the public library and drew out Edwin Durning-Lawrence's *Bacon is Shakespeare*.[1] The next day I *did* know what I was talking about, and I must have made life miserable for Miss Graves for the next month or two. Durning-Lawrence had analyzed act five, scene one of *Love's Labours Lost,* proving that the word *honorificabilitudinitatibus* was a cipher which, when properly interpreted, read, "These works, the offspring of Francis Bacon, are preserved for the world." To my amazement I discovered that the same act and scene in *As You Like It* was also cryptic. The philosopher Touchstone (who else but Bacon?) is disputing with the simple William (who else but Shakespeare?) for the possession of the fair Audrey (what else but the authorship of the plays?). The clincher was that William says that he was born in the Forest of Arden, and Shakespeare's mother's name was Arden. (O, the lovely adolescent obscenity of that "forest"!) I have long since lost interest in the Bacon-Shakespeare controversy, but in my defensive zeal I read biographies of Bacon, summaries of his philosophical position, and a good deal of *The Advancement of Learning* and *Novum Organum*. How much it meant to me at the age of 14 or 15 I cannot say, but Francis Bacon will turn up again in this story.

Miss Graves was probably responsible for the fact that in college I majored in English literature and afterwards embarked upon a career as a writer, and probably also for the fact that I have dabbled in art. I have never painted or sculpted really well, but I have enjoyed trying to do so.

My father had played the trumpet (then called the cornet) in a small orchestra, but he gave it up when he married. I never heard him play more than a few notes; he had "lost his lip." My mother played the piano well and had an excellent contralto voice. She sang at weddings and funerals—and the same songs at both. I still have her copy of J.C. Bartlett's "A Dream." It begins, "Last night I was dreaming of thee, love, was dreaming...." A sacred text for use at funerals is added in her own hand: "Come, Jesus, Redeemer, abide thou with me-e...." At the age of 8 or 9 I studied the piano for a year with an old man who sucked Sens-sens and jabbed me in the ribs with a sharp pencil whenever I made a mistake. For a while I gave up the piano in favor of the saxophone. My father was then local attorney for the Erie Railroad, and he arranged for me to play with an employee's band. We never got beyond "Poet and Peasant," "Morning Noon and Night in Vienna," and other overtures by von Suppe, but I learned to love ensemble playing. I played in a jazz band during my high school years. When I returned to the piano again, a friend of the family who taught piano noticed that I was limited to my mother's sentimental music and a few volumes of *Piano Pieces the Whole World Loves,* and she sent me a copy of Mozart's Fourth Sonata. Shortly afterward I bought all the Mozart sonatas, playing at first only short passages here and there. Later I came to play them all through once a year in a kind of ritual.

I was never physically punished by my father and only once by my mother. She washed my mouth out with soap and water because I had used a bad word. My father never missed an opportunity, however, to inform me of the punishments which were waiting if I turned out to have a criminal mind. He once took me through the county jail, and on a summer vacation I was taken to a lecture with colored slides describing life in Sing Sing. As a result I am afraid of the police and buy too many tickets to their annual dances.

My mother was quick to take alarm if I showed any deviation from what was "right." Her technique of control was to say "tut-tut" and to ask "What will people think?" I can easily recall the consternation in my family when in second grade I brought home a report card on which, under "Deportment," the phrase "Annoys others" had been checked. Many things which were not "right" still haunt me. I was allowed to play in the cemetery next door, but it was not "right" to step on a grave. Recently in a cathedral I found myself executing a series of smart right-angle detours to avoid the engraved stones on the floor. I was taught to "respect books," and it is only with a twinge that I can today crack the spine of a book to make it stay open on the piano.

My Grandmother Skinner made sure that I understood the concept of hell by showing me the glowing bed of coals in the parlor stove. In a traveling magician's show I saw a devil complete with horns and barbed tail, and I lay awake all that night in an agony of fear. Miss Graves, though a devout Christian, was liberal. She explained, for example, that one might interpret the miracles in the Bible as figures of speech. Shortly after I reached puberty, I had a mystical experience. I lost a watch which I had just been given by my family, and I was afraid to go home ("You would lose your head if it were not screwed on"). I took my bicycle and rode up along the river and followed the creek up to our shack. I was miserably unhappy. Suddenly it occurred to me that happiness and unhappiness must cancel out and that if I were unhappy now I would necessarily be happy later. I was tremendously relieved. The principle came with the force of a revelation. In a mood of intense exaltation I started down along the creek. Halfway to the road, in a nest of dried grass beside the path, lay my watch. I have no explanation; I had certainly "lost" it in town. I took this as a Sign. I hurried home and wrote an account in biblical language and purple ink. (The ink I had made by dissolving the lead from an indelible pencil, and it had an appropriate golden sheen.) No other signs followed, however, and my new testament remained only one chapter in length. Within a year I had gone to Miss Graves to tell her that I no longer believed in God. "I know," she said, "I have been through that myself." But her strategy misfired: I never went *through* it.

COLLEGE

A friend of the family recommended Hamilton College, and I did not think of going anywhere else. It was then at the nadir of its long career. I took an absurd program of courses, but in some curious way I have made good use of every one of them. I majored in English and had good courses in Anglo-Saxon, Chaucer (for which I wrote a modern translation of "The Pardoner's Tale"), Shakespeare, Restoration drama, and Romantic poetry. I minored in Romance languages. Hamilton was proud of its reputation for public speaking, and I had 4 thin compulsory years of that. I elected biology as my freshman science and went on to advanced courses in embryology and cat anatomy.

The most important thing that happened to me at Hamilton was getting to know the Saunders family. They were abroad during my freshman year, recovering from the tragic death of their elder son, a brilliant student who had been killed in a hazing accident the year before. All the Saunders children were prepared for college at home; and when the family returned, they asked my mathematics professor to suggest a tutor for their younger son. I agreed to serve.

Percy Saunders was then dean. Hamilton College students called him "Stink" because he taught chemistry, but his great love was hybrid peonies. He and his family lived in a large frame house alongside the campus. It was full of books, pictures, sculpture, musical instruments, and huge bouquets of peonies in season. Dean Saunders played the violin, and there were string quartets at least one night a week. Louise Saunders took in a few students each year to prepare them for college, among them usually a pretty girl with whom I would fall in love. We would walk through the Root Woods, returning for tea before a fire in the music room in the late afternoon. Once in a while on a clear night a telescope would be set up among the peonies, and we would look for the moons of Mars or Saturn's rings. Interesting people came to stay—writers, musicians, and artists. Beside my chair as I listened to Schubert or Beethoven I might find a copy of the avant-garde *Broom* or a letter from Ezra Pound. I remember a page from the score of George Antheil's *Ballet Mécanique* with the words COMPLETELY PERCUS-SIVE printed diagonally across it. Percy and Louise Saunders made an art of living, something I had not known was possible.

I never fitted into student life at Hamilton. I joined a fraternity without knowing what it was all about. I was not good at sports and suffered acutely as my shins were cracked in ice hockey or better players bounced basketballs off my cranium—all in the name of what was ironically called "physical education." In a paper I wrote at the end of my freshman year, I complained that the college was pushing me around with unnecessary requirements (one of them daily chapel) and that almost no intellectual interest was shown by most of the students. By my senior year I was in open revolt.

John K. Hutchens and I began that year with a hoax. Our professor of English composition, Paul Fancher, was a great name-dropper in the field of the theater. Hutchens and I had posters printed reading, in part: "Charles Chaplin, the famous cinema comedian, will deliver his lecture 'Moving Pictures as a Career' in the Hamilton College Chapel on Friday, October 9." The lecture was said to be under Fancher's auspices. In the early hours of October 9 we went down to the village, plastered the posters on store windows and telephone poles, threw a few into lobbies of apartment houses, and went back to bed. That morning Hutchens called the afternoon paper in Utica, the nearest city, and told them that the president had announced the lecture at morning chapel. By noon the thing was completely out of hand. The paper ran Chaplin's picture on the front page and even guessed at the time he would arrive at Union Station, which, I am ashamed to say, was swarming with children at the appointed hour. In spite of police roadblocks it was estimated that 400 cars got through to the campus. A football pep meeting was mistaken for a Chaplin rally, and a great throng began to mill around the gymnasium. The editorial which appeared next day in the college paper ("No man with the slightest regard for his alma mater would have done it") was one of the best things Hutchens ever wrote.

As a nihilistic gesture, the hoax was only the beginning. Through the student publications we began to attack the faculty and various local sacred cows. I published a parody of the bumbling manner in which the professor of public speaking would review student performances at the end of a class. I wrote an editorial attacking Phi Beta Kappa. At commencement time I was in charge of Class Day exercises, which were held in the gymnasium, and with the help of another student (Alf Evers, later a well-known illustrator) I covered the walls with bitter caricatures of the faculty.

One of the most sacred of Hamilton institutions was the Clark Prize Oration. Students submitted written orations, six of which were selected to be spoken in an evening contest, from which a winner was chosen by a committee of judges. Four of us decided to wreck the institution. We submitted orations which we thought would be selected but which were potentially so bombastic that we could convert the evening into an uproarious farce. We misjudged the judges, however. Only mine was selected. I found myself on the program with five serious speakers. I decided there was nothing for it but to go through with the joke alone, hoping that my friends would understand. Very few did. We also made a shambles of the commencement ceremonies, and at intermission the president warned us sternly that we would not get our degrees if we did not settle down.

LITERARY INTERLUDE

My Hamilton College activities seemed to be pointing toward a career as a writer. As a child I had had an old typewriter and a small printing press, and during my grade school years I wrote poems and stories and typed or printed them "artistically." I started a novel or two—sentimental stuff on the model of James Oliver Curwood: Pierre, an old trapper, lived in the woods of colonial Pennsylvania with his lovely daughter, Marie (how they got down from Quebec I never thought it necessary to explain). In high school I worked for the local *Transcript*. In the morning before school I would crib national and international news from the Binghamton papers which had come in on the morning train. Occasionally I did a feature story or published a poem in the manner of Edgar Guest. When I got to college I contributed serious poems to the *Hamilton Literary Magazine*. Free verse was coming in, and I tried my hand at it. Here is a sample:

Concupiscence

An old man, sowing in a field,
Walks with a slow, uneasy rhythm.
He tears handfuls of seed from his vitals,
Caressing the wind with the sweep of this hand.
At night he stops, breathless,
Murmuring to his earthly consort,
"Love exhausts me!"

And I had not yet heard of Freud. Once, when in love, I wrote five or six rather derivative Shakespearean sonnets and enjoyed the strange excitement of emitting whole lines ready-made, properly scanned and rhymed.

The summer before my senior year I attended the Middlebury School of English at Breadloaf, Vermont. I took a course with Sidney Cox, who one day invited me to have lunch with Robert Frost. Frost asked me to send him some of my work, and I sent him three short stories. His comments came the following April. The letter is printed in the *Selected Letters of Robert Frost*, edited by Lawrence Thompson.[2] It was encouraging, and on the strength of it I definitely decided that I would be a writer. My father had always hoped that I would study law and come into his office. My birth had been announced in the local paper in that vein: "The town has a new law firm: Wm. A. Skinner & Son." I had taken a course in political science my senior year just in case I might indeed go into law. My father was naturally unhappy that I had decided against it. He thought I should prepare myself to earn a living—say, as a lawyer—and *then* try my hand at writing. He eventually agreed, however, that I should live at home (in Scranton, Pennsylvania, to which my family had moved) and write for a year or two. I built a small study in the attic and set to work. The results were disastrous. I frittered away my time. I read aimlessly, built model ships, played the piano, listened to the newly invented radio, contributed to the humorous column of a local paper but wrote almost nothing else, and thought about seeing a psychiatrist.

Before the year was out, I rescued myself and my self-respect by taking on a hack job. The FBI has occasionally expressed interest in that 2-year gap in my educational history, but I was not writing for the *Daily Worker*. On the contrary, I was way out on the right wing. In 1904, after a bitter coal strike, President Theodore Roosevelt had set up a Board of Conciliation to settle grievances brought by unions and companies. The decisions which had since been handed down were increasingly cited as precedents, and the coal companies wanted them digested so that their lawyers could prepare cases more effectively. I read and abstracted thousands of decisions and classified them for ready reference. My book was privately printed under the title *A Digest of Decisions of the Anthracite Board of Conciliation*. (My father was listed as coauthor, but for prestige only.) The book was intended to give the coal companies an advantage, but the lawyer who prepared all the union cases had a copy within the year.

After I had finished the book, I went to New York for 6 months of bohemian living in Greenwich Village, then to Europe for the summer, and on to Harvard in the fall to begin the study of psychology. In New York I worked in a book shop, dined at Chumley's, and drank hot rum Punchinos at Jimmy's, a speakeasy on Barrow Street. My friends were liberal and even intellectual. On Saturday nights 8 or 10 of us would somehow manage to have an all-night party on 1 quart of prohibition gin. That summer Paris was full of literary expatriates and I met some of them, but a violent reaction against all things literary was setting in.

I had failed as a writer because I had had nothing important to say, but I could not accept that explanation. It was literature which must be at fault. A girl I had played tennis with in high school—a devout Catholic who later became a nun—had once quoted Chesterton's remark about a character of Thackeray's: "Thackeray didn't know it but she drank." I generalized the principle to all literature. A writer might portray human behavior accurately, but he did not therefore understand it. I was to remain interested in human behavior, but the literary method had failed me; I would turn to the scientific. Alf Evers, the artist, had eased the transition. "Science," he once told me, "is the art of the 20th century." The relevant science appeared to be psychology, though I had only the vaguest idea of what that meant.

TOWARD PSYCHOLOGY

Many odds and ends contributed to my decision. I had long been interested in animal behavior. We had no household pets, but I caught and kept turtles, snakes, toads, lizards, and chipmunks. I read Thornton Burgess and Ernest Thompson Seton and was interested in folk wisdom about animals. The man who kept the livery stable once explained that the cowboys in the rodeo let themselves be thrown just before "breaking the spirit" of the bucking broncos to avoid spoiling them for future performances. At a county fair I saw a troupe of performing pigeons. The scene was the facade of a building. Smoke appeared from the roof, and a presumably female pigeon poked her head out of an upper window. A team of pigeons came on stage pulling a fire engine, smoke pouring from its boiler. Other pigeons with red fire hats rode on the engine, one of them pulling a string which rang a bell. Somehow a ladder was put up against the building, and one of the firepigeons climbed it and came back down followed by the pigeon from the upper window.

Human behavior also interested me. A man in Binghamton who gave me advanced lessons on the saxophone had entertained soldiers during the war with a vaudeville act. He wrote the alphabet forward with his right hand and backward with his left while adding a column of figures and answering questions—all at the same time. It gave him a headache. I remember being puzzled by an episode at some kind of church fair where there was a booth in which you could throw baseballs at dolls mounted on a rack. The dolls were restored to their place by pulling a rope from the front of the booth. When the woman who ran the concession was gathering balls near the dolls, some wag pulled the rope. Everyone laughed as the woman dropped to the ground in alarm. Why had she confused the sound of the rack with the sound of a ball?

Some of the things I built had a bearing on human behavior. I was not allowed to smoke, so I made a gadget incorporating an atomizer bulb with which I could "smoke" cigarettes and blow smoke rings hygienically. (There might be a demand for it today.) At one time my mother started a campaign to teach me to hang up my pajamas. Every morning while I was eating breakfast, she would go up to my room, discover that my pajamas were not hung up, and call to me to come up immediately. She continued this for weeks. When the aversive stimulation grew unbearable, I constructed a

mechanical device that solved my problem. A special hook in the closet of
my room was connected by a string-and-pulley system to a sign hanging
above the door to the room. When my pajamas were in place on the hook,
the sign was held high above the door out of the way. When the pajamas
were off the hook, the sign hung squarely in the middle of the door frame. It
read: "Hang up your pajamas!"

My earliest interest in psychology was philosophical. In high school I
began a treatise entitled "Nova Principia Orbis Terrarum." (That sounds
pretentious, but at least I got it out of my system early. Clark Hull published
his Principia at the age of 59.) Two pages of this great work survive. It begins:
"Our soul consists of our mind, our power of reasoning, thinking, imagining,
weighing, our power to receive impressions, and stimulate action of our
body; and our conscience, our inner knowledge of write (sic)." I engaged in
a good deal of self-observation, and I kept notes. Once in a rather noisy street
I was trying to talk to a friend in a store window. Though I strained to hear
him, I could not make out what he was saying. Then I discovered that there
was no glass in the window and that his voice was reaching me loud and
clear. I had dismissed it as part of the ambient noise and was listening for a
fainter signal.

College did little to further my interest in psychology. The only formal
instruction I received lasted 10 minutes. Our professor of philosophy (who
had actually studied under Wundt) once drew a pair of dividers from his
desk drawer (the first Brass Instrument I had ever seen) and demonstrated
the two-point limen. My term paper for a course in Shakespeare was a study
of Hamlet's madness. I read rather extensively on schizophrenia, but I
should not care to have the paper published today. At Breadloaf I wrote a
one-act play about a quack who changed people's personalities with
endocrines, a subject which was then beginning to attract attention in the
newspapers.

After college my literary interests carried me steadily toward psychology.
Proust's *A La Recherche du temps perdu* was just being translated. I read all
that was available in English and then carried on in French. (I bought part
VIII, *Le Temps retrouvé*, in Algiers in 1928. The uncut pages indicate that I
abandoned literature on page 96.) Proust intensified my habit of self-
observation and of noting and recording many tricks of perception and
memory. Before going to Harvard I bought Parson's book on perception,
and I suppose it was only my extraordinary luck which kept me from
becoming a Gestalt or (so help me) a cognitive psychologist.

The competing theme which saved me was suggested by "Bugsy"
Morrell, my biology teacher at Hamilton. He had called my attention to
Jacques Loeb's *Physiology of the Brain and Comparative Psychology,*[3] and
later he showed me Pavlov's *Conditioned Reflexes.*[4] I bought Pavlov's book
and read it while living in Greenwich Village. The literary magazine called

The Dial, to which I subscribed, was publishing articles by Bertrand Russell, and they led me to Russell's book, *Philosophy,* published in 1925,[5] in which he devoted a good deal of time to John B. Watson's *Behaviorism,*[6] emphasizing its epistemological implications. I got hold of Watson's *Behaviorism* (but not his *Psychology from the Standpoint of a Behaviorist*),[7] and in the bookstore in New York I read the store's copy of his *Psychological Care of Infant and Child*[8] between customers.

The Department of Psychology at Harvard did not strengthen any particular part of this hodgepodge of interests, but two graduate students did. Fred S. Keller, who was teaching part time at Tufts, was a sophisticated behaviorist in every sense of the word. I had seen the regal name of Charles K. Trueblood spread across the pages of *The Dial,* for which he wrote many reviews. Now I found Trueblood himself, in white coat and gumshoes, moving silently through the corridors of Emerson Hall carrying cages of rats, the performances of which he was studying in a rotated maze. I welcomed the support of another renegade from literature.

At Harvard I entered upon the first strict regimen of my life. I had done what was expected of me in high school and college but had seldom worked hard. Aware that I was far behind in a new field, I now set up a rigorous schedule and maintained it for almost 2 years. I would rise at six, study until breakfast, go to classes, laboratories, and libraries with no more than 15 minutes unscheduled during the day, study until exactly 9:00 at night, and go to bed. I saw no movies or plays, seldom went to concerts, had scarcely any dates, and read nothing but psychology and physiology.[9]

My program in the department was not heavy. Boring was on leave, writing his history. Troland gave a course, but I found it unbearably dull and withdrew after the first day. Carroll Pratt taught psychophysical methods and was always available for discussions. I took Harry Murray's course in Abnormal Psychology the first year he gave it. I could read French but needed German as well, so I took an intensive course which met 5 days a week. To pass statistics I simply read G. Udney Yule's *An Introduction to the Theory of Statistics.*[10] His use of Greek letters to refer to the absence of attributes explains my symbols S^D and S^Δ, the awkwardness of which has plagued many psychologists since.

The intellectual life around the department was of a high order. A weekly colloquium, loosely structured, was always exciting and challenging. We argued with Pratt, Beebe-Center, and Murray on even terms. The informality is shown by a letter which I wrote to Harry Murray, of which he recently reminded me. He had given a colloquium on his theory of "regnancy." I wrote to tell him that there were some things about himself I felt he ought to know. When he was a child, he had obviously been led to believe that it was urine which entered the female in sexual intercourse. This had wreaked havoc in his scientific thinking, and he was still trying to separate *p* from *pregnancy.*

A joint reception for new students in philosophy and psychology was held each year at Professor Hocking's. My first year I turned up at the appointed hour, which was, of course, too early. A little old man with a shiny bald head and deep-set eyes soon arrived and came straight toward me in the friendliest way. He wore a wing collar and ascot tie. He stammered slightly and spoke with an English accent. I sized him up as a clergyman—perhaps an imported preacher in one of the better Boston churches. He asked me where I had gone to college and what philosophy I had studied. He had never heard the name of my professor and was only puzzled when I tried to help by explaining that he was an Edwardian (meaning a disciple of Jonathan Edwards). He told me that a young psychologist should keep an eye on philosophy, and I told *him*, fresh from my contact with Bertrand Russell, that it was quite the other way around: We needed a psychological epistemology. This went on for 15 or 20 minutes, as the room filled up. Others began to speak to my new friend. Finally a student edged in beside me, explaining that he wanted to get as close to the professor as possible. "Professor who?" I asked. "Professor Whitehead," he said.

My thesis had only the vaguest of Harvard connections. Through a friend who had come to Harvard to study under Percy Bridgman I got to know the *Logic of Modern Physics.*[11] I read Poincaré and Mach. I began to spend a good deal of time in the Boston Medical Library and in the summer of 1930 wrote a paper on the concept of the reflex, adopting the semihistorical method from Mach's *Science of Mechanics.*[12] Early that fall I was discussing my future with Beebe-Center. I outlined the work I intended to cover in my thesis. His comment was typical: "Who do you think you are? Helmholtz?" He encouraged me to get a thesis in at once. I was already well along in my work on changes in rate of eating and had written two short papers on drive and reflex strength. I combined these with my paper on the reflex and submitted them as a thesis to Professor Boring, who was now back in residence. I still have his long reply. He was bothered by my selective use of history. A thesis on the history of the reflex should be quite different. He suggested an alternative outline. I felt that he had missed my point, and I resubmitted the thesis without change. Suspecting that he was bothered by my behavioristic leanings, I attached a quotation from Thomas Hood:

> Owning her weakness,
> Her evil behavior,
> And leaving, with meekness,
> Her sins to her Savior.

Boring accepted the role of Savior. He appointed a thesis committee of which he himself was not a member; the thesis was approved, and I passed my orals at the end of the fall term of 1930–31. I stayed in my laboratory, supported by the balance of a Harvard Fellowship, until June.

Meanwhile I had come into close contact with W.J. Crozier and Hudson Hoagland. Hoagland had taken his Ph.D. in psychology but was teaching in Crozier's Department of General Physiology. It was felt, I think, that Crozier was stealing students from psychology. He certainly offered enthusiastic encouragement, and after I got my degree he put me up for National Research Council Fellowhips for 2 years, but I was never under any pressure to adopt his principles or move into his field. During my first postdoctoral year I spent every other day working on the central nervous system at the medical school under Alexander Forbes and Hallowell Davis. For the rest of my time Crozier offered me a subterranean laboratory in the new biology building. I moved my animal equipment into it and worked there for 5 years, the last 3 as a Junior Fellow in the Harvard Society of Fellows.

I have traced the development of my research in detail elsewhere. Russell and Watson had given me no glimpse of experimental method, but Pavlov had: Control the environment and you will see order in behavior. In a course with Hoagland I discovered Sherrington and Magnus. I read *Körperstellung*[13] and proposed to do a translation (fortunately I failed to find a publisher). I felt that my thesis had exorcised the physiological ghosts from Sherrington's[14] synapse, and I could therefore maintain contact with these earlier workers. In writing *The Behavior of Organisms* (1938) I held doggedly to the term "reflex." Certain characteristics of operant behavior were, however, becoming clear. My first papers were challenged by two Polish physiologists, Konorski and Miller. It was in my answer to them that I first used the word "operant." Its function, then as now, was to identify behavior traceable to reinforcing contingencies rather than to eliciting stimuli.

MINNESOTA

In the spring of 1936, the low point of the depression, the end of my Junior Fellowship was approaching and I had no job. The best offer the Department of Psychology could pass along to me was from a YMCA college; but Walter Hunter was teaching that summer at Minnesota, and he mentioned me to R.M. Elliott, who was looking for someone to teach small sections of a big introductory course. The beginning salary was $1900.

At Minnesota I not only taught for the first time, I began to learn college psychology, keeping a jump or two ahead of my students in Woodworth's text. I chose two sections of 20 students each from about 800 in the beginning course. Many of them were already committed to particular careers, such as medicine, law, journalism, and engineering, but 5 percent of the students I had during 5 years went on to get Ph.D.'s in psychology and many more to get M.A.'s. I stole W.K. Estes from engineering and Norman Guttman from philosophy. My teaching has never again been so richly reinforced.

VERBAL BEHAVIOR

I did not quite give up literature. At Harvard I met I.A. Richards, who managed somehow to blend psychology and literary criticism, and I discussed books and techniques with other literary friends. I wrote an article for the *Atlantic Monthly* under the editor's title of "Has Gertrude Stein a Secret?" In it I showed that a paper which Gertrude Stein had published when at Radcliffe contained samples of her own automatic writing which resembled material she later published as literature. Gertrude Stein wrote to the editor in reply: "No, it is not so automatic as he thinks. If there is anything secret it is the other way too. I think I achieve by xtra consciousness, xcess, but then what is the use of telling him that, he being a psychologist and I having been one."

I began to look at literature, not as a medium for portraying human behavior, but as a field of behavior to be analyzed. A discussion with Whitehead after dinner at the Society of Fellows set me to work on my book *Verbal Behavior* (1957). The chairman of the Society, L.J. Henderson, cautioned me that such a book might take 5 years. The following summer he sent a postcard from France: "A motto for your book— 'Car le mot, ç'est le verbe, et le verbe, ç'est Dieu'—Victor Hugo."

As a boy I knew two interesting cases of verbal behavior. My Grandmother Skinner was an almost pathological talker. My grandfather had stopped listening to her while still a young man, and when any visitor came to her house she would begin talking and would repeat, without pausing, a string of anecdotes and stereotyped comments which we all knew by heart. More predictable verbal behavior I have never seen. The other case was Professor Bowles, the principal of my high school, who taught mathematics. He had a long list of favorite topics, and almost any stimulus would set him off on a digression. He would eventually return to mathematics with a perfunctory bow to the comment which had first set him off. One day I made running notes of the topics he was touching upon. There were two long harangues that day, and to my surprise he concluded the second by returning to the topic with which he had begun and concluded the first!

When I was in the Society of Fellows, another verbal phenomenon came to my attention. On a beautiful Sunday morning I was in my subterranean, soundproofed laboratory writing notes against a background of rhythmic noise from my apparatus. Suddenly I found myself joining in the rhythm, saying silently, "You'll never get out, you'll never get out, you'll never get out." The relevance of the remark seemed worth investigating. I built a phonographic system in which patterns of vowels (separated by glottal stops) could be repeated as often as desired. Playing each sample softly to a subject, I could maintain the illusion that it was actual speech and could collect a large sample of "projective" verbal responses. Harry Murray supplied me with subjects from his research on thematic apperception.

My renewed interest in literature was encouraged by my marriage in 1936 to Yvonne Blue. She had majored in English at the University of Chicago, where she had taken a course in English composition with Thornton Wilder. She is an active reader (and a rapid one—she reads exactly twice as fast as I), and there were always new books around the house. When I had a chance to give a summer school course in the psychology of literature, she attended my lectures and reinforced me appropriately. I gave the course again and broadcast it over an educational radio station. To fill out the term I roamed rather widely, from *The Meaning of Meaning*[15] through psychoanalysis, and thus explored the field of verbal behavior rather more widely than I should otherwise have done. As a rule the material in which I had least confidence proved to be most popular, but I did not wholly abandon my scientific principles. After several persuasive demonstrations of alliteration as a verbal process, for example, I became suspicious and made a statistical analysis of 100 of Shakespeare's sonnets. I found that, although an occasional line might have as many as four stressed initial *s*'s, such lines occurred almost exactly as often as one would predict from chance. (A similar study of Swinburne, I was glad to find, not only demonstrated alliteration, but showed an alliterative tendency extending over several syllables.)

In the fall of 1941 on a Guggenheim Fellowship I began to write a final draft of *Verbal Behavior*. The war intervened, but I picked up the Fellowship again in 1944-45 and finished the greater part of the manuscript. I gave a course from it in the summer of 1947 at Columbia, and my William James Lectures at Harvard that fall were based on it. I put off a final version in order to write *Science and Human Behavior* (1953). *Verbal Behavior* was published, not 5, as Henderson had predicted, but 23 years after it was begun, in 1957. It was completed under heavy competition from research and from another book, *Schedules of Reinforcement* (1957), which Charles Ferster and I published at about the same time.

PROJECT PIGEON

By the end of the 1930s the Nazis had demonstrated the power of the airplane as an offensive weapon. On a train from Minneapolis to Chicago in the spring of 1939, I was speculating rather idly about surface-to-air missiles as a possible means of defense. How could they be controlled? I knew nothing about radar, of course, but infrared radiation from the exhaust of the engines seemed a possibility. Was visible radiation out of the question? I noticed a flock of birds flying alongside the train, and it suddenly occurred to me that I might have the answer in my own research. Why not teach animals to guide missiles? I went back to Minneapolis and bought some pigeons. The rest of the story of Project Pigeon has already been told.[16]

THE "BABY BOX"

Toward the end of the Second World War, we decided to have a second child. My wife remarked that she did not mind bearing children but that the first 2 years were hard to take. I suggested that we mechanize the care of a baby. There is nothing natural about a crib. Wrapping a baby in several layers of cloth—undershirt, nightie, sheets, and blankets, with a mattress under-neath—is an inefficient way of maintaining a proper temperature, and it greatly restricts the child's movements. I built, instead, an enclosed space in which the baby, wearing only a diaper, could lie on a tightly stretched woven plastic sheet, the surface of which feels rather like linen and through which warm air rises, moved by convection or a fan, depending on the outside temperature.

When our second daughter, Deborah, came home from the hospital, she went directly into the device and used it as sleeping space for 2½ years. I reported our happy experience in an article in the *Ladies' Home Journal*, and many hundreds of babies have been raised in what is now called an Aircrib. Child care is conservative, and the method has been adopted fairly slowly, but medical and behavioral advantages should be studied. Predictions and tales of dire consequences have not been supported. Deborah broke her leg in a skiing accident but presumably not because of "the box." Otherwise she has had remarkably good health. She is now in college, interested in art and music from Bach to Beatle, and she usually beats me at chess. To complete the story of the shoemaker's children, our older daughter, Julie, is married to a sociologist, Ernest Vargas, and is finishing her work for a Ph.D. in educational research. Their first child, Lisa, is, of course, being raised in an Aircrib.[17]

WALDEN TWO

In the spring of 1945 at a dinner party in Minneapolis, I sat next to a friend who had a son and a son-in-law in the South Pacific. I expressed regret that when the war was over they would come back and take up their old way of life, abandoning their present crusading spirit. She asked me what I would have them do instead, and I began to discuss an experimental attitude toward life. I said that some of the communities of the 19th century repre-sented a healthy attitude. She pressed me for details and later insisted that I publish them. I was unaware that I was taking her seriously. A paper on "The Operational Analysis of Psychological Terms" (1945) was due on June 1, and I met that deadline. Then, to my surprise, I began to write *Walden Two* (1948). It began simply as a description of a feasible design for community living. I chose the unoriginal utopian strategy of having a few people visit a community. The characters soon took over.

In general I write very slowly and in longhand. It took me 2 minutes to write each word of my thesis and that is still about my rate. From 3 or 4 hours of writing each day I eventually salvage about 100 publishable words. *Walden Two* was an entirely different experience. I wrote it on the typewriter in 7 weeks. It is pretty obviously a venture in self-therapy, in which I was struggling to reconcile two aspects of my own behavior represented by Burris and Frazier. Some of it was written with great emotion. The scene in Frazier's room, in which Frazier defends *Walden Two* while admitting that he himself is not a likeable person or fit for communal life, I worked out while walking the streets near our house in St. Paul. I came back and typed it out in white heat.

I receive a steady trickle of letters from people who have read *Walden Two,* want to know whether such a community has ever been established, and, if so, how they can join. At one time I seriously considered an actual experiment. It could be one of the most dramatic adventures in the 20th century. It needs a younger man, however, and I am unwilling to give up the opportunity to do other things which in the long run may well advance the principles of *Walden Two* more rapidly. A conference organized to consider an actual experiment was recently attended by nearly 100 people.[18]

INDIANA

In the fall of 1945 I became chairman of the Department of Psychology at Indiana. I took with me from Minnesota the unfinished manuscript of *Verbal Behavior,* the manuscript of *Walden Two,* the Aircrib with its lovely occupant, and a miscellaneous lot of apparatus. I was inexperienced as an administrator, but the department survived my brief chairmanship. I did no undergraduate teaching, but the chapter in *Science and Human Behavior* on self-control is to a large extent the joint product of a seminar in which, for almost the only time in my life, I successfully managed group thinking. In spite of my administrative responsibilities I ran a number of experiments— all with pigeons—on reaction time, differential reinforcement of slow responding, two operanda, and matching-to-sample. These studies are mostly reported in "Are Theories of Learning Necessary?" (1950).

THE EXPERIMENTAL ANALYSIS OF BEHAVIOR

Other people were now beginning to do research along the same lines. W.K. Estes, who went on to get a Ph.D. at Minnesota, wrote a thesis on the effects of punishment which became a classic. At Columbia Fred Keller was teaching graduate students from *The Behavior of Organisms* and, with W.N. Schoenfeld, was planning a revolutionary introductory course in the college. A problem in communication arose, and Keller and I started what became a series of annual conferences on the experimental analysis of behavior. Those who attended the first of these at Indiana in the spring of 1946 are pictured in volume 5 (1962) of the *Journal of the Experimental Analysis of Behavior*. Eventually we began to meet at the same time as the American Psychological Association and later as part of its program. When Division 3 could no longer provide space or arrange time for our expanding activities, we took the probably inevitable step of forming a separate division— Division 25.

Meanwhile, the need for a special journal had become clear. I proposed an inexpensive newsletter, but more constructive opinions prevailed. A small holding society was formed and the *Journal of the Experimental Analysis of Behavior* founded. The history of the discipline can also be traced in the increasing availability of excellent apparatus, reflecting the growing complexity and subtlety of the contingencies of reinforcement under analysis.[19]

HARVARD AGAIN

While giving the William James Lectures at Harvard in 1947, I was asked to become a permanent member of the department, and we moved to Cambridge in 1948. Remembering my introductory teaching at Minnesota, I proposed to add a course in human behavior to the Harvard list. The first year was nearly a disaster. More than 400 students, anticipating a "gut" course, signed up. I had no appropriate text and could only supply hastily prepared mimeographed sheets. My section men were loyal but puzzled. Later the course was incorporated into the General Education program and gradually improved. By 1953 *Science and Human Behavior* was available as a text.

Meanwhile I had set up a pigeon laboratory in which Charles Ferster and I worked very happily together for more than 5 years. It was the high point in my research history. Scarcely a week went by without some exciting discovery. Perhaps the behavior we dealt with most effectively was our own. Near the end of our collaboration we found ourselves with a vast quantity of unanalyzed and unpublished data, and we proceeded to design an environment in which we could scarcely help writing a book. In it we both worked as we had never worked before. In one spring term and one long hot summer we wrote a text and a glossary and prepared over 1000 figures, more than 900 of which were published.

The success of my laboratory in the 1950s and early 1960s was due in large part to many excellent graduate students, not all of them under my direction, of whom I may mention Douglas G. Anger, James E. Anliker, Donald S. Blough, Richard J. Herrnstein (now my colleague on the Harvard faculty), Alfredo V. Lagmay, William H. Morse, Nathan H. Azrin, Ogden R. Lindsley, Lewis R. Gollub, Matthew L. Israel, Harlan L. Lane, George S.

Reynolds, A. Charles Catania, Herbert S. Terrace, and Neil J. Peterson. With very little direct help from me they all made and are continuing to make important contributions.

TECHNOLOGICAL APPLICATIONS

At Minnesota W.T. Heron and I had studied the effects of certain drugs on operant behavior. In the 1950s a strong interest in psychopharmacology suddenly developed. Almost all the large drug companies set up operant laboratories, some only for the screening of new compounds but many providing an opportunity for basic research. Much of this interest was generated by Joseph V. Brady of the Walter Reed Army Medical Center. Peter Dews of the Department of Pharmacology in the Harvard Medical School began to work in close cooperation with my laboratory and soon organized an active program in his own department.

In the early 1950s Dr. Harry Solomon, then chairman of the Department of Psychiatry at the Harvard Medical School, helped me set up a laboratory for the study of the operant behavior of psychotics at the Metropolitan State Hospital in Waltham, Massachusetts. Ogden R. Lindsley took over, and the work he initiated there has now been carried forward in many other laboratories. Azrin and others have extended operant principles to the management of psychotic patients in hospital wards, and there is increasing interest in applications to personal therapy.[20]

Sporadic research on operant behavior in children goes back to the 1930s. Sidney Bijou, among others, has been particularly active in applying the principles of an experimental analysis to the behavior of children in nursery schools, clinics, and the home. Ferster turned from our work on schedules to the study of autistic children, and there are now many operant laboratories for the study of retardates. Almost all these practical applications have contributed to our understanding of behavior. Fortunately, they have not overshadowed the basic science; many laboratories continue to study operant behavior apart from technological significances.

In the late 1930s, looking ahead to the education of our first child, I began to write a book called *Something to Think About.* It was never completed, though I got as far as having an artist work on the illustrations. It contained examples of what later came to be called programmed instruction. When our daughters went to school, I showed the usual interest as a parent but carefully refrained from speaking as a specialist in the field of learning. In 1953 our younger daughter was in fourth grade in a private school in Cambridge. On November 11, as a Visiting Father, I was sitting in the back of the room in an arithmetic class. Suddenly the situation seemed perfectly absurd. Here were 20 extremely valuable organisms. Through no fault of her own the teacher was violating almost everything we knew about the learning process.

I began to analyze the contingencies of reinforcement which might be useful in teaching school subjects and designed a series of teaching machines which would permit the teacher to provide such contingencies for individual students. At a conference on current trends in psychology at the University of Pittsburgh in the spring of 1954 I demonstrated a machine to teach spelling and arithmetic. Within a year I found myself caught up in the teaching machine movement. A series of projects at Harvard led eventually to a Committee on Programmed Instruction, in which I had the invaluable collaboration of James G. Holland.[21]

Economics, government, and religion are farther from psychology than linguistics, psychotherapy, or education, and few people have the kind of joint interest needed for an examination of common principles. I have seen myself moving slowly in this direction, however, and I am now working under a Career Award from the National Institutes of Health which will permit me to explore the social sciences from the point of view of an experimental analysis of behavior.[22]

MY BEHAVIOR AS A SCIENTIST

It is often said that behaviorists do not view themselves as they view their subjects—for example, that they regard what they say as true in some sense which does not apply to the statements of the people they study. On the contrary, I believe that my behavior in writing *Verbal Behavior,* for example, was precisely the sort of behavior the book discusses. Whether from narcissism or scientific curiosity, I have been as much interested in myself as in rats and pigeons. I have applied the same formulations, I have looked for the same kinds of causal relations, and I have manipulated behavior in the same way and sometimes with comparable success. I would not publish personal facts of this sort if I did not believe that they throw some light on my life as a scientist.

I was taught to fear God, the police, and what people will think. As a result I usually do what I have to do with no great struggle. I try not to let any day "slip useless away." I have studied when I did not feel like studying, taught when I did not want to teach. I have taken care of animals and run experiments as the animals dictated. (Some of my first cumulative records are stamped December 25th and January 1st.) I have met deadlines for papers and reports. In both my writing and my research I have fought hard against deceiving myself. I avoid metaphors which are effective at the cost of obscuring issues. I avoid rhetorical devices which give unwarranted plausibility to an argument (and I sometimes reassure myself by making lists of the devices so used by others). I avoid the unwarranted prestige conferred by mathematics, even, I am afraid, when mathematics would be helpful. I do not spin impressive physiological theories from my data, as I could easily do.

I never convert an exploratory experiment into an *experimentum crucis* by inventing a hypothesis after the fact. I write and rewrite a paper until, so far as possible, it says exactly what I have to say. (A constant search for causes seems to be another product of that early environment. When my wife or one of my daughters tells me that she has a headache, I am likely to say "Perhaps you have not been eating wisely" or "You may have been out in the sun too much." It is an almost intolerable trait in a husband, father, or friend, but it is an invaluable scientific practice.)

I must admit that all these characteristics have been helpful. Max Weber could be right about the Protestant Ethic. But its effect is only cautionary or restrictive. Much more important in explaining my scientific behavior are certain positive reinforcements which support Feuer's[23] answer to Weber in which he shows that almost all noted scientists follow a "hedonistic ethic." I have been powerfully reinforced by many things: food, sex, music, art, and literature—and my scientific results. I have built apparatuses as I have painted pictures or modeled figures in clay. I have conducted experiments as I have played the piano. I have written scientific papers and books as I have written stories and poems. I have *never* designed and conducted an experiment because I felt I ought to do so, or to meet a deadline, or to pass a course, or to "publish rather than perish." I dislike experimental designs which call for the compulsive collection of data and, particularly, data which will not be reinforcing until they have been exhaustively analyzed. I freely change my plans when richer reinforcements beckon. My thesis was written before I knew it was a thesis. *Walden Two* was not planned at all. I may practice self-management for Protestant reasons, but I do so in such a way as to maximize non-Protestant reinforcements. I emphasize positive contingencies. For example, I induce myself to write by making production as conspicuous as possible (actually, in a cumulative record). In short, I arrange an environment in which what would otherwise be hard work is actually effortless.

I could not have predicted that among the reinforcers which explain my scientific behavior the opinions of others would not rank high, but that seems to be the case. Exceptions are easily traced to my history. I take a silly pride in the fact that "Freedom and the Control of Men" (1955-56) appears as an example of good contemporary prose in textbooks written for college freshmen; Miss Graves would have been pleased. But in general my effects on other people have been far less important than my effects on rats and pigeons—or on people as experimental subjects. That is why I was able to work for almost 20 years with practically no professional recognition. People supported me, but not my line of work; only my rats and pigeons supported *that*. I was never in any doubt as to its importance, however, and when it began to attract attention, I was wary of the effect rather than pleased.

Many notes in my files comment on the fact that I have been depressed or frightened by so-called honors. I forego honors which would take time away from my work or unduly reinforce specific aspects of it. That I have never been interested in critical reactions, either positive or negative, is probably part of the same pattern. I have never actually read more than a dozen pages of Chomsky's famous review of *Verbal Behavior*. (A quotation from it which I have used I got from I.A. Richards.) When Rochelle Johnson sent me a reprint of her reply to Scrivin's criticism of my position, it only reminded me that I had never read Scrivin. Clark Hull used to say that I did not make hypotheses because I was afraid of being wrong. Verbal statements are, indeed, right or wrong, and in some sense I want my statements to be right. But I am much more interested in measures for the control of a subject matter. Some relevant measures are verbal, but even so they are not so much right or wrong as effective or ineffective, and arguments are of no avail. For the same reason I am not interested in psychological theories, in rational equations, in factor analyses, in mathematical models, in hypothetico-deductive systems, or in other verbal systems which must be *proved* right.

Much of this attitude is Baconian. Whether my early and quite accidental contact with Bacon is responsible or not, I have followed his principles closely. I reject verbal authority. I have "studied nature not books," asking questions of the organism rather than of those who have studied the organism. I think it can be said, as it was said of Bacon, that I get my books out of life, not out of other books. I have followed Bacon in organizing my data. I do not collect facts in random "botanizing," for there are principles which dictate what Poincaré called *le choix des faits,* and they are not, as Poincaré argued, hypotheses. I classify not for the sake of classification but to reveal properties.

I also follow Bacon in distinguishing between observation and experimentation. Bacon no doubt underestimated the importance of extending the range of human sense organs with instruments, but he did so in emphasizing that knowledge is more than sensory contact. I would put it this way: *Observation* overemphasizes stimuli; *experimentation* includes the rest of the contingencies which generate effective repertoires. I have also satisfied myself that Bacon's four Idols can be translated into an acceptable behavioral analysis of faulty thinking.

My position as a behaviorist came from other sources. Perhaps, like Jeremy Bentham and his theory of fictions, I have tried to resolve my early fear of theological ghosts. Perhaps I have answered my mother's question, "What will people think?" by proving that they do not think at all (but the question might as well have been "What will people *say?*"). I used to toy with the notion that a behavioristic epistemology was a form of intellectual suicide, but there is no suicide because there is no corpse. What perishes is the homunculus—the spontaneous, creative inner man to whom, ironically, we once attributed the very scientific activities which led to his demise.

To me behaviorism is a special case of philosophy of science which first took shape in the writings of Ernst Mach, Henri Poincaré, and Percy Bridgman. Bridgman himself could never make the extension to behavior. He is one man I *did* argue with. When he published *The Way Things Are*,[24] he sent me a copy with a note: "Here it is. Now do your damnedest!" I was busy with other things and did nothing. But I could never have convinced him, for it is not a matter of conviction. Behaviorism is a formulation which makes possible an effective experimental approach to human behavior. It is a working hypothesis about the nature of a subject matter. It may need to be clarified, but it does not need to be argued. I have no doubt of the eventual triumph of the position—not that it will eventually be proved right, but that it will provide the most direct route to a successful science of Man.

I have acknowledged my indebtedness to Bertrand Russell, Watson, and Pavlov. I never met or even saw Watson, but his influence was, of course, important. Thorndike (not a behaviorist but still an important figure in a science of behavior) I met briefly. He knew of my interest in verbal behavior and sent me his *Studies in the Psychology of Language*.[25] When I wrote to thank him, I told him about my analysis of alliteration and added, "Hilgard's review of my book [*The Behavior of Organisms*] in the *Bulletin* has reminded me of how much of your work in the same vein I failed to acknowledge....I seem to have identified your point of view with the modern psychological view taken as a whole. It has always been obvious that I was merely carrying on your puzzle box experiments but it never occurred to me to remind my readers of the fact." Thorndike replied, "I am better satisfied to have been of service to workers like yourself than if I had founded a 'school.'"

Walter Hunter I knew well. He gave me professional advice. I recall his wry smile as he told me, "It only takes one little idea to be a success in American psychology." (He measured the idea with thumb and forefinger.) Clark Hull visited my laboratory in Cambridge and made suggestions, which I never followed. I talked to his seminar at Yale and was invited to the unveiling of his portrait shortly before he died. I have a bound volume of my papers which was once on his shelves under the title *Experimental Studies in Learning*.

Tolman taught summer school at Harvard in 1931, and we had many long discussions. I had been analyzing the concept of hunger as a drive. In my thesis I had called it a "third" variable—that is, a variable in addition to stimulus and response occupying the intervening position of Sherrington's synaptic states. I have always felt that Tolman's later formulation was very similar. When *The Behavior of Organisms* appeared, he wrote:

I think the two words *operant* and *respondent* are swell....I do think, as I have said so many times before, that what you ought to do next is to put in two levers and see what relationships the functions obtained from such a discrimination set up will bear to your purified functions where you have only one lever. No doubt you were right that the "behavior-ratio" is a clumsy thing for getting the fundamental laws, but it is a thing that has finally to be predicted and someone must show the relation between it and your fundamental analysis. I congratulate you on coming through Harvard so beautifully unscathed!...

P.S. And, of course, I was pleased as Hell to be mentioned in the Preface.

Another behaviorist whose friendship I have valued is J.R. Kantor. In many discussions with him at Indiana I profited from his extraordinary scholarship. He convinced me that I had not wholly exorcised all the "spooks" in my thinking.

THE CONTROL OF BEHAVIOR

I learned another Baconian principle very slowly: "Nature to be commanded must be obeyed." Frazier in *Walden Two* speaks for me here:

I remember the rage I used to feel when a prediction went awry. I could have shouted at the subjects of my experiments, "Behave, damn you! Behave as you ought!" Eventually I realized that the subjects were always right. They always behaved as they should have behaved. It was I who was wrong. I had made a bad prediction.

But that coin has another face: Once obeyed, nature can be commanded. The point of Solomon's House in the *New Atlantis,* as of The Royal Society founded on Bacon's model, was that knowledge should be useful. A hundred years later—in an epoch in which I feel especially at home— Diderot developed the theme in his *Encyclopédie.* A hundred years after that, the notion of progress took on new significance in the theory of evolution. *Walden Two* is my *New Atlantis;* I suppose it could also be said that in applying an experimental analysis to education I returned to a motto which Bacon as a child saw in his father's house: *Moniti Meliora* (instruction brings progress). I believe in progress, and I have always been alert to practical significances in my research.

I began to talk explicitly about the control of human behavior after I had written *Walden Two.* Control was definitely in the air during my brief stay at Indiana. In *Science and Human Behavior* and the course for which it was written, I elaborated on the theme. In the summer of 1955, on the island of Monhegan, Maine, where we had a cottage, I wrote "Freedom and the Control of Men" for a special issue of the *American Scholar.* In it I took a much stronger stand on freedom and determinism. My position has been rather bitterly attacked, especially by people in the humanities, who feel that it is in conflict with Western democratic ideas and that it plays down the role of the individual. I have been called Machiavellian, a Communist, a Fascist, and many other names. The fact is, I accept the ends of a democratic philosophy, but I disagree with the means which are at the moment most commonly employed. I see no virtue in accident or in the chaos from which somehow we have reached our present position. I believe that we must now plan our own future and that we must take every advantage of a science of behavior in solving the problems which will necessarily arise. The great danger is not that science will be misused by despots for selfish purposes but that so-called democratic principles will prevent people of goodwill from using it in their advance toward humane goals. I continue to be an optimist, but there are moments of sadness. I find the following in my notebook, dated August 5, 1963.

End of an Era

Last night Deborah and I went to the Gardner Cox's for some music in their garden. A group of young people, mostly current or former Harvard and Radcliffe students, sang a Mass by William Byrd. It was *a cappella* and, for most of the singers, sight reading. Very well done. The night was pleasant. Ragged clouds moved across the sky, one of them dropping briefly a fine mist. The garden has a circular lawn surrounded by shrubs and a few old trees. Half a dozen lights burned among green branches. Several kittens played on the grass. We sat in small groups, in folding chairs. Except for a few jet planes the night was quiet and the music delightful. *Kyrie eleison...* I thought of *Walden Two* and the B-minor Mass scene. And of the fact that this kind of harmless, beautiful, sensitive pleasure was probably nearing the end of its run. This was Watermusic, floating down the Thames and out to sea. And why?

Phyllis Cox may have answered the question. As I said good night, she motioned toward the young man who had conducted the music and said, "You know, he thinks you are a terrible person. Teaching machines... a fascist...."

Possibly our only hope of maintaining any given way of life now lies with science, particularly a science of human behavior and the technology to be derived from it. We need not worry about the scientific way of life; it will take care of itself. It would be tragic, however, if other ways of life, not concerned with the practice of science as such, were to forego the same kind of support through a misunderstanding of the role of science in human affairs.

The garden we sat in that evening once belonged to Asa Gray. In high school I studied Botany from a text by Gray, called, as I remember it, *How Plants Grow.* One passage impressed me so much that I made a copy which I have kept among my notes for nearly 50 years. It is the story of a radish. I would reject its purposivism today but not its poetry, for it suggests to me a reasonable place for the individual in a natural scheme of things.

So the biennial root becomes large and heavy, being a storehouse of nourishing matter, which man and animals are glad to use for food. In it, in the form of starch, sugar, mucilage, and in other nourishing and savory products, the plant (expending nothing in flowers or in show) has laid up the avails of its whole summer's work. For what purpose? This plainly appears when the next season's growth begins. Then, fed by this great stock of nourishment, a stem shoots forth rapidly and strongly, divides into branches, bears flowers abundantly, and ripens seeds, almost wholly at the expense of the nourishment accumulated in the root, which is now light, empty, and dead; and so is the whole plant by the time the seeds are ripe.

REFERENCES AND NOTES

[1]Durning-Lawrence, E. *Bacon is Shakespeare.* London: Gay and Hancock, 1910.

[2]Thompson, L. (Ed.). *Selected letters of Robert Frost.* New York: Holt, Rinehart & Winston, 1964.

[3]Loeb, J. *Physiology of the brain and comparative psychology.* New York: Putnam, 1900.

[4]Pavlov, I. *Conditioned reflexes.* London: Oxford, 1927.

[5]Russell, B. *Philosophy.* New York: Norton, 1925.

[6]Watson, J.B. *Behaviorism.* New York: People's Institute, 1924.

[7]Watson, J.B. *Psychology from the standpoint of a behaviorist.* Philadelphia: Lippincott, 1919.

[8]Watson, J.B. *Psychological care of infant and child.* New York: Norton, 1928.

[9]Extant documents do not fully confirm the Spartan character of this period.

[10]Yule, G. *An introduction to the theory of statistics.* London: Griffin, 1911.

[11]Bridgman, P. *The logic of modern physics.* New York: Macmillan, 1927.

[12]Mach, E. *The science of mechanics, a critical and historical account of its development.* Chicago: Open Court, 1893.

[13]Magnus, R. *Körperstellung.* Berlin: Springer, 1924.

[14]Sherrington, C.S. *The integrative action of the nervous system.* New York: Charles Scribner's Sons, 1906.

[15]Richards, I.A., & Ogden, C.K. *The meaning of meaning.* New York: Harcourt, Brace & World, 1923.

[16]See Chapter 12.

[17]More of the story: Julie and Ernie are both professors in the School of Education at West Virginia University. Lisa, who now calls herself Kris, is at boarding school. Her younger sister, Justine, is in school at home. Deborah, a successful artist, is married to Barry Buzan, who teaches International Studies at Warwick University. They live in London. See Chapter 14 in this volume for more of the original story.

[18]A number of communities inspired by *Walden Two,* though not always closely resembling it, are in existence in the United States, Canada, and Mexico.

[19]The Division of the Experimental Analysis of Behavior of the American Psychological Association was created in 1964. The Association for Behavior Analysis was founded in 1974. Both of these organizations are concerned both with basic and applied parts of the field.

[20]The *Journal of Applied Behavior Analysis* was founded in 1968, and more than 20 related journals have been founded since.

[21]Holland and Skinner programmed part of Skinner's undergraduate course at Harvard and published it as *The Analysis of Behavior* in 1961. Skinner surveyed the field in a book called *The Technology of Teaching*, published in 1968. The Pittsburgh paper appears as Chapter 10 in this book.

[22]This exploration led in 1971 to the publication of *Beyond Freedom and Dignity*. See the Postscript to this chapter.

[23]Feuer, L. *The scientific intellectual.* New York: Basic Books, 1963.

[24]Bridgman, P. *The way things are.* Cambridge: Harvard University Press, 1959.

[25]Thorndike, E.L. Studies in the psychology of language. *Archives of Psychology,* 1938, No. 231.

POSTSCRIPT

In 1964, at the invitation of the Division of Social Psychology of the American Psychological Association, I gave an address called "The Science of Behavior and Human Dignity." In it I stated a theme to which I was to give most of the next 6 years—the apparent encroachment of a science of behavior upon the freedom and dignity of the individual. The question of freedom had had a long history—many philosophers, theologians, and behavioral scientists were determinists—but the question of the feeling of dignity or worth had received much less attention. We are usually willing to attribute our shortcomings to our environment, but we want credit for our achievements. Nevertheless, as a scientific analysis traces our behavior to our genetic and personal histories, less and less seems to remain for which we ourselves are responsible.

That became the theme of *Beyond Freedom and Dignity*, which I published in 1971. Possibly because the book appeared at the conclusion of a decade in which young people had broken free from almost all societal control, it attracted a good deal of attention. *Time* magazine did a cover story on it, and it was on the best-seller lists for many months. Reactions were both positive and negative, the negative in many cases quite violent. The *Time* cover had me asserting that "We can't afford freedom," and my title convinced those who did not read the book that I was indeed against freedom and dignity. But in spite of the scientific evidence that we are not in any way responsible for our behavior, it is important that we should *feel* free and worthy, and I argued that by recognizing the scientific facts we could move more rapidly to a world in which people would feel as free and worthy as possible. What lay "beyond" the freedom and dignity of the individual was the survival of the species or, more immediately, of a way of life in which the potential of the species was more fully realized.

The negative reactions to *Beyond Freedom and Dignity* made it clear that many people misunderstood the behavioristic position. The reviewers tended to recall the behaviorism they had learned about in courses in psychology. Behavior was said to be a matter of responses to stimuli; people were treated as if they were rats and pigeons, creative thinking was not accounted for, and so on. Many psychologists were dashing off in what I thought were unprofitable directions. It seemed necessary to restate the behavioristic position, and in an effort to do so, I published *About Behaviorism* in 1974. The central theme was simple: Philosophers and most psychologists were egocentric. A person was said to perceive the world, form concepts about it, engage in thought processes, and act upon the world intentionally or purposefully. The behavioristic position was just the opposite: A person comes under the control of a stimulating environment, responds to subtle properties of that environment, and responds to it in many complex ways because of the consequences contingent upon earlier responses. The environment *selects* behavior and, on the analogy of natural selection, takes over the role of creative thought, purpose, and plans. The cognitive processes which had become so popular a subject of psychology were really misrepresentations of the role of contingencies of reinforcement. They were inferred from behavior in relation to the environment. They could not be directly observed because "there were no nerves going to the right places in the brain."

At the same time I began to write a book on the future. Overpopulation, the exhaustion of resources, the pollution of the environment, and the growing probability of a nuclear holocaust also lay "beyond freedom and dignity" unless something was done about them. I wrote a book-length manuscript and brought a revision up to the same length, but decided not to publish it. Instead I gave several lectures on the subject, the title of one of them, "Are We Free to Have a Future?" indicating its relation to *Beyond Freedom and Dignity*. I am currently at work on a further statement of the position.

Many of the attacks on *Beyond Freedom and Dignity* were personal. Reviews were accompanied by portraits of me in which my head was attached to the bodies of rats and pigeons. On one campus I was hanged in effigy. I decided that it was time to "report me and my cause aright," and that I should write an autobiography. I began with a few rules. Whenever possible, I would use documentary evidence rather than recollection. I would tell the story as it happened with as little contemporary interpretation as possible. I would include personal details but allow the reader to infer their connections with my life as a psychologist. The first volume, *Particulars of My Life*, brings the story up to the point at which I left for Harvard to become a graduate student in psychology. The second, *The Shaping of a Behaviorist*, covers the ensuing

20 years, when I returned to Harvard as a professor. A third volume will, I hope, complete the story.

In 1964 I received a Career Award from the National Institute of Mental Health. For 5 years, renewable for another 5, it would free me from all commitments to the University and allow me to devote myself to an analysis of cultural practices from the point of view of an experimental analysis of behavior. Of the four books written during those 10 years, *Beyond Freedom and Dignity* was closest to the assigned theme. The grant terminated upon my retirement in 1974, but I have continued to work in the same vein.

The arrival of a new graduate student, Robert Epstein, made a change. He edited a volume composed of papers I had recently published, which was called *Reflections on Behaviorism and Society.* He also discovered that I had written thousands of notes over the years and edited a selection of them under the title *Notebooks.*

As a more drastic change, he persuaded me to return to laboratory experimentation. I was ready to do so because I thought tremendous opportunities were being neglected in the field of the experimental analysis of behavior. Few people seemed to understand the role of contingencies of reinforcement in shaping and maintaining the behavior of such an organism as a pigeon, but it was those contingencies which, I had argued in *About Behaviorism,* were the factual side of so-called cognitive processes. We collaborated on a variety of research, including a 3-year project which we eventually called "Columban [Pigeon] Simulation." Through careful construction of complex contingencies of reinforcement, we were able to get pigeons to exhibit behavior said to show "symbolic communication," "spontaneous use of memoranda," "self-concept," "insight," and other so-called cognitive or creative processes.

PART ONE

Research

C H A P T E R 1

Are Theories of Learning Necessary?

EDITOR'S NOTE

The article was first published in *Psychological Review* (1950, 57, 193-216)
and has been republished in *Cumulative Record* and elsewhere. Its title
has led many people to believe that Skinner is against theorizing, but the
article is critical of only a certain *kind* of theorizing. Clark Hull and
Edward C. Tolman had constructed elaborate theories of the "intervening
variables" that were said to mediate changes in behavior. Such theories
contributed nothing, as far as Skinner was concerned, to our ability to
discover order in behavior. Hull's work, in particular, was so theory-laden,
according to Skinner, that it impeded the search for order. In a critical
review of Hull's *Principles of Behavior* (published in *The American
Journal of Psychology*, 1944, 57, 276-281), Skinner noted Hull's "autistic
tendency to create appropriate data (one-third of the graphs represent
hypothetical cases)" and complained that at one point "three
experimental points [were described] with an equation containing three
constants!" Skinner did not discuss his own alternative in the review; he
does so in the following paper.

The three types of learning theories to which Skinner objects are:
physiological, mental, and conceptual. A science of behavior should
provide an account of behavior in terms of manipulable variables;
physiological, mental, and conceptual theories do not provide such
variables and indeed often impede the search for them. Traditional
measures of learning, such as latency or percent correct, are inadequate.
Rate of responding has a number of advantages: It reveals orderly
moment-to-moment changes in behavior, is sensitive to change over a
great range, and corresponds to what we usually mean by learning, as
well as to the concept of *probability* of response. Rate of responding is
affected by variables such as level of motivation and difficulty of response.
Skinner shows the effects of such variables and discusses the nature of
reinforcement and extinction, largely by describing a large body of
research he conducted with rats and pigeons.

The following are among the more notable results reported:
"Periodic" and "aperiodic" (later called "fixed-interval" and "variable-interval") schedules of intermittent reinforcement produce characteristic rates and patterns of responding, as well as characteristic patterns of extinction. Complex learning, often dealt with under the rubric of "preference," "choice," "discrimination," and so on, is also amenable to an objective laboratory analysis. "Choice" has been studied, for example, by examining the responses of a pigeon to two concurrently available stimuli. If pecks to the two stimuli produce different rates of reinforcement, one finds that "tendencies to respond eventually correspond to the probabilities of reinforcement" at the alternatives. "Preference" at any point in time might be expressed as the "relative rates of responding to the two keys." Complex discriminations have been studied using a "matching-to-sample" procedure in which, for example, a pigeon is confonted by some "sample stimulus" and then by several other stimuli from which it must select the corresponding one.

There is a need for theory in the sense of "a formal representation of the data reduced to a minimal number of terms," but "[we] do not seem to be ready for theory in this sense." There is, Skinner concludes, a great deal of basic research that must first be done. Premature equations "will have so many arbitrary constants that a good fit will be a matter of course and cause for very little satisfaction."

Skinner's own work is virtually devoid of the kinds of theories he rejects in this paper but is rich with a kind of informal, tentative theory, distinctive in its close ties to data. In 1969 he published a book entitled *Contingencies of Reinforcement: A **Theoretical** Analysis* and has published many theoretically oriented papers (e.g., see Part Two of this book). For further explication of his rejection of mathematical models, see the Hull review or his review of Bush and Mosteller's *Stochastic Models for Learning* (*Contemporary Psychology,* 1956, *1,* 101-103).

Certain basic assumptions, essential to any scientific activity, are sometimes called theories. That nature is orderly rather than capricious is an example. Certain statements are also theories simply to the extent that they are not yet facts. A scientist may guess at the result of an experiment before the experiment is carried out. The prediction and the later statement of result may be composed of the same terms in the same syntactic arrangement, the difference being in the degree of confidence. No empirical statement is wholly nontheoretical in this sense because evidence is never complete, nor is any prediction probably ever made wholly without evidence. The term *theory* will not refer here to statements of these sorts but rather to any explanation of an observed fact which appeals to events taking place somewhere else, at some other level of observation, described in different terms, and measured, if at all, in different dimensions.

Three types of theory in the field of learning satisfy this definition. The most characteristic is to be found in the field of physiological psychology. We are all familiar with the changes which are supposed to take place in the nervous system when an organism learns. Synaptic connections are made or broken, electrical fields are disrupted or reorganized, concentrations of ions are built up or allowed to diffuse away, and so on. In the science of neurophysiology statements of this sort are not necessarily theories in the present sense. But in a science of behavior, where we are concerned with whether or not an organism secretes saliva when a bell rings, or jumps toward a gray triangle, or says *bik* when a card reads *tuz*, or loves someone who resembles its mother, all statements about the nervous system are theories in the sense that they are not expressed in the same terms and could not be confirmed with the same methods of observation as the facts for which they are said to account.

A second type of learning theory is in practice not far from the physiological, although there is less agreement about the method of direct observation. Theories of this type have always dominated the field of human behavior. They consist of references to "mental" events, as in saying that an organism learns to behave in a certain way because it "finds something pleasant" or because it "expects something to happen." To the mentalistic psychologist these explanatory events are no more theoretical than synaptic connections to the neurophysiologist, but in a science of behavior they are theories because the methods and terms appropriate to the events to be explained differ from the methods and terms appropriate to the explaining events.

In a third type of learning theory the explanatory events are not directly observed. The writer's suggestion [in *The Behavior of Organisms*] that the letters *CNS* be regarded as representing, not the Central Nervous System, but the Conceptual Nervous System seems to have been taken seriously. Many theorists point out that they are not talking about the nervous system as an actual structure undergoing physiological or biochemical changes but only as a system with a certain dynamic output. Theories of this sort are multiplying fast, and so are parallel operational versions of mental events. A purely behavioral definition of expectancy has the advantage that the problem of mental observation is avoided and with it the problem of how a mental event can cause a physical one. But such theories do not go so far as to assert that the explanatory events are identical with the behavioral facts which they purport to explain. A statement about behavior may support such a theory but will never resemble it in terms or syntax. Postulates are good examples. True postulates cannot become facts. Theorems may be deduced from them which, as tentative statements about behavior, may or may not be confirmed, but theorems are not theories in the present sense. Postulates remain theories to the end.

It is not the purpose of this paper to show that any of these theories cannot be put in good scientific order, or that the events to which they refer may not actually occur or be studied by appropriate sciences. It would be foolhardy to deny the achievements of theories of this sort in the history of science. The question of whether they are necessary, however, has other implications and is worth asking. If the answer is No, then it may be possible to argue effectively against theory in the field of learning. A science of behavior must eventually deal with behavior in its relation to certain manipulable variables. Theories—whether neural, mental, or conceptual— talk about intervening steps in these relationships. But instead of prompting us to search for and explore relevant variables, they frequently have quite the opposite effect. When we attribute behavior to a neural or mental event, real or conceptual, we are likely to forget that we still have the task of accounting for the neural or mental event. When we assert that an animal acts in a given way because it expects to receive food, then what began as the task of accounting for learned behavior becomes the task of accounting for expectancy. The problem is at least equally complex and probably more difficult. We are likely to close our eyes to it and to use the theory to give us answers in place of the answers we might find through further study. It might be argued that the principal function of learning theory to date has been, not to suggest appropriate research, but to create a false sense of security, an unwarranted satisfaction with the status quo.

Research designed with respect to theory is also likely to be wasteful. That a theory generates research does not prove its value unless the research is valuable. Much useless experimentation results from theories, and much energy and skill are absorbed by them. Most theories are eventually overthrown, and the greater part of the associated research is discarded. This could be justified if it were true that productive research requires a theory— as is, of course, often claimed. It is argued that research would be aimless and disorganized without a theory to guide it. The view is supported by psychological texts which take their cue from the logicians rather than empirical science and describe thinking as necessarily involving stages of hypothesis, deduction, experimental test, and confirmation. But this is not the way most scientists actually work. It is possible to design significant experiments for other reasons, and the possibility to be examined is that such research will lead more directly to the kind of information which a science usually accumulates.

The alternatives are at least worth considering. How much can be done without theory? What other sorts of scientific activity are possible? And what light do alternative practices throw upon our present preoccupation with theory?

It would be inconsistent to try to answer these questions at a theoretical level. Let us therefore turn to some experimental material in three areas in which theories of learning now flourish and raise the question of the function of theory in a more concrete fashion.

THE BASIC DATUM IN LEARNING

What actually happens when an organism learns is not an easy question to answer. Those who are interested in a science of behavior will insist that learning is a change in behavior, but they tend to avoid explicit references to responses or acts as such. "Learning is adjustment or adaptation to a situation." But of what stuff are adjustments and adaptations made? Are they data, or inferences from data? "Learning is improvement." But improvement in what? And from whose point of view? "Learning is restoration of equilibrium." But what is in equilibrium and how is it put there? "Learning is problem solving." But what are the physical dimensions of a problem—or of a solution? Definitions of this sort show an unwillingness to take what appears before the eyes in a learning experiment as a basic datum. Particular observations seem too trivial. An error score falls; but we are not ready to say that this is learning rather than merely the result of learning. An organism meets a criterion of 10 successful trials; but an arbitrary criterion is at variance with our conception of the generality of the learning process.

This is where theory steps in. If it is not the time required to get out of a puzzle box which changes in learning, but rather the strength of a bond, or the conductivity of a neural pathway, or the excitatory potential of a habit, then problems seem to vanish. Getting out of a box faster and faster is not learning; it is merely performance. The learning goes on somewhere else, in a different dimensional system. And although the time required depends upon arbitrary conditions, often varies discontinuously, and is subject to reversal of magnitude, we feel sure that the learning process itself is continuous, orderly, and beyond the accidents of measurement. Nothing could better illustrate the use of theory as a refuge from the data.

But we must eventually get back to an observable datum. If learning is the process we suppose it to be, then it must appear so in the situations in which we study it. Even if the basic process belongs to some other dimensional system, our measures must have relevant and comparable properties. But productive experimental situations are hard to find, particularly if we accept certain plausible restrictions. To show an orderly change in the behavior of the *average* rat or ape or child is not enough, since learning is a process in the behavior of the individual. To record the beginning and end of learning of a few discrete steps will not suffice, since a series of cross sections will not give complete coverage of a continuous process. The dimensions of the change must spring from the behavior itself; they must not be imposed by an external judgment of success or failure or an external criterion of completeness. But when we review the literature with these requirements in mind, we find little justification for the theoretical process in which we take so much comfort.

The energy level or work-output of behavior, for example, does not change in appropriate ways. In the sort of behavior adapted to the Pavlovian experiment (respondent behavior) there may be a progressive increase in the magnitude of response during learning. But we do not shout our responses louder and louder as we learn verbal material, nor does a rat press a lever harder and harder as conditioning proceeds. In operant behavior the energy or magnitude of response changes significantly only when some arbitrary value is differentially reinforced—when such a change is what is learned.

The emergence of a right response in competition with wrong responses is another datum frequently used in the study of learning. The maze and the discrimination box yield results which may be reduced to these terms. But a behavior-ratio of right vs. wrong cannot yield a continuously changing measure in a single experiment on a single organism. The point at which one response takes precedence over another cannot give us the whole history of the change in either response. Averaging curves for groups of trials or organisms will not solve this problem.

Increasing attention has recently been given to latency, the relevance of which, like that of energy level, is suggested by the properties of conditioned and unconditioned reflexes. But in operant behavior the relation to a stimulus is different. A measure of latency involves other considerations, as inspection of any case will show. Most operant responses may be emitted in the absence of what is regarded as a relevant stimulus. In such a case the response is likely to appear before the stimulus is presented. It is no solution to escape this embarrassment by locking a lever so that an organism cannot press it until the stimulus is presented, since we can scarcely be content with temporal relations which have been forced into compliance with our expectations. Runway latencies are subject to this objection. In a typical experiment the door of a starting box is opened and the time which elapses before a rat leaves the box is measured. Opening the door is not only a stimulus, it is a change in the situation which makes the response possible for the first time. The time measured is by no means as simple as a latency and requires another formulation. A great deal depends upon what the rat is doing at the moment the stimulus is presented. Some experimenters wait until the rat is facing the door, but to do so is to tamper with the measurement being taken. If, on the other hand, the door is opened without reference to what the rat is doing, the first major effect is the conditioning of favorable waiting behavior. The rat eventually stays near and facing the door. The resulting shorter starting-time is not due to a reduction in the latency of a response, but to the conditioning of favorable preliminary behavior.

Latencies in a single organism do not follow a simple learning process. Relevant data on this point were obtained as part of an extensive study of reaction time. A pigeon, enclosed in a box, is conditioned to peck at a recessed disc in one wall. Food is presented as reinforcement by exposing a hopper through a hole below the disc. If responses are reinforced only after a stimulus has been presented, responses at other times disappear. Very short reaction times are obtained by differentially reinforcing responses which occur very soon after the stimulus.[1] But responses also come to be made very quickly without differential reinforcement. Inspection shows that this is due to the development of effective waiting. The bird comes to stand before the disc with its head in good striking position. Under optimal conditions, without differential reinforcement, the mean time between stimulus and response will be of the order of 1/3 second. This is not a true reflex latency, since the stimulus is discriminative rather than eliciting, but it is a fair example of the latency used in the study of learning. The point is that this measure does not vary continuously or in an orderly fashion. By giving the bird more food, for example, we induce a condition in which it does not always respond. But the responses which occur show approximately the same temporal relation to the stimulus (Figure 1, middle curve). In extinction, of special interest here, there is a scattering of latencies because lack of reinforcement generates an emotional condition. Some responses occur sooner and others are delayed, but the commonest value remains unchanged (bottom curve in Figure 1). The longer latencies are easily explained by inspection. Emotional behavior, of which examples will be

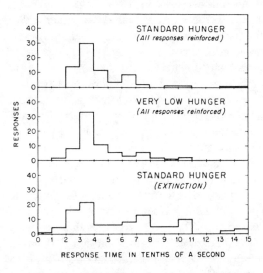

Figure 1

mentioned later, is likely to be in progress when the ready-signal is presented. It is often not discontinued before the "go" signal is presented, and the result is a long starting-time. Cases also begin to appear in which the bird simply does not respond at all during a specified time. If we average a large number of readings, either from one bird or many, we may create what looks like a progressive lengthening of latency. But the data for an individual organism do not show a continuous process.

Another datum to be examined is the rate at which a response is emitted. Fortunately the story here is different. We study this rate by designing a situation in which a response may be freely repeated, choosing a response (for example, touching or pressing a small lever or key) which may be easily observed and counted. The responses may be recorded on a polygraph, but a more convenient form is a cumulative curve from which rate of responding is immediately read as slope. The rate at which a response is emitted in such a situation comes close to our preconception of the learning process. As the organism learns, the rate rises. As it unlearns (for example, in extinction) the rate falls. Various sorts of discriminative stimuli may be brought into control of the response with corresponding modifications of the rate. Motivational changes alter the rate in a sensitive way. So do those events which we speak of as generating emotion. The range through which the rate varies significantly may be as great as of the order of 1000:1. Changes in rate are satisfactorily smooth in the individual case, so that it is not necessary to average cases. A given value is often quite stable: In the pigeon a rate of 4000 or 5000 responses per hour may be maintained without interruption for as long as 15 hours.

Rate of responding appears to be the only datum which varies significantly and in the expected direction under conditions which are relevant to the "learning process." We may, therefore, be tempted to accept it as our long-sought-for measure of strength of bond, excitatory potential, etc. Once in possession of an effective datum, however, we may feel little need for any theoretical construct of this sort. Progress in a scientific field usually waits upon the discovery of a satisfactory dependent variable. Until such a variable has been discovered, we resort to theory. The entities which have figured so prominently in learning theory have served mainly as substitutes for a directly observable and productive datum. They have little reason to survive when such a datum has been found.

It is no accident that rate of responding is successful as a datum because it is particularly appropriate to the fundamental task of a science of behavior. If we are to predict behavior (and possibly to control it), we must deal with *probability of response*. The business of a science of behavior is to evaluate this probability and explore the conditions which determine it. Strength of bond, expectancy, excitatory potential, and so on, carry the notion of probability in an easily imagined form, but the additional properties suggested by these terms have hindered the search for suitable measures. Rate of responding is not a "measure" of probability, but it is the only appropriate datum in a formulation in these terms.

As other scientific disciplines can attest, probabilities are not easy to handle. We wish to make statements about the likelihood of occurrence of a single future response, but our data are in the form of frequencies of responses which have already occurred. These responses were presumably similar to each other and to the response to be predicted. But this raises the troublesome problem of response-instance vs. response-class. Precisely what responses are we to take into account in predicting a future instance? Certainly not the responses made by a population of different organisms, for such a statistical datum raises more problems than it solves. To consider the frequency of repeated responses in an individual demands something like the experimental situation just described.

This solution of the problem of a basic datum is based upon the view that operant behavior is essentially an emissive phenomenon. Latency and magnitude of response fail as measures because they do not take this into account. They are concepts appropriate to the field of the reflex, where the all but invariable control exercised by the eliciting stimulus makes the notion of probability of response trivial. Consider, for example, the case of latency. Because of our acquaintance with simple reflexes we infer that a response which is more likely to be emitted will be emitted more quickly. But is this true? What can the word *quickly* mean? Probability of response, as well as prediction of response, is concerned with the moment of emission. This is a point in time, but it does not have the temporal dimension of a latency. The execution may take time after the response has been initiated, but the moment of occurrence has no duration.[2] In recognizing the emissive character of operant behavior and the central position of probability of response as a datum, latency is seen to be irrelevant to our present task.

Various objections have been made to the use of rate of responding as a basic datum. For example, such a program may seem to bar us from dealing with many events which are unique occurrences in the life of the individual. One does not decide upon a career, get married, make a million dollars, or get killed in an accident often enough to make a rate of response meaningful. But these activities are not responses. They are not simple unitary events lending themselves to prediction as such. If we are to predict marriage, success, accidents, and so on, in anything more than statistical terms, we must deal with the smaller units of behavior which lead to and compose these unitary episodes. If the units appear in repeatable form, the present analysis may be applied. In the field of learning a similar objection takes the form of asking how the present analysis may be extended to experimental situations in which it is impossible to observe frequencies. It does not follow that learning is not taking place in such situations. The notion of probability is usually extrapolated to cases in which a frequency analysis cannot be carried out. In the field of behavior we arrange a situation in which frequencies are available as data, but we use the notion of probability in analyzing and formulating instances or even types of behavior which are not susceptible to this analysis.

Another common objection is that a rate of response is just a set of latencies and hence not a new datum at all. This is easily shown to be wrong. When we measure the time elapsing between two responses, we are in no doubt as to what the organism was doing when we started our clock. We know that it was just executing a response. This is a natural zero—quite unlike the arbitrary point from which latencies are measured. The free repetition of a response yields a rhythmic or periodic datum very different from latency. Many periodic physical processes suggest parallels.

We do not choose rate of responding as a basic datum merely from an analysis of the fundamental task of a science of behavior. The ultimate appeal is to its success in an experimental science. The material which follows is offered as a sample of what can be done. It is not intended as a complete demonstration, but it should confirm the fact that when we are in possession of a datum which varies in a significant fashion, we are less likely to resort to theoretical entities carrying the notion of probability of response.

WHY LEARNING OCCURS

We may define learning as a change in probability of response, but we must also specify the conditions under which it comes about. To do this we must survey some of the independent variables of which probability of response is a function. Here we meet another kind of learning theory.

An effective classroom demonstration of the Law of Effect may be arranged in the following way. A pigeon, reduced to 80 percent of its *ad lib* weight, is habituated to a small, semicircular amphitheatre and is fed there for several days from a food hopper, which the experimenter presents by closing a hand switch. The demonstration consists of establishing a selected response by suitable reinforcement with food. For example, by sighting across the amphitheatre at a scale on the opposite wall, it is possible to present the hopper whenever the top of the pigeon's head rises above a given mark. Higher and higher marks are chosen until, within a few minutes, the pigeon is walking about the cage with its head held as high as possible. In another demonstration the bird is conditioned to strike a marble placed on the floor of the amphitheatre. This may be done in a few minutes by reinforcing successive steps. Food is presented first when the bird is merely moving near the marble, later when it looks down in the direction of the marble, later still when it moves its head toward the marble, and finally when it pecks it. Anyone who has seen such a demonstration knows that the Law of

Effect is no theory. It simply specifies a procedure for altering the probability of a chosen response.

But when we try to say *why* reinforcement has this effect, theories arise. Learning is said to take place because the reinforcement is pleasant, satisfying, tension reducing, and so on. The converse process of extinction is explained with comparable theories. If the rate of responding is first raised to a high point by reinforcement and reinforcement is then withheld, the response is observed to occur less and less frequently thereafter. One common theory explains this by asserting that a state is built up which suppresses the behavior. This "experimental inhibition" or "reaction inhibition" must be assigned to a different dimensional system, since nothing at the level of behavior corresponds to opposed processes of excitation and inhibition. Rate of responding is simply increased by one operation and decreased by another. Certain effects commonly interpreted as showing release from a suppressing force may be interpreted in other ways. Disinhibition, for example, is not necessarily the uncovering of suppressed strength: It may be a sign of supplementary strength from an extraneous variable. The process of spontaneous recovery, often cited to support the notion of suppression, has an alternative explanation, to be noted in a moment.

Let us evaluate the question of why learning takes place by turning again to some data. Since conditioning is usually too rapid to be easily followed, the process of extinction will provide us with a more useful case. A number of different types of curves have been consistently obtained from rats and pigeons using various schedules of prior reinforcement. By considering some of the relevant conditions we may see what room is left for theoretical processes.

The mere passage of time between conditioning and extinction is a variable which has surprisingly little effect. The rat is too short-lived to make an extended experiment feasible, but the pigeon, which may live 10 or 15 years, is an ideal subject. More than 5 years ago, 20 pigeons were conditioned to strike a large translucent key upon which a complex visual pattern was projected. Reinforcement was contingent upon the maintenance of a high and steady rate of responding and upon striking a particular feature of the visual pattern. These birds were set aside in order to study retention. They were transferred to the usual living quarters, where they served as breeders. Small groups were tested for extinction at the end of 6 months, 1 year, 2 years, and 4 years. Before the test each bird was transferred to a separate living cage. A controlled feeding schedule was used to reduce the weight to approximately 80 percent of the *ad lib* weight. The bird was then fed in the dimly lighted experimental apparatus in the absence of the key for several days, during which emotional responses to the apparatus disappeared. On the day of the test the bird was placed in the darkened box. The translucent key was present but not lighted. No responses were made. When the pattern was projected upon the key, each bird responded quickly and extensively. Figure 2 shows the largest curve obtained. This bird struck the key within 2 seconds after presentation of a visual pattern which it had not seen for 4 years, and at the precise spot upon which differential reinforcement had previously been based. It continued to respond for the next hour, emitting about 700 responses. This is of the order of one-half to one-quarter of the responses it would have emitted if extinction had not been delayed 4 years, but otherwise the curve is fairly typical.

Level of motivation is another variable to be taken into account. An example of the effect of hunger has been reported elsewhere.[3] The response of pressing a lever was established in eight rats with a schedule of periodic reinforcement. They were fed the main part of their ration on alternate days so that the rates of responding on successive days were alternately high and low. Two subgroups of four rats each were matched on the basis of the rate maintained under periodic reinforcement under these conditions. The response was then extinguished—in one group on alternate days when the hunger was high, in the other group on alternate days when the hunger was low. (The same amount of food was eaten on the nonexperimental days as before.) The result is shown in Figure 3. The upper graph gives the raw data. The levels of hunger are indicated by the points at P on the abscissa, the rates prevailing under periodic reinforcement. The subsequent points show the decline in extinction. If we multiply the lower curve through by a factor chosen to superimpose the points at P, the curves are reasonably closely superimposed, as shown in the lower graph. Several other experiments on both rats and pigeons have confirmed this general principle. If a given ratio of responding prevails under periodic reinforcement, the slopes of later extinction curves show the same ratio. Level of hunger determines the slope of the extinction curve but not its curvature.

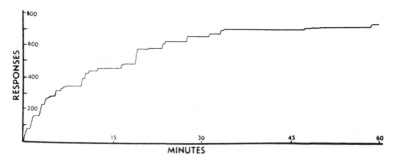

Figure 2

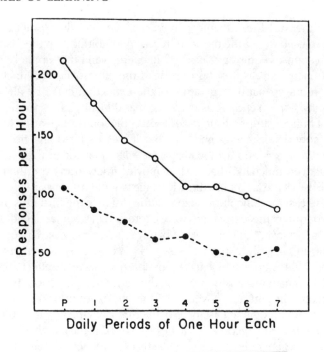

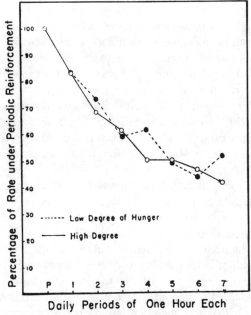

Figure 3

Another variable, difficulty of response, is especially relevant because it has been used to test the theory of reaction inhibition,[4] on the assumption that a response requiring considerable energy will build up more reaction inhibition than an easy response and lead, therefore, to faster extinction. The theory requires that the curvature of the extinction curve be altered, not merely its slope. Yet there is evidence that difficulty of response acts like level of hunger simply to alter the slope. A pigeon is suspended in a jacket which confines its wings and legs but leaves its head and neck free to respond to a key and a food magazine.[5] Its behavior in this situation is quantitatively much like that of a bird moving freely in an experimental box, but the use of the jacket has the advantage that the response to the key may be made easy or difficult by changing the distance the bird must reach. In one experiment these distances were expressed in seven equal but arbitrary units. At Distance 7 the bird could barely reach the key, at 3 it could strike without appreciably extending its neck. Periodic reinforcement gave a straight baseline upon which it was possible to observe the effect of difficulty by quickly changing position during the experimental period. Each of the five records in Figure 4 covers a 15-minute experimental period under periodic reinforcement. Distances of the bird from the key are indicated by numerals above the records. It will be observed that the rate of responding at Distance 7 is generally quite low while that at Distance 3 is high. Intermediate distances produce intermediate slopes. It should also be noted that the change from one position to another is felt immediately. If repeated responding in a difficult position were to build a considerable amount of reaction inhibition, we should expect the rate to be low for some little time after returning to an easy response. Contrariwise, if an easy response were to build little reaction inhibition, we should expect a fairly high rate of responding for some time after a difficult position is assumed. Nothing like this occurs. The "more rapid extinction" of a difficult response is an ambigious expression. The slope constant is affected and with it the number of responses in extinction to a criterion, but there may be no effect upon curvature.

One way of considering the question of why extinction curves are curved is to regard extinction as a process of exhaustion comparable to the loss of heat from source to sink or the fall in the level of a reservoir when an outlet is opened. Conditioning builds up a predisposition to respond—a "reserve"—which extinction exhausts. This is perhaps a defensible description at the level of behavior. The reserve is not necessarily a theory in the present sense, since it is not assigned to a different dimensional system. It could be operationally defined as a predicted extinction curve, even though, linguistically, it makes a statement about the momentary condition of a response. But it is not a particularly useful concept, nor does the view that

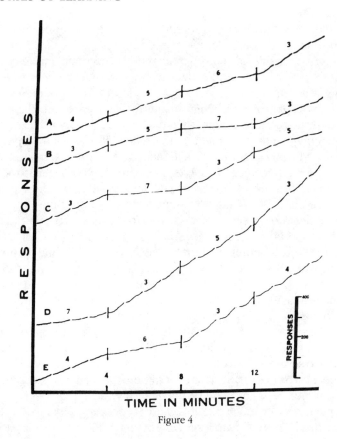

TIME IN MINUTES

Figure 4

extinction is a process of exhaustion add much to the observed fact that extinction curves are curved in a certain way.

There are, however, two variables which affect the rate, both of which operate during extinction to alter the curvature. One of these falls within the field of emotion. When we fail to reinforce a response which has previously been reinforced, we not only initiate a process of extinction, we set up an emotional response—perhaps what is often meant by frustration. The pigeon coos in an identifiable pattern, moves rapidly about the cage, defecates, or flaps its wings rapidly in a squatting position which suggests treading (mating) behavior. This competes with the response of striking a key and is perhaps enough to account for the decline in rate in early extinction. It is also possible that the probability of a response based upon food deprivation is directly reduced as part of such an emotional reaction. Whatever its nature, the effect of this variable is eliminated through adaptation. Repeated extinction curves become smoother, and in some of the schedules to be described shortly there is little or no evidence of an emotional modification of rate.

A second variable has a much more serious effect. Maximal responding during extinction is obtained only when the conditions under which the response was reinforced are precisely reproduced. A rat conditioned in the presence of a light will not extinguish fully in the absence of the light. It will begin to respond more rapidly when the light is again introduced. This is true for other kinds of stimuli, as the following classroom experiment illustrates. Nine pigeons were conditioned to strike a yellow triangle under intermittent reinforcement. In the session represented by Figure 5 the birds were first reinforced on this schedule for 30 minutes. The combined cumulative curve is essentially a straight line, showing more than 1100 responses per bird during this period. A red triangle was then substituted for the yellow and no responses were reinforced thereafter. The effect was a sharp drop in responding, with only a slight recovery during the next 15 minutes. When the yellow triangle was replaced, rapid responding began immediately, and the usual extinction curve followed. Similar experiments have shown that the pitch of an incidental tone, the shape of a pattern being struck, or the size of a pattern, if present during conditioning, will to some extent control the rate of responding during extinction. Some properties are more effective than others, and a quantitative evaluation is possible. By changing to several values of a stimulus in random order repeatedly during the extinction process, the gradient for stimulus generalization may be read directly in the rates of responding under each value.

Something very much like this must go on during extinction. Let us suppose that all responses to a key have been reinforced and that each has been followed by a short period of eating. When we extinguish the behavior, we create a situation in which responses are not reinforced, in which no eating takes place, and in which there are probably new emotional responses. The situation could easily be as novel as a red triangle after a yellow. If so, it could explain the decline in rate during extinction. We might have obtained a smooth curve, *shaped like an extinction curve,* between the vertical lines in Figure 5 by *gradually* changing the color of the triangle from yellow to red. This might have happened even though no other sort of extinction were taking place. The very conditions of extinction seem to presuppose a growing novelty in the experimental situation. Is this why the extinction curve is curved?

Some evidence comes from the data of "spontaneous recovery." Even after prolonged extinction an organism will often respond at a higher rate for at least a few moments at the beginning of another session. One theory contends that this shows spontaneous recovery from some sort of inhibition, but another explanation is possible. No matter how carefully an animal is

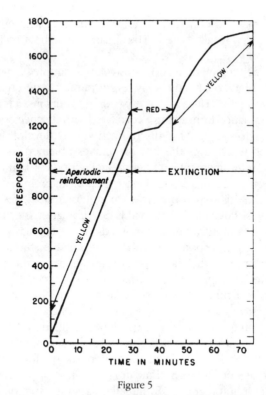

Figure 5

handled, the stimulation coincident with the beginning of an experiment must be extensive and unlike anything occurring in the later part of an experimental period. Responses have been reinforced in the presence of, or shortly following, this stimulation. In extinction it is present for only a few moments. When the organism is again placed in the experimental situation the stimulation is restored; further responses are emitted as in the case of the yellow triangle. The only way to achieve full extinction in the presence of the stimulation of starting an experiment is to start the experiment repeatedly.

Other evidence of the effect of novelty comes from the study of periodic reinforcement. The fact that intermittent reinforcement produces bigger extinction curves than continuous reinforcement is a troublesome difficulty for those who expect a simple relation between number of reinforcements and number of responses in extinction. But this relation is actually quite complex. One result of periodic reinforcement is that emotional changes adapt out. This may be responsible for the smoothness of subsequent extinction curves but probably not for their greater extent. The latter may be attributed to the lack of novelty in the extinction situation. Under periodic reinforcement many responses are made without reinforcement and when no eating has recently taken place. The situation in extinction is therefore not wholly novel.

Periodic reinforcement is not, however, a simple solution. If we reinforce on a regular schedule—say, every minute—the organism soon forms a discrimination. Little or no responding occurs just after reinforcement, since stimulation from eating is correlated with absence of subsequent reinforcement. How rapidly the discrimination may develop is shown in Figure 6, which reproduces the first five curves obtained from a pigeon under periodic reinforcement in experimental periods of 15 minutes each. In the fifth period (or after about 1 hour of periodic reinforcement) the discrimination yields a pause after each reinforcement, resulting in a markedly stepwise curve. As a result of this discrimination the bird is almost always responding rapidly when reinforced. This is the basis for another discrimination. Rapid responding becomes a favorable stimulating condition. A good example of the effect upon the subsequent extinction curve is shown in Figure 7. This pigeon's pecks had been reinforced once every minute during daily experimental periods of 15 minutes each for several weeks. In the extinction curve shown, the bird begins to respond at the rate prevailing under the preceding schedule. A quick positive acceleration at the start is lost in the reduction of the record. The pigeon quickly reaches and sustains a rate which is higher than the overall rate during periodic reinforcement. During this period the pigeon creates a stimulating condition previously optimally correlated with reinforcement. Eventually, as some sort of exhaustion intervenes, the rate falls off rapidly to a much lower but fairly stable value and then to practically zero. A condition then prevails under which a response is

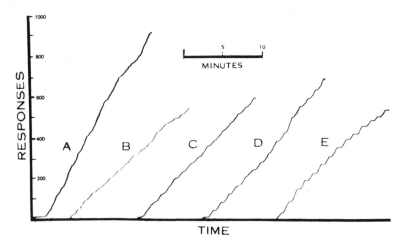

Figure 6

not normally reinforced. The bird is therefore not likely to begin to respond again. When it does respond, however, the situation is slightly improved and, if it continues to respond, the conditions rapidly become similar to those under which reinforcement has been received. Under this "autocatalysis" a high rate is quickly reached, and more than 500 responses are emitted in a second burst. The rate then declines quickly and fairly smoothly, again to nearly zero. This curve is not by any means disorderly. Most of the curvature is smooth. But the burst of responding at 45 minutes shows a considerable residual strength which, if extinction were merely exhaustion, should have appeared earlier in the curve. The curve may be reasonably accounted for by assuming that the bird is largely controlled by the preceding spurious correlation between reinforcement and rapid responding.

This assumption may be checked by constructing a schedule of reinforcement in which a differential contingency between rate of responding and reinforcement is impossible. In one such schedule of what may be called "aperiodic reinforcement" one interval between successive reinforced responses is so short that no unreinforced responses intervene, while the longest interval is about 2 minutes.[6] Other intervals are distributed arithmetically between these values, the average remaining 1 minute. The intervals are roughly randomized to compose a program of reinforcement. Under this program the probability of reinforcement does not change with respect to previous reinforcements, and the curves never acquire the stepwise character of Curve E in Figure 6. (Figure 9 shows curves from a similar program.) As a result no correlation between different rates of responding and different probabilities of reinforcement can develop.

An extinction curve following a brief exposure to aperiodic reinforcement is shown in Figure 8. It begins characteristically at the rate prevailing under aperiodic reinforcement and, unlike the curve following regular

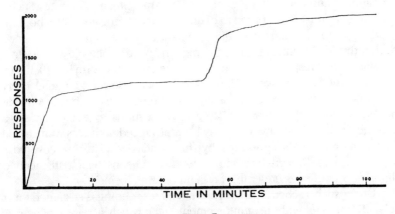

Figure 7

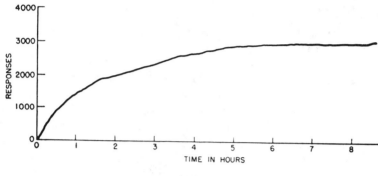

Figure 8

periodic reinforcement, does not accelerate to a higher overall rate. There is no evidence of the "autocatalytic" production of an optimal stimulating condition. Also characteristically, there are no significant discontinuities or sudden changes in rate in either direction. The curve extends over a period of 8 hours, as against not quite 2 hours in Figure 7, and seems to represent a single orderly process. The total number of responses is higher, perhaps because of the greater time allowed for emission. All of this can be explained by the single fact that we have made it impossible for the pigeon to form a pair of discriminations based, first, upon stimulation from eating and, second, upon stimulation from rapid responding.

Since the longest interval between reinforcement was only 2 minutes, a certain novelty must still have been introduced as time passed. Whether this explains the curvature in Figure 8 may be tested to some extent with other programs of reinforcement containing much longer intervals. A geometric progression was constructed by beginning with 10 seconds as the shortest interval and repeatedly multiplying by 1.54. This yielded a set of intervals averaging 5 minutes, the longest of which was more than 21 minutes. Such a set was randomized in a program of reinforcement repeated every hour. In changing to this program from the arithmetic series, the rates first declined during the longer intervals, but the pigeons were soon able to sustain a constant rate of responding under it. Two records in the form in which they were recorded are shown in Figure 9. (The pen resets to zero after every thousand responses. In order to obtain a single cumulative curve it would be necessary to cut the record and piece the sections together to yield a continuous line. The raw form may be reproduced with less reduction.) Each reinforcement is represented by a horizontal dash. The time covered is about 3 hours. Records are shown for two pigeons which maintained different overall rates under this program of reinforcement.

Under such a schedule a constant rate of responding is sustained for at least 21 minutes without reinforcement, after which a reinforcement is

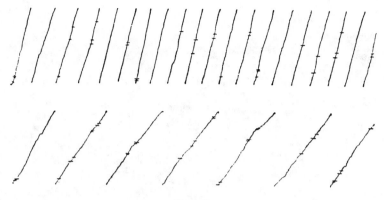

Figure 9

received. Less novelty should therefore develop during succeeding extinction. In Curve 1 of Figure 10 the pigeon had been exposed to several sessions of several hours each with this geometric set of intervals. The number of responses emitted in extinction is about twice that of the curve in Figure 8 after the arithmetic set of intervals averaging 1 minute, but the curves are otherwise much alike. Further exposure to the geometric schedule builds up longer runs during which the rate does not change significantly. Curve 2 followed Curve 1 after 2½ hours of further aperiodic reinforcement. On the day shown in Curve 2 a few aperiodic reinforcements were first given, as marked at the beginning of the curve. When reinforcement was discontinued, a fairly constant rate of responding prevailed for several thousand responses. After another experimental session of 2½ hours with the geometric series, Curve 3 was recorded. This session also began with a short series of aperiodic reinforcements, followed by a sustained run of more than 6000 unreinforced responses with little change in rate (A). There seems to be no reason why other series averaging perhaps more than 5 minutes per interval and containing much longer exceptional intervals would not carry such a straight line much further.

In this attack upon the problem of extinction we create a schedule of reinforcement which is so much like the conditions which will prevail during extinction that no decline in rate takes place for a long time. In other words we generate extinction with no curvature. Eventually some kind of exhaustion sets in, but it is not approached gradually. The last part of Curve 3 (unfortunately much reduced in the figure) may possibly suggest exhaustion in the slight overall curvature, but it is a small part of the whole process. The record is composed mainly of runs of a few hundred responses each, most of them at approximately the same rate as that maintained under periodic reinforcement. The pigeon stops abruptly; when it starts to respond again, it quickly reaches the rate of responding under which it was

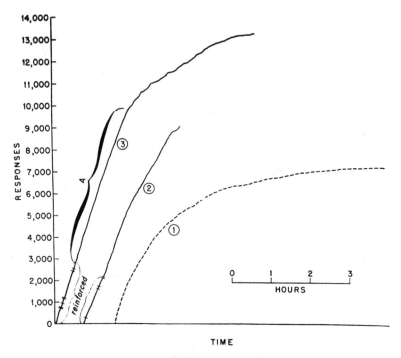

Figure 10

reinforced. This recalls the spurious correlation between rapid responding and reinforcement under regular reinforcement. We have not, of course, entirely eliminated this correlation. Even though there is no longer a differential reinforcement of high against low rates, practically all reinforcements have occurred under a constant rate of responding.

Further study of reinforcing schedules may or may not answer the question of whether the novelty appearing in the extinction situation is entirely responsible for the curvature. It would appear to be necessary to make the conditions prevailing during extinction identical with the conditions prevailing during conditioning. This may be impossible, but in that case the question is academic. The hypothesis, meanwhile, is not a theory in the present sense, since it makes no statements about a parallel process in any other universe of discourse.

It is true that it appeals to stimulation generated in part by the pigeon's own behavior. This may be difficult to specify or manipulate, but it is not theoretical in the present sense. So long as we are willing to assume a one-to-one correspondence between action and stimulation, a physical specification is possible.

The study of extinction after different schedules of aperiodic reinforcement is not addressed wholly to this hypothesis. The object is an economical description of the conditions prevailing during reinforcement and extinction and of the relations between them. In using rate of responding as a basic datum we may appeal to conditions which are observable and manipulable and we may express the relations between them in objective terms. To the extent that our datum makes this possible, it reduces the need for theory. When we observe a pigeon emitting 7000 responses at a constant rate without reinforcement, we are not likely to explain an extinction curve containing perhaps a few hundred responses by appeal to the piling up of reaction inhibition or any other fatigue product. Research which is conducted without commitment to theory is more likely to carry the study of extinction into new areas and new orders of magnitude. By hastening the accumulation of data, we speed the departure of theories. If the theories have played no part in the design of our experiments, we need not be sorry to see them go.

COMPLEX LEARNING

A third type of learning theory is illustrated by terms like *preferring, choosing, discriminating,* and *matching.* An effort may be made to define these solely in terms of behavior, but in traditional practice they refer to processes in another dimensional system. A response to one of two available stimuli may be called choice, but it is commoner to say that it is the result of choice, meaning by the latter a theoretical pre-behavioral activity. The higher mental processes are the best examples of theories of this sort; neurological parallels have not been well worked out. The appeal to theory is encouraged by the fact that choosing (like discriminating, matching, and so on) is not a particular piece of behavior. It is not a response or an act with specified topography. The term characterizes a larger segment of behavior in relation to other variables or events. Can we formulate and study the behavior to which these terms would usually be applied without recourse to the theories which generally accompany them?

Discrimination is a relatively simple case. Suppose we find that the probability of emission of a given response is not significantly affected by changing from one of two stimuli to the other. We then make reinforcement of the response contingent upon the presence of one of them. The well-established result is that the probability of response remains high under this stimulus and reaches a very low point under the other. We say that the organism now discriminates between the stimuli. But discrimination is not itself an action, or necessarily even a unique process. Problems in the field of discrimination may be stated in other terms. How much induction obtains between stimuli of different magnitudes or classes? What are the smallest differences in stimuli which yield a difference in control? And so on. Questions of this sort do not presuppose theoretical activities in other dimensional systems.

A somewhat larger segment must be specified in dealing with the behavior of choosing one of two concurrent stimuli. This has been studied in the pigeon by examining responses to two keys differing in position (right or left) or in some property like color randomized with respect to position. By occasionally reinforcing a response on one key or the other without favoring either key, we obtain equal rates of responding on the two keys. The behavior approaches a simple alternation from one key to the other. This follows the rule that tendencies to respond eventually correspond to the probabilities of reinforcement. Given a system in which one key or the other is occasionally connected with the magazine by an external clock, then if the right key has just been struck, the probability of reinforcement via the left key is higher than that via the right since a greater interval of time has elapsed during which the clock may have closed the circuit to the left key. But the bird's behavior does not correspond to this probability merely out of respect for mathematics. The specific result of such a contingency of reinforcement is that changing-to-the-other-key-and-striking is more often reinforced than striking-the-same-key-a-second-time. We are no longer dealing with just two responses. In order to analyze "choice" we must consider a single final response, striking, without respect to the position or color of the key, and in addition the responses of changing from one key or color to the other.

Quantitative results are compatible with this analysis. If we periodically reinforce responses to the right key only, the rate of responding on the right will rise while that on the left will fall. The response of changing-from-right-to-left is never reinforced while the response of changing-from-left-to-right is occasionally so. When the bird is striking on the right, there is no great tendency to change keys; when it is striking on the left, there is a strong tendency to change. Many more responses come to be made to the right key. The need for considering the behavior of changing over is clearly shown if we now reverse these conditions and reinforce responses to the left key only. The ultimate result is a high rate of responding on the left key and a low rate on the right. By reversing the conditions again the high rate can be shifted back to the right key. In Figure 11 a group of eight curves has been averaged to follow this change during six experimental periods of 45 minutes each. Beginning on the second day in the graph responses to the right key (R^R) decline in extinction while responses to the left key (R^L) increase through periodic reinforcement. The mean rate shows no significant variation, since periodic reinforcement is continued on the same schedule. The mean rate shows the condition of strength of the response of striking a key regardless of position. The distribution of responses between right and left depends upon the relative strength of the responses of changing over. If this were simply a case of the extinction of one response and the concurrent reconditioning of another, the mean curve would not remain approximately horizontal since reconditioning occurs much more rapidly than extinction. (Two topographically independent responses, capable of emission at the same time and hence not requiring changeover, show separate processes of reconditioning and extinction, and the combined rate of responding varies.)

The rate with which the bird changes from one key to the other depends upon the distance between the keys. This distance is a rough measure of the stimulus-difference between the two keys. It also determines the scope of the response of changing over, with an implied difference in sensory feedback. It also modifies the spread of reinforcement to responses supposedly not reinforced, since if the keys are close together, a response reinforced on one side may occur sooner after a preceding response on the other side. In Figure 11 the two keys were about 1 inch apart. They were therefore fairly similar with respect to position in the experimental box. Changing from one to the other involved a minimum of sensory feedback, and reinforcement of a response to one key could follow very shortly upon a response to the other. When the keys are separated by as much as 4 inches, the change in strength is much more rapid. Figure 12 shows two curves recorded simultaneously from a single pigeon during one experimental period of about 40 minutes. A high rate to the right key and a low rate to the left had previously been established. In the figure no responses to the

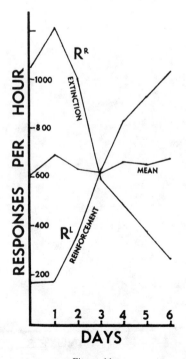

Figure 11

right were reinforced, but those to the left were reinforced every 2 minutes as indicated by the vertical dashes above curve L. The slope of R declines in a fairly smooth fashion while that of L increases, also fairly smoothly, to a value comparable to the initial value of R. The bird has conformed to the changed contingency within a single experimental period. The mean rate of responding is shown by a dotted line, which again shows no significant curvature.

What is called "preference" enters into this formulation. At any stage of the process shown in Figure 12 preference might be expressed in terms of the relative rates of responding to the two keys. This preference, however, is not in striking a key but in changing from one key to the other. The probability that the bird will strike a key regardless of its identifying properties behaves independently of the preferential response of changing from one key to the other. Several experiments have revealed an additional fact. A preference remains fixed if reinforcement is withheld. Figure 13 is an example. It shows simultaneous extinction curves from two keys during seven daily experimental periods of 1 hour each. Prior to extinction the relative strength of the responses of changing-to-R and changing-to-L yielded a "preference" of about 3 to 1 for R. The constancy of the rate throughout the process of extinction has been shown in the figure by multiplying L through

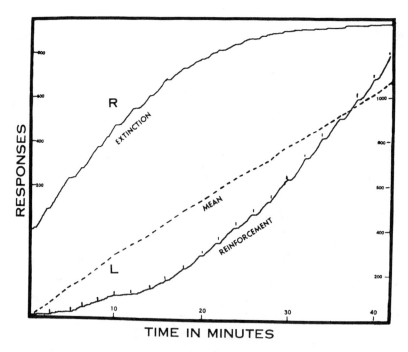

TIME IN MINUTES

Figure 12

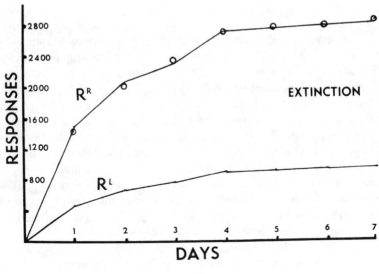

Figure 13

by a suitable constant and entering the points as small circles on R. If extinction altered the preference, the two curves could not be superimposed in this way.

These formulations of discrimination and choosing enable us to deal with what is generally regarded as a much more complex process—matching to sample. Suppose we arrange three translucent keys, each of which may be illuminated with red or green light. The middle key functions as the sample, and we color it either red or green in random order. We color the two side keys one red and one green, also in random order. The "problem" is to strike the side key which corresponds in color to the middle key. There are only four three-key patterns in such a case, and it is possible that a pigeon could learn to make an appropriate response to each pattern. This does not happen, at least within the temporal span of the experiments to date. If we simply present a series of settings of the three colors and reinforce successful responses, the pigeon will strike the side keys without respect to color or pattern and be reinforced 50 percent of the time. This is, in effect, a schedule of "fixed ratio" reinforcement which is adequate to maintain a high rate of responding.

Nevertheless it is possible to get a pigeon to match to sample by reinforcing the discriminative responses of striking-red-after-being-stimulated-by-red and striking-green-after-being-stimulated-by-green while extinguishing the other two possibilities. The difficulty is in arranging the proper stimulation at the time of the response. The sample might be made conspicious—for example, by having the sample color in the general illumination of the experimental box. In such a case the pigeon would learn to strike red keys in a red light and green keys in a green light (assuming a neutral illumination of the background of the keys). But a procedure which holds more closely to the notion of matching is to induce the pigeon to "look at the sample" by means of a separate reinforcement. We may do this by presenting the color on the middle key first, leaving the side keys uncolored. A response to the middle key is then reinforced (secondarily) by illuminating the side keys. The pigeon learns to make two responses in quick succession—to the middle key and then to one side key. The response to the side key follows quickly upon the visual stimulation from the middle key, which is the requisite condition for a discrimination. Successful matching was readily established in all 10 pigeons tested with this technique. Choosing the opposite is also easily set up. The discriminative response of striking-red-after-being-stimulated-by-red is apparently no easier to establish than striking-red-after-being-stimulated-by-green. When the response is to a key of the same color, however, generalization may make it possible for the bird to match a new color. This is an extension of the notion of matching which has not yet been studied with this method.

Even when matching behavior has been well established, the bird will not respond correctly if all three keys are now presented at the same time. The bird does not possess strong behavior of looking at the sample. The experimenter must maintain a separate reinforcement to keep this behavior in strength. In monkeys, apes, and human subjects the ultimate success in choosing is apparently sufficient to reinforce and maintain the behavior of looking at the sample. It is possible that this species difference is simply a difference in the temporal relations required for reinforcement.

The behavior of matching survives unchanged when all reinforcement is withheld. An intermediate case has been established in which the correct matching response is only periodically reinforced. In one experiment one color appeared on the middle key for 1 minute; it was then changed or not changed, at random, to the other color. A response to this key illuminated the side keys, one red and one green, in random order. A response to a side key cut off the illumination to both side keys until the middle key had again been struck. The apparatus recorded all matching responses on one graph and all nonmatching on another. Pigeons which have acquired matching behavior under continuous reinforcement have maintained this behavior when reinforced no oftener than once per minute on the average. They may make thousands of matching responses per hour while being reinforced for no more than 60 of them. This schedule will not necessarily develop matching behavior in a naive bird, for the problem can be solved in three ways. The bird will receive practically as many reinforcements if it responds to (1) only one key or (2) only one color, since the programming of the experiment makes any persistent response eventually the correct one.

A sample of the data obtained in a complex experiment of this sort is given in Figure 14. Although this pigeon had learned to match color under continuous reinforcement, it changed to the spurious solution of a color preference under periodic reinforcement. Whenever the sample was red, it struck both the sample and the red side key and received all reinforcements. When the sample was green, it did not respond and the side keys were not illuminated. The result shown at the beginning of the graph in Figure 14 is a high rate of responding on the upper graph, which records matching responses. (The record is actually step-wise, following the presence or absence of the red sample, but this is lost in the reduction in the figure.) A color preference, however, is not a solution to the problem of opposites. By changing to this problem, it was possible to change the bird's behavior as shown between the two vertical lines in the figure. The upper curve between these lines shows the decline in matching responses which had resulted from the color preference. The lower curve between the same lines shows the development of responding to and matching the opposite color. At the second vertical line the reinforcement was again made contingent upon matching. The upper curve shows the reestablishment of matching behavior while the lower curve shows a decline in striking the opposite color. The

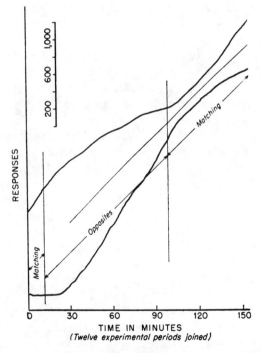

Figure 14

result was a true solution: The pigeon struck the sample, no matter what its color, and then the corresonding side key. The lighter line connects the means of a series of points on the two curves. It seems to follow the same rule as in the case of choosing: Changes in the distribution of responses between two keys do not involve the overall rate of responding to a key. This mean rate will not remain constant under the spurious solution achieved with a color preference, as at the beginning of this figure.

These experiments on a few higher processes have necessarily been very briefly described. They are not offered as proving that theories of learning are not necessary, but they may suggest an alternative program in this difficult area. The data in the field of the higher mental processes transcend single responses or single stimulus-response relationships. But they appear to be susceptible to formulation in terms of the differentiation of concurrent responses, the discrimination of stimuli, the establishment of various sequences of responses, and so on. There seems to be no a priori reason why a complete account is not possible without appeal to theoretical processes in other dimensional systems.

CONCLUSION

Perhaps to do without theories altogether is a *tour de force* which is too much to expect as a general practice. Theories are fun. But it is possible that the most rapid progress toward an understanding of learning may be made by research which is not designed to test theories. An adequate impetus is supplied by the inclination to obtain data showing orderly changes characteristic of the learning process. An acceptable scientific program is to collect data of this sort and to relate them to manipulable variables, selected for study through a common-sense exploration of the field.

This does not exclude the possibility of theory in another sense. Beyond the collection of uniform relationships lies the need for a formal representation of the data reduced to a minimal number of terms. A theoretical construction may yield greater generality than any assemblage of facts. But such a construction will not refer to another dimensional system and will not, therefore, fall within our present definition. It will not stand in the way of our search for functional relations because it will arise only after relevant variables have been found and studied. Though it may be difficult to understand, it will not be easily misunderstood, and it will have none of the objectionable effects of the theories here considered.

We do not seem to be ready for theory in this sense. At the moment we make little effective use of empirical, let alone rational, equations. A few of the present curves could have been fairly closely fitted. But the most elementary preliminary research shows that there are many relevant variables, and until their importance has been experimentally determined, an equation which allows for them will have so many arbitrary constants that a good fit will be a matter of course and cause for very little satisfaction.

REFERENCES AND NOTES

[1]An experiment on "differential reinforcement with respect to time" was reported at a meeting of the American Psychological Association, September, 1946. An abstract appears in the *American Psychologist*, 1946, *1*, 274-275.

[2]It cannot, in fact, be shortened or lengthened. Where a latency appears to be forced toward a minimal value by differential reinforcement, another interpretation is called for. Although we may differentially reinforce more energetic behavior or the faster execution of behavior after it begins, it is meaningless to speak of differentially reinforcing responses with short or long latencies. What we actually reinforce differentially are (a) favorable waiting behavior and (b) more vigorous responses. In a human reaction-time experiment, to respond "as soon as possible" is essentially (a) to carry out as much of the response as possible without actually reaching the criterion of emission, (b) to do as little else as possible, and (c) to respond energetically after the stimulus has been given. This may yield a minimal measurable time between stimulus and response, but this time is not necessarily a basic datum nor have our instructions altered it as such. A parallel interpretation of the differential reinforcement of long "latencies" is required. This is easily established by inspection. In the experiments with pigeons previously cited, preliminary behavior is conditioned which postpones the response to the key until the proper time. Behavior which "marks time" is usually conspicuous.

[3]The experiment from which the following data are taken was reported at a meeting of the American Psychological Association, September, 1940. An abstract appears in the *Psychological Bulletin*, 1940, *37*, 423.

[4]Mowrer, O.H., & Jones, H.M. Extinction and behavior variability as functions of effortfulness of task. *Journal of Experimental Psychology*, 1943, *33*, 369-386.

[5]This experiment was reported at a meeting of the Midwestern Psychological Association, March, 1946. An abstract appears in the *American Psychologist*, 1946, *1*, 462.

[6]What is called "periodic reinforcement" in this paper has since come to be known as "fixed-interval reinforcement" and "aperiodic" as "variable-interval." (See *Schedules of Reinforcement.*)

POSTSCRIPT

My title was suggested by a book by James Thurber and E.B. White called "Is Sex Necessary?" One could hardly answer No, as much as one might at times be inclined to do so. The paper defined the kind of theory I was questioning as "any explanation of an observed fact which appeals to events taking place somewhere else, at some other level of observation, described in different terms, and measured, if at all, in different dimensions." I had in mind physiological and mental theories. Those who knew the paper only by title assumed that I meant all theory, and I was soon called "a Grand Antitheoretician."

I gave the paper as a Presidential Address at a meeting of the Midwestern Psychological Association and took the occasion to report previously unpublished research. Some of it was done with my colleagues, Keller Breland and Norman Guttman, on Project Pigeon (see Chapter 12); some at Indiana, when I was much too busy being chairman to spend much time in the laboratory; and some during my first year at Harvard in 1948.

The point of the paper is simple enough: We want to believe that there are orderly learning processes. We average our data to get smooth curves, but we cannot conceal the fact that the individual organism is not behaving in a very orderly way. We therefore invent orderly learning processes which we locate in the nervous system or the mind. By contrast, the data of an experimental analysis of behavior are orderly enough to make an appeal to a theory for that purpose unnecessary.

C H A P T E R 2

A Case History in Scientific Method

EDITOR'S NOTE

The article was first published in *American Psychologist* (1956, *11*, 221-233) and has been republished in *Psychology: A Study of a Science* (Vol. 2), edited by Sigmund Koch (New York: McGraw-Hill, 1959, pp. 359-379), all editions of *Cumulative Record,* and elsewhere. It was unique in 1956 in at least three respects: It was Skinner's first autobiographical publication; it gave the public a glimpse of Skinner's wit; and it traced for the first time the early history of operant psychology.

It begins with an indictment of "formal reconstructions" of scientific method and then traces the rather circuitous route by which Skinner's own discoveries occurred. As a new graduate student at Harvard in 1928, Skinner, a gifted tinkerer, rapidly designed, built, modified, and discarded one piece of apparatus after another in a search for order in behavior. He first built a silent release box to study the way a rat adapted to a novel stimulus. As the rat would emerge from the box Skinner would sound a click, the rat would retreat, and Skinner would record how long it took for the rat to reemerge. Skinner reports: "The major result of this experiment was that some of my rats had babies." He abandoned the box and began to study postural reflexes in baby rats. Several uninteresting experiments and pieces of apparatus later, Skinner was recording the pattern of vibrations made when a rat was startled by a click during a run down an 8-foot wooden runway. Eventually, to save himself the trouble of replacing the rat at the beginning of the runway, he added a back alley. At the end of the runway the rat would find some food and then return to the beginning of the runway through the alley. Skinner noted that the pauses after the rat ate changed in an orderly fashion as a function of how much it had eaten; he dropped his previous investigation to study this effect alone. He built a new apparatus in which the rat dispensed its own food by completing one run around the course (Figure 8 in the article). This is the precursor to what is now commonly called the "Skinner box."

Eventually, Skinner saw that the runway was unnecessary. The rat was placed in a small chamber and could obtain food by pushing open a door. The apparatus and first results are described in Skinner's first substantive publication ("On the Conditions of Elicitation of Certain Eating Reflexes," 1930). A lever soon took the place of the door (see "Drive and Reflex Strength: II," 1932). This apparatus, modified to suit the animal and topic being studied, has become one of psychology's most popular laboratory instruments.

Skinner enumerates four informal and rather unconventional "principles" of scientific method that led him to his discoveries: (1) "When you run onto something interesting, drop everything else and study it." (2) "Some ways of doing research are easier than others." (3) "Some people are lucky." (4) "Apparatuses sometimes break down."

In the latter half of the article Skinner discusses some of the more important events in his early career (for example, the publication of his first book, *The Behavior of Organisms*) and some of the major research findings of a number of his students and colleagues. The end of the article includes the famous Columbia *Jester* cartoon and a notable passage from *Walden Two*.

Skinner's early scientific career is further elaborated in *The Shaping of a Behaviorist* (1979).

It has been said that college teaching is the only profession for which there is no professional training, and it is commonly argued that this is because our graduate schools train scholars and scientists rather than teachers. We are more concerned with the discovery of knowledge than with its dissemination. But can we justify ourselves quite so easily? It is a bold thing to say that we know how to train a person to be a scientist. Scientific thinking is the most complex and probably the most subtle of all human activities. Do we actually know how to shape up such behavior, or do we simply mean that some of the people who attend our graduate schools eventually become scientists?

Except for a laboratory course which acquaints the student with standard apparatus and standard procedures, the only explicit training in scientific method generally received by a young psychologist is a course in statistics— not the introductory course, which is often required of so many kinds of students that it is scarcely scientific at all, but an advanced course which includes "model building," "theory construction," and "experimental design." But it is a mistake to identify scientific practice with the formalized constructions of statistics and scientific method. These disciplines have their place, but it does not coincide with the place of scientific research. They offer *a* method of science but not, as is so often implied, *the* method. As formal disciplines they arose very late in the history of science, and most of the facts of science have been discovered without their aid. It takes a great deal of skill to fit Faraday with his wires and magnets into the picture which statistics gives us of scientific thinking. And most current scientific practice would be equally refractory, especially in the important initial stages. It is no wonder that laboratory scientists are puzzled and often dismayed when they discover how their behavior has been reconstructed in the formal analyses of scientific method. They are likely to protest that this is not at all a fair representation of what they do.

But their protest is not likely to be heard. For the prestige of statistics and scientific methodology is enormous. Much of it is borrowed from the high repute of mathematics and logic, but much of it derives from the flourishing state of the art itself. Some statisticians are professional people employed by scientific and commercial enterprises. Some are teachers and pure researchers who give their colleagues the same kind of service for nothing—or at most a note of acknowledgment. Many are zealous people who, with the best of intentions, are anxious to show nonstatistical scientists how they can do their job more efficiently and assess their results more accurately. There are strong professional societies devoted to the advancement of statistics, and hundreds of technical books and journals are published annually.

Against this, practicing scientists have very little to offer. They cannot refer young psychologists to a book which will tell them how to find out all there is to know about a subject matter, how to have the good hunch which will lead them to devise a suitable piece of apparatus, how to develop an efficient experimental routine, how to abandon an unprofitable line of attack, how to move on most rapidly to later stages of their research. The work habits which have become second nature to them have not been formalized by anyone, and they may feel that they possibly never will be. As Richter[1] has pointed out, "Some of the most important discoveries have been made without any plan of research" (p. 91), and "there are researchers who do not work on a verbal plane, who cannot put into words what they are doing" (p. 92).

If we are interested in perpetuating the practices responsible for the present corpus of scientific knowledge, we must keep in mind that some very important parts of the scientific process do not now lend themselves to mathematical, logical, or any other formal treatment. We do not know enough about human behavior to know how scientists do what they do. Although statisticians and methodologists may seem to tell us, or at least imply, how the mind works—how problems arise, how hypotheses are formed, deductions made, and crucial experiments designed—we as psychologists are in a position to remind them that they do not have methods appropriate to the empirical observation or the functional analysis of such data. These are aspects of human behavior, and no one knows better than we how little can at the moment be said about them.

Some day we shall be better able to express the distinction between empirical analysis and formal reconstruction, for we shall have an alternative account of the behavior of Man Thinking. Such an account will not only plausibly reconstruct what a particular scientist did in any given case, it will permit us to evaluate practices and, I believe, to teach scientific thinking. But that day is some little distance in the future. Meanwhile we can only fall back on examples.

When the director of Project A of the American Psychological Association asked me to describe and analyze my activities as a research psychologist, I went through a trunkful of old notes and records and, for my pains, reread some of my earlier publications. This has made me all the more aware of the contrast between the reconstructions of formalized scientific method and at least one case of actual practice. Instead of amplifying the points I have just made by resorting to a generalized account (principally because it is not available), I should like to discuss a case history. It is not one of the case histories we should most like to have, but what it lacks in importance is perhaps somewhat offset by accessibility. I therefore ask you to imagine that you are all clinical psychologists—a task which becomes easier and easier as the years go by—while I sit across the desk from you or stretch out upon this comfortable leather couch.

The first thing I can remember happened when I was only 22 years old. Shortly after I was graduated from college Bertrand Russell published a series of articles in the old *Dial* magazine on the epistemology of John B. Watson's behaviorism. I had had no psychology as an undergraduate but I had had a lot of biology, and two of the books which my biology professor had put into my hands were Loeb's *Physiology of the Brain* and the newly published Oxford edition of Pavlov's *Conditioned Reflexes*. And now here was Russell extrapolating the principles of an objective formulation of behavior to the problem of knowledge! Many years later when I told Lord Russell that his articles were responsible for my interest in behavior, he could only exclaim, "Good heavens! I had always supposed that those articles had demolished behaviorism!" But at any rate he had taken Watson seriously, and so did I.

When I arrived at Harvard for graduate study, the air was not exactly full of behavior, but Walter Hunter was coming in once a week from Clark University to give a seminar, and Fred Keller, also a graduate student, was an expert in both the technical details and the sophistry of behaviorism. Many a time he saved me as I sank into the quicksands of an amateurish discussion of "What is an image?" or "Where is red?" I soon came into contact with W.J. Crozier, who had studied under Loeb. It had been said of Loeb, and might have been said of Crozier, that he "resented the nervous system." Whether this was true or not, the fact was that both these men talked about animal behavior without mentioning the nervous system and with surprising success. So far as I was concerned, they canceled out the physiological theorizing of Pavlov and Sherrington and thus clarified what remained of the work of these men as the beginnings of an independent science of behavior. My doctoral thesis was in part an operational analysis of Sherrington's synapse, in which behavioral laws were substituted for supposed states of the central nervous system.

But the part of my thesis at issue here was experimental. So far as I can see, I began simply by looking for lawful processes in the behavior of the intact organism. Pavlov had shown the way; but I could not then, as I cannot now, move without a jolt from salivary reflexes to the important business of the organism in everyday life. Sherrington and Magnus had found order in surgical segments of the organism. Could not something of the same sort be found, to use Loeb's phrase, in "the organism as a whole"? I had the clue from Pavlov: Control your conditions and you will see order.

It is not surprising that my first gadget was a silent release box, operated by compressed air and designed to eliminate disturbances when introducing a rat into an apparatus. I used this first in studying the way a rat adapted to a novel stimulus. I built a soundproofed box containing a specially structured space. A rat was released, pneumatically, at the far end of a darkened tunnel from which it emerged in exploratory fashion into a well-lighted area. To accentuate its progress and to facilitate recording, the tunnel was placed at the top of a flight of steps, something like a functional Parthenon (Figure 1).

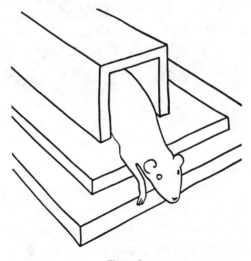

Figure 1

The rat would peek out from the tunnel, perhaps glancing suspiciously at the one-way window through which I was watching it, then stretch itself cautiously down the steps. A soft click (carefully calibrated, of course) would cause it to pull back into the tunnel and remain there for some time. But repeated clicks had less and less of an effect. I recorded the rat's advances and retreats by moving a pen back and forth across a moving paper tape.

The major result of this experiment was that some of my rats had babies. I began to watch young rats. I saw them right themselves and crawl about very much like the decerebrate or thalamic cats and rabbits of Magnus. So I set about studying the postural reflexes of young rats. Here was a first principle not formally recognized by scientific methodologists: When you run onto something interesting, drop everything else and study it. I tore up the Parthenon and started over.

If you hold a young rat on one hand and pull it gently by the tail, it will resist you by pulling forward and then, with a sudden sharp spring which usually disengages its tail, it will leap out into space. I decided to study this behavior quantitatively. I built a light platform covered with cloth and mounted it on tightly stretched piano wires (Figure 2). Here was a version of Sherrington's torsion-wire myograph, originally designed to record the isometric contraction of the *tibialis anticus* of a cat, but here adapted to the response of a whole organism. When the tail of the young rat was gently pulled, the rat clung to the cloth floor and tugged forward. By amplifying the fine movements of the platform, it was possible to get a good kymograph record of the tremor in this motion and then, as the pull against the tail was increased, of the desperate spring into the air (Figure 3).

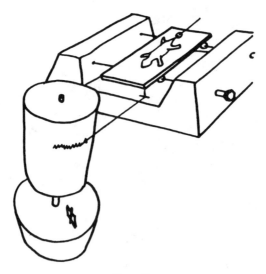

Figure 2

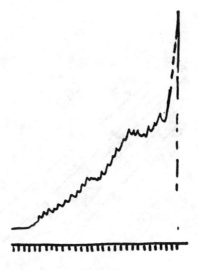

Figure 3

Now, baby rats have very little future, except as adult rats. Their behavior is literally infantile and cannot be usefully extrapolated to everyday life. But if this technique would work with a baby, why not try it on a mature rat? To avoid attaching anything to the rat, it should be possible to record, not a pull against the substrate, but the ballistic thrust exerted as the rat runs forward or suddenly stops in response to my calibrated click. So, invoking the first principle of scientific practice again, I threw away the piano-wire platform and built a runway, 8 feet long. This was constructed of light wood, in the form of a U girder, mounted rigidly on vertical glass plates, the elasticity of which permitted a very slight longitudinal movement (Figure 4). The runway became the floor of a long tunnel, not shown, at one end of which I placed my soundless release box and at the other end myself, prepared to reinforce the rat for coming down the runway by giving it a bit of wet mash, to sound a click from time to time when it had reached the middle of the runway, and to harvest kymograph records of the vibrations of the substrate.

Now for a second unformalized principle of scientific practice: Some ways of doing research are easier than others. I got tired of carrying the rat back to the other end of the runway. A back alley was therefore added (Figure 5). Now the rat could eat a bit of mash at point C, go down the back alley A, around the end as shown, and back home by runway B. The experimenter at E could collect records from the kymograph at D in comfort. In this way a great many records were made of the forces exerted against the substratum as rats ran down the alley and occasionally stopped dead in their tracks as a click sounded (Figure 6).

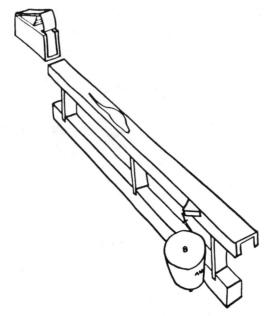

Figure 4

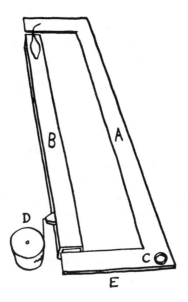

Figure 5

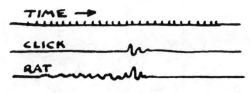

Figure 6

There was one annoying detail, however. The rat would often wait an inordinately long time at C before starting down the back alley on the next run. There seemed to be no explanation for this. When I timed these delays with a stop watch, however, and plotted them, they seemed to show orderly changes (Figure 7). This was, of course, the kind of thing I was looking for. I forgot all about the movements of the substratum and began to run rats for the sake of the delay measurements alone. But there was now no reason why the runway had to be 8 feet long and, as the second principle came into play again, I saw no reason why the rat could not deliver its own reinforcement.

A new apparatus was built. In Figure 8 we see the rat eating a piece of food just after completing a run. It produced the food by its own action. As it ran down the back alley A to the far end of the rectangular runway, its weight caused the whole runway to tilt slightly on the axis C and this movement turned the wooden disc D, permitting a piece of food in one of the holes around its perimeter to drop through a funnel into a food dish. The food was pearl tapioca, the only kind I could find in the grocery stores in reasonably uniform pieces. The rat had only to complete its journey by coming down the homestretch B to enjoy its reward. The experimenter was able to enjoy *his* reward at the same time, for he had only to load the magazine, put in a rat, and relax. Each tilt was recorded on a slowly moving kymograph.

A third unformalized principle of scientific practice: Some people are lucky. The disc of wood from which I had fashioned the food magazine was taken from a storeroom of discarded apparatus. It happened to have a central spindle, which fortunately I had not bothered to cut off. One day it occurred to me that if I wound a string around the spindle and allowed it to unwind as the magazine was emptied (Figure 9), I would get a different kind of record.

Figure 7

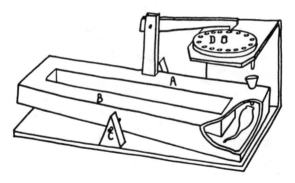

Figure 8

Instead of a mere report of the up-and-down movement of the runway, as a series of pips as in a polygraph, I would get a *curve*. And I knew that science made great use of curves, although, so far as I could discover, very little of pips on a polygram. The difference between the old type of record at A (Figure 10) and the new at B may not seem great, but as it turned out the curve revealed things in the rate of responding, and in changes in that rate, which would certainly otherwise have been missed. By allowing the string to unwind rather than to wind, I had got my curve in an awkward Cartesian quadrant, but that was easily remedied. Psychologists have adopted cumulative curves only very slowly, but I think it is fair to say that they have become an indispensable tool for certain purposes of analysis.

Eventually, of course, the runway was seen to be unnecessary. The rat could simply reach into a covered tray for pieces of food, and each movement of the cover could operate a solenoid to move a pen one step in a cumulative curve. The first major change in rate observed in this way was due to indigestion. Curves showing how the rate of eating declined with the time

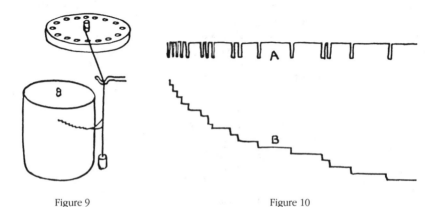

Figure 9   Figure 10

of eating comprised the other part of my thesis. But a refinement was needed. The behavior of the rat in pushing open the door was not a normal part of the ingestive behavior of *Rattus rattus*. The act was obviously learned but its status as part of the final performance was not clear. It seemed wise to add an initial conditioned response connected with ingestion in a quite arbitrary way. I chose the first device which came to hand—a horizontal bar or lever placed where it could be conveniently depressed by the rat to close a switch which operated a magnetic magazine. Ingestion curves obtained with this initial response in the chain were found to have the same properties as those without it.

Now, as soon as you begin to complicate an apparatus, you necessarily invoke a fourth principle of scientific practice: Apparatuses sometimes break down. I had only to wait for the food magazine to jam to get an extinction curve. At first I treated this as a defect and hastened to remedy the difficulty. But eventually, of course, I deliberately disconnected the magazine. I can easily recall the excitement of that first complete extinction curve (Figure 11). I had made contact with Pavlov at last! Here was a curve uncorrupted by the physiological process of ingestion. It was an orderly change due to nothing more than a special contingency of reinforcement. It was pure behavior! I am not saying that I would not have got around to extinction curves without a breakdown in the apparatus; Pavlov had given too strong a lead in that direction. But it is still no exaggeration to say that some of the most interesting and surprising results have turned up first because of similar accidents. Foolproof apparatus is no doubt highly desirable, but Charles Ferster and I, in recently reviewing the data from a 5-year program of research, found many occasions to congratulate ourselves on the fallibility of relays and vacuum tubes.

I then built four soundproofed ventilated boxes, each containing a lever and a food magazine and supplied with a cumulative recorder, and was on my way to an intensive study of conditioned reflexes in skeletal behavior. I would reinforce every response for several days and then extinguish for a day or two, varying the number of reinforcements, the amount of previous magazine training, and so on.

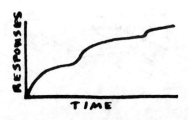

Figure 11

At this point I made my first use of the deductive method. I had long since given up pearl tapioca as too unbalanced a diet for steady use. A neighborhood druggist had shown me his pill machine, and I had had one made along the same lines (Figure 12). It consisted of a fluted brass bed across which one laid a long cylinder of stiff paste (in my case a MacCollum formula for an adequate rat diet). A similarly fluted cutter was then lowered onto the cylinder and rolled slowly back and forth, converting the paste into about a dozen spherical pellets. These were dried for a day or so before use. The procedure was painstaking and laborious. Eight rats eating 100 pellets each per day could easily keep up with production. One pleasant Saturday afternoon I surveyed my supply of dry pellets and, appealing to certain elemental theorems in arithmetic, deduced that unless I spent the rest of that afternoon and evening at the pill machine, the supply would be exhausted by 10:30 Monday morning.

Since I do not wish to deprecate the hypothetico-deductive method, I am glad to testify here to its usefulness. It led me to apply our second principle of unformalized scientific method and to ask myself why *every* press of the lever had to be reinforced. I was not then aware of what had happened at the Brown laboratories, as Harold Schlosberg later told the story. A graduate student had been given the task of running a cat through a difficult discrimination experiment. One Sunday the student found the supply of cat food exhausted. The stores were closed, and so, with a beautiful faith in the frequency-theory of learning, he ran the cat as usual and took it back to its living cage unrewarded. Schlosberg reports that the cat howled its protest continuously for nearly 48 hours. Unaware of this I decided to reinforce a response only once every minute and to allow all other responses to go unreinforced. There were two results: (a) my supply of pellets lasted almost indefinitely; and (b) each rat stabilized at a fairly constant rate of responding.[2]

Now, a steady state was something I was familiar with from physical chemistry, and I therefore embarked upon the study of periodic reinforcement. I soon found that the constant rate at which the rat stabilized

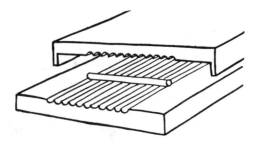

Figure 12

depended upon how hungry it was. Hungry rat, high rate; less hungry rat, lower rate. At that time I was bothered by the practical problem of controlling food deprivation. I was working half time at the medical school (on chronaxie of subordination!) and could not maintain a good schedule in working with the rats. The rate of responding under periodic reinforcement suggested a scheme for keeping a rat at a constant level of deprivation. The argument went like this: Suppose you reinforce, not at the end of a given period, but when the rat has completed the number of responses ordinarily emitted in that period. And suppose you use substantial pellets of food and give the rat continuous access to the lever. Then, except for periods when the rat sleeps, it should operate the lever at a constant rate around the clock. For, whenever it grows slightly hungrier, it will work faster, get food faster, and become less hungry, while whenever it grows slightly less hungry, it will respond at a lower rate, get less food, and grow hungrier. By setting the reinforcement at a given number of responses it should even be possible to hold the rat at any given level of deprivation. I visualized a machine with a dial which one could set to make available, at any time of day or night, a rat in a given state of deprivation. Of course, nothing of the sort happens. This is "fixed-ratio" rather than "fixed-interval" reinforcement and, as I soon found out, it produces a very different type of performance. This is an example of a fifth unformalized principle of scientific practice, but one which has at least been named. Walter Cannon described it with a word invented by Horace Walpole: *serendipity*—the art of finding one thing while looking for something else.

This account of my scientific behavior up to the point at which I published my results in a book called *The Behavior of Organisms* is as exact in letter and spirit as I can now make it. The notes, data, and publications which I have examined do not show that I ever behaved in the manner of Man Thinking as described by John Stuart Mill or John Dewey or in reconstructions of scientific behavior by other philosophers of science. I never faced a Problem which was more than the eternal problem of finding order. I never attacked a problem by constructing a Hypothesis. I never deduced Theorems or submitted them to Experimental Check. So far as I can see, I had no preconceived Model of behavior—certainly not a physiological or mentalistic one and, I believe, not a conceptual one. The "reflex reserve" was an abortive, though operational, concept which was retracted a year or so after publication in a paper at the Philadelphia meeting of the APA. It lived up to my opinion of theories in general by proving utterly worthless in suggesting further experiments. Of course, I was working on a basic Assumption—that there was order in behavior if I could only discover it—but such an assumption is not to be confused with the hypotheses of deductive theory. It is also true that I exercised a certain Selection of Facts, but not because of relevance to theory but because one fact was more orderly than another. If I engaged in Experimental Design at all, it was simply to complete or extend some evidence of order already observed.

Most of the experiments described in *The Behavior of Organisms* were done with groups of four rats. A fairly common reaction to the book was that such groups were too small. How did I know that other groups of four rats would do the same thing? Keller, in defending the book, countered with the charge that groups of four were too *big*. Unfortunately, however, I allowed myself to be persuaded of the contrary. This was due in part to my association at the University of Minnesota with W.T. Heron. Through him I came into close contact for the first time with traditional animal psychology. Heron was interested in inherited maze behavior, inherited activity, and certain drugs— the effects of which could then be detected only through the use of fairly large groups. We did an experiment together on the effect of starvation on the rate of pressing a lever and started the new era with a group of 16 rats. But we had only 4 boxes, and this was so inconvenient that Heron applied for a grant and built a battery of 24 lever-boxes and cumulative recorders. I supplied an attachment which would record, not only the mean performance of all 24 rats in a single averaged curve, but mean curves for 4 subgroups of 12 rats each and 4 subgroups of 6 rats each.[3] We thus provided for the design of experiments according to the principles of R.A. Fisher, which were then coming into vogue. We had, so to speak, mechanized the Latin square.

With this apparatus Heron and I published a study of extinction in maze-bright and maze-dull rats using 95 subjects. Later I published mean extinction curves for groups of 24, and W.K. Estes and I did our work on anxiety with groups of the same size. But although Heron and I could properly voice the hope that "the possibility of using large groups of animals greatly improves upon the method as previously reported, since tests of significance are provided for and properties of behavior not apparent in single cases may be more easily detected," in actual practice that is not what happened. The experiments I have just mentioned are almost all we have to show for this elaborate battery of boxes. Undoubtedly more work could be done with it and would have its place, but something had happened to the natural growth of the method. You cannot easily make a change in the conditions of an experiment when 24 apparatuses have to be altered. Any gain in rigor is more than matched by a loss in flexibility. We were forced to confine ourselves to processes which could be studied with the baselines already developed in earlier work. We could not move on to the discovery of other processes or even to a more refined analysis of those we were working with. No matter how significant might be the relations we actually demonstrated, our statistical Leviathan had swum aground. The art of the method had stuck at a particular stage of its development.

Another accident rescued me from mechanized statistics and brought me back to an even more intensive concentration on the single case.[4] In essence, I suddenly found myself face to face with the engineering problem of the animal trainer. When you have the responsibility of making absolutely sure that a given organism will engage in a given sort of behavior at a given time, you quickly grow impatient with theories of learning. Principles, hypotheses, theorems, satisfactory proof at the .05 level of significance that behavior at a choice point shows the effect of secondary reinforcement— nothing could be more irrelevant. No one goes to the circus to see the average dog jump through a hoop significantly oftener than untrained dogs raised under the same circumstances, or to see an elephant demonstrate a principle of behavior.

Perhaps I can illustrate this without giving aid and comfort to the enemy by describing a Russian device which the Germans found quite formidable. The Russians used dogs to blow up tanks. A dog was trained to hide behind a tree or wall in low brush or other cover. As a tank approached and passed, the dog ran swiftly alongside it, and a small magnetic mine attached to the dog's back was sufficient to cripple the tank or set it afire. The dog, of course, had to be replaced.

Now I ask you to consider some of the technical problems which the psychologist faces in preparing a dog for such an act of unintentional heroism. The dog must wait behind the tree for an indefinite length of time. Very well, waiting must be intermittently reinforced. But what schedule will achieve the highest probability of waiting? If the reinforcement is to be food, what is the absolutely optimal schedule of deprivation consistent with the health of the dog? The dog must run to the tank—that can be arranged by reinforcing runs to a practice tank—but it must start instantly if it is to overtake a swift tank, and how do you differentially reinforce short reaction times, especially in counteracting the reinforcement for sitting and waiting? The dog must react only to tanks, not to a refugee driving an oxcart along the road, but what are the defining properties of a tank so far as a dog is concerned?

I think it can be said that a functional analysis proved adequate in its technological application. Manipulation of environmental conditions alone made possible a wholly unexpected practical control. Behavior could be shaped up according to specifications and maintained indefinitely almost at will. One behavioral technologist who worked with me at the time (Keller Breland) is now specializing in the production of behavior as a salable commodity and has described this new profession in the *American Psychologist.*[5]

There are many useful applications within psychology itself. Ratliff and Blough have recently conditioned pigeons to serve as psychophysical observers. In their experiment a pigeon may adjust one of two spots of light until the two are equally bright or it may hold a spot of light at the absolute threshold during dark adaptation. The techniques which they have developed to induce pigeons to do this are only indirectly related to the point of their experiments and hence exemplify the application of a behavioral science.[6] The field in which a better technology of behavior is perhaps most urgently needed is education. I cannot describe here the applications which are now possible, but perhaps I can indicate my enthusiasm by hazarding the guess that educational techniques at all age levels are on the threshold of revolutionary changes.

The effect of a behavioral technology on scientific practice is the issue here. Faced with practical problems in behavior, you necessarily emphasize the refinement of *experimental* variables. As a result, some of the standard procedures of statistics appear to be circumvented. Let me illustrate. Suppose that measurements have been made on two groups of subjects differing in some detail of experimental treatment. Means and standard deviations for the two groups are determined, and any difference due to the treatment is evaluated. If the difference is in the expected direction but is not statistically significant, the almost universal recommendation would be to study larger groups. But our experience with practical control suggests that we may reduce the troublesome variability by changing the conditions of the experiment. By discovering, elaborating, and fully exploiting every relevant variable, we may eliminate *in advance of measurement* the individual differences which obscure the difference under analysis. This will achieve the same result as increasing the size of groups, and it will almost certainly yield a bonus in the discovery of new variables which would not have been identified in the statistical treatment.

The same may be said of smooth curves. In our study of anxiety, Estes and I published several curves, the reasonable smoothness of which was obtained by averaging the performances of 12 rats for each curve. The individual curves published at that time show that the mean curves do not faithfully represent the behavior of any one rat. They show a certain tendency toward a change in slope which supported the point we were making, and they may have appeared to warrant averaging for that reason.

But an alternative method would have been to explore the individual case until an equally smooth curve could be obtained. This would have meant not only rejecting the temptation to produce smoothness by averaging cases, but manipulating all relevant conditions as we later learned to manipulate them for practical purposes. The individual curves which we published at that time point to the need not for larger groups but for improvement in experimental technique. Here, for example, is a curve the smoothness of which is characteristic of current practice. Such curves were shown in the making in a demonstration which Ferster and I arranged at the Cleveland meeting of the American Psychological Association (Figure 13). Here, in a single organism, three different schedules of reinforcement are yielding corresponding performances with great uniformity under appro-

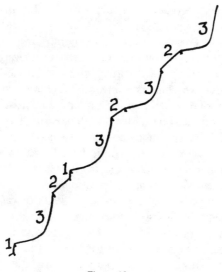

Figure 13

priate stimuli alternating at random. One does not reach this kind of order through the application of statistical methods.

In *The Behavior of Organisms* I was content to deal with the overall slopes and curvature of cumulative curves and could make only a rough classification of the properties of behavior shown by the finer grain. The grain has now been improved. The resolving power of the microscope has been greatly increased, and we can see fundamental processes of behavior in sharper and sharper detail. In choosing rate of responding as a basic datum and in recording this conveniently in a cumulative curve, we make important temporal aspects of behavior *visible*. Once this has happened, our scientific practice is reduced to simple looking. A new world is opened to inspection. We use such curves as we use a microscope, X-ray camera, or telescope. This is well exemplified by recent extensions of the method. These are no longer part of my case history, but perhaps you will permit me to consult you about what some critics have described as a *folie à deux* or group neurosis.

An early application of the method to the behavior of avoidance and escape was made by Keller in studying the light aversion of the rat. This was brilliantly extended by Murray Sidman in his shock-avoidance experiments. It is no longer necessary to describe avoidance and escape by appeal to "principles," for we may *watch* the behavior develop when we have arranged the proper contingencies of reinforcement, as we later watch it change as these contingencies are changed.

Hunt and Brady have extended the use of a stable rate in the study of anxiety-producing stimuli and have shown that the depression in rate is eliminated by electroconvulsive shock and by other measures which are effective in reducing anxiety in human patients. O.R. Lindsley has found the same thing for dogs, using insulin-shock therapy and sedatives. Brady has refined the method by exploring the relevance of various schedules of reinforcement in tracing the return of the conditioned depression after treatment. In these experiments you *see* the effect of a treatment as directly as you see the constriction of a capillary under the microscope.

Early work with rats on caffeine and Benzedrine has been extended by Lindsley with dogs. A special technique for evaluating several effects of a drug in a single short experimental period yields a record of behavior which can be read as a specialist reads an electrocardiogram. Dr. Peter Dews of the Department of Pharmacology at the Harvard Medical School is investigating dose-response curves and the types and effects of various drugs, using pigeons as subjects. In the Psychological Laboratories at Harvard additional work on drugs is being carried out by Morse, Herrnstein, and Marshall, and the technique is being adopted by drug manufacturers. There could scarcely be a better demonstration of the experimental treatment of variability. In a *single* experimental session with a *single* organism one observes the onset, duration, and decline of the effects of a drug.

The direct observation of *defective* behavior is particularly important. Clinical or experimental damage to an organism is characteristically unique. Hence the value of a method which permits the direct observation of the behavior of the individual. Lindsley has studied the effects of near-lethal irradiation, and the effects of prolonged anesthesia and anoxia are currently being examined by Thomas Lohr in co-operation with Dr. Henry Beecher of the Massachusetts General Hospital. The technique is being applied to neurological variables in the monkey by Dr. Karl Pribram at the Hartford Institute. The pattern of such research is simple: Establish the behavior in which you are interested, submit the organism to a particular treatment, and then look again at the behavior. An excellent example of the use of experimental control in the study of *motivation* is some work on obesity by J.E. Anliker in collaboration with Dr. Jean Mayer of the Harvard School of Public Health, where abnormalities of ingestive behavior in several types of obese mice can be compared by direct inspection.

There is perhaps no field in which behavior is customarily described more indirectly than psychiatry. In an experiment at the Massachusetts State Hospital, O.R. Lindsley is carrying out an extensive program which might be characterized as a quantitative study of the temporal properties of psychotic behavior.[7] Here again it is a question of making certain characteristics of the behavior visible.

The extent to which we can eliminate sources of variability before measurement is shown by a result which has an unexpected significance for comparative psychology and the study of individual differences. Figure 14 shows tracings of three curves which report behavior in response to a

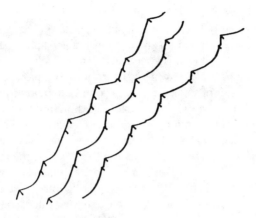

Figure 14

multiple fixed-interval fixed-ratio schedule. The hatches mark reinforcements. Separating them in some cases are short, steep lines showing a high constant rate on a fixed-ratio schedule and, in others, somewhat longer "scallops" showing a smooth acceleration as the organism shifts from a very low rate just after reinforcement to a higher rate at the end of the fixed interval. The values of the intervals and ratios, the states of deprivation, and the exposures to the schedules were different in the three cases, but except for these details the curves are quite similar. Now, one of them was made by a *pigeon* in some experiments by Ferster and me, one was made by a *rat* in an experiment on anoxia by Lohr, and the third was made by a *monkey* in Karl Pribram's laboratory at the Hartford Institute. Pigeon, rat, monkey, which is which? It doesn't matter. Of course, these three species have behavioral repertoires which are as different as their anatomies. But once you have allowed for differences in the ways in which they make contact with the environment, and in the ways in which they act upon the environment, what remains of their behavior shows astonishingly similar properties. Mice, cats, dogs, and human children could have added other curves to this figure. And when organisms which differ as widely as this nevertheless show similar properties of behavior, differences between members of the same species may be viewed more hopefully. Difficult problems of idiosyncrasy or individuality will always arise as products of biological and cultural processes, but it is the very business of the experimental analysis of behavior to devise techniques which reduce their effects except when they are explicitly under investigation.

We are within reach of a science of the individual. This will be achieved, not by resorting to some special theory of knowledge in which intuition or understanding takes the place of observation and analysis, but through an increasing grasp of relevant conditions to produce order in the individual case.

A second consequence of an improved technology is the effect upon behavior theory. As I have pointed out elsewhere, it is the function of learning theory to create an imaginary world of law and order and thus to console us for the disorder we observe in behavior itself. Scores on a T-maze or jumping-stand hop about from trial to trial almost capriciously. Therefore we argue that if learning is, as we hope, a continuous and orderly process, it must be occurring in some other system of dimensions—perhaps in the nervous system, or in the mind, or in a conceptual model of behavior. Both the statistical treatment of group means and the averaging of curves encourage the belief that we are somehow going behind the individual case to an otherwise inaccessible, but more fundamental, process. The whole tenor of our paper on anxiety, for example, was to imply that the change we observed was not necessarily a property of behavior, but of some theoretical state of the organism ("anxiety") which was merely *reflected* in a slight modification of performance.

When we have achieved a practical control over the organism, theories of behavior lose their point. In representing and managing relevant variables, a conceptual model is useless; we come to grips with behavior itself. When behavior shows order and consistency, we are much less likely to be concerned with physiological or mentalistic causes. A datum emerges which takes the place of theoretical fantasy. In the experimental analysis of behavior we address ourselves to a subject matter which is not only manifestly the behavior of an individual and hence accessible without the usual statistical aids but also "objective" and "actual" without recourse to deductive theorizing.

Statistical techniques serve a useful function, but they have acquired a purely honorific status which may be troublesome. Their presence or absence has become a shibboleth to be used in distinguishing between good and bad work. Because measures of behavior have been highly variable, we have come to trust only results obtained from large numbers of subjects. Because some workers have intentionally or unconsciously reported only selected favorable instances, we have come to put a high value on research which is planned in advance and reported in its entirety. Because measures have behaved capriciously, we have come to value skillful deductive theories which restore order. But although large groups, planned experiments, and valid theorizing are associated with significant scientific results, it does not follow that nothing can be achieved in their absence. Here are two brief examples of the choice before us.

How can we determine the course of dark adaptation in a pigeon? We move a pigeon from a bright light to a dark room. What happens? Presumably the bird is able to see fainter and fainter patches of light as the process of adaptation takes place, but how can we follow this process? One way would be to set up a discrimination apparatus in which choices would be made at specific intervals after the beginning of dark adaptation. The test patches of light could be varied over a wide range, and the percentages of correct choices at each value would enable us eventually to locate the threshold fairly accurately. But hundreds of observations would be needed to establish only a few points on the curve and to prove that these show an actual change in sensitivity. In the experiment by Blough already mentioned, the pigeon holds a spot of light close to the threshold throughout the experimental period. A single curve, such as the one sketched in Figure 15, yields as much information as hundreds of readings, together with the means and standard deviations derived from them. The information is more accurate because it applies to a single organism in a single experimental session. Yet many psychologists who would accept the first as a finished experiment because of the tables of means and standard deviations would boggle at the second or call it a preliminary study. The direct evidence of one's senses in observing a process of behavior is not trusted.

As another example, consider the behavior of several types of obese mice. Do they all suffer from a single abnormality in their eating behavior or are there differences? One might attempt to answer this with some such measure of hunger as an obstruction apparatus. The numbers of crossings of a grid to get to food, counted after different periods of free access to food, would be the data. Large numbers of readings would be needed, and the resulting mean values would possibly not describe the behavior of any one mouse in any experimental period. A much better picture may be obtained with one mouse of each kind in single experimental sessions, as Anliker and Mayer have shown.[8] In an experiment reported roughly in Figure 16, each mouse was reinforced with a small piece of food after completing a short "ratio" of responses. The hypothalamic-obese mouse shows an exaggerated

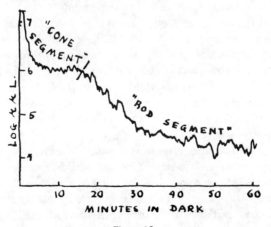

Figure 15

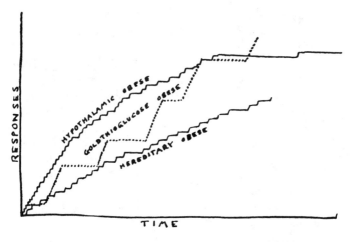

Figure 16

but otherwise normal ingestion curve. The hereditary-obese mouse eats slowly but for an indefinite length of time and with little change in rate. The gold-poisoned obese mouse shows a sharp oscillation between periods of very rapid responding and no responding at all. These three individual curves contain more information than could probably every be generated with measures requiring statistical treatment, yet they will be viewed with suspicion by many psychologists because they are single cases.

It is perhaps natural that psychologists should awaken only slowly to the possibility that behavioral processes may be directly observed, or that they should only gradually put the older statistical and theoretical techniques in their proper perspective. But it is time to insist that science does not progress by carefully designed steps called "experiments," each of which has a well-defined beginning and end. Science is a continuous and often a disorderly and accidental process. We shall not do the young psychologist any favor if we agree to reconstruct our practices to fit the pattern demanded by current scientific methodology. What statisticians mean by the design of experiments is design which yields the kind of data to which *their* techniques are applicable. They do not mean the behavior of scientists in their laboratories devising research for their own immediate and possibly inscrutable purposes.

The organism whose behavior is most extensively modified and most completely controlled in research of the sort I have described is the experimenter. The point was well made by a cartoonist in the Columbia *Jester* (Figure 17). The caption read: "Boy, have I got this guy conditioned! Every time I press the bar down he drops in a piece of food." The subjects we study reinforce our behavior much more effectively than we reinforce theirs.

Figure 17

I have been telling you simply how I have been conditioned to behave. And of course it is a mistake to argue too much from one case history. My behavior would not have been shaped as it was were it not for personal characteristics which all psychologists fortunately do not share. Freud has had something to say about the motivation of scientists and has given us some insight into the type of person who achieves the fullest satisfaction from precise experimental design and the intricacies of deductive systems. Such people tend to be more concerned with their success as scientists than with their subject matter, as is shown by the fact that they often assume the role of a roving ambassador. If this seems unfair, let me hasten to characterize my own motivation in equally unflattering terms. Several years ago I spent a pleasant summer writing a novel called *Walden Two*. One of the characters, Frazier, said many things which I was not yet ready to say myself. Among them was this:

> I have only one important characteristic, Burris: I'm stubborn. I've had only one idea in my life—a true *idée fixe*...to put it as bluntly as possible, the idea of having my own way. "Control" expresses it, I think. The control of human behavior, Burris. In my early experimental days it was a frenzied, selfish desire to dominate. I remember the rage I used to feel when a prediction went awry. I could have shouted at the subjects of my experiments, "Behave, damn you, behave as you ought!" Eventually I realized that the subjects were always right. They always behaved as they ought. It was I who was wrong. I had made a bad prediction.

(In fairness to Frazier and the rest of myself, I want to add his next remark: "And what a strange discovery for a would-be tyrant, that the only effective technique of control is unselfish." Frazier means, of course, positive reinforcement.)

We have no more reason to say that all psychologists should behave as I have behaved than that they should all behave like R.A. Fisher. Scientists, like other organisms, are the products of unique histories. The practices which they find most appropriate will depend in part upon those histories.

Fortunately, personal idiosyncrasies usually leave a negligible mark on science as public property. They are important only when we are concerned with the encouragement of scientists and the prosecution of research. When we have at last an adequate empirical account of the behavior of Man Thinking, we shall understand all this. Until then, it may be best not to try to fit all scientists into any single mold.

REFERENCES AND NOTES

[1]Richter, C.P. Free research versus design research. *Science,* 1953, *118,* 91-93.

[2]The reference is to Project Pigeon, described in Chapter 12. The project was still classified when this paper was published.

[3]Heron, W.T., & Skinner, B.F. An apparatus for the study of animal behavior. *Psychological Record,* 1939, *3,* 166-176.

[4]*The Shaping of a Behaviorist* (1979) tells a slightly different story. See page 97 of that book.

[5]Breland, K., & Breland, M. A field of applied animal psychology. *American Psychologist,* 1951, *6,* 202-204.

[6]Ratliff, F., & Blough, D.S. Behavior studies of visual processes in the pigeon (Report of Contract N50ri-07663). Cambridge: Harvard University, Psychological Laboratories, September 1954.

[7]Lindsley, O. Operant conditioning methods applied to research in chronic schizophrenia. *Psychiatric Research Reports,* 1956, *5,* 118-139.

[8]Anliker, J., & Mayer, J. Operant conditioning technique for studying feeding-fasting patterns in normal and obese mice. *Journal of Applied Physiology,* 1956, *8,* 667-670.

POSTSCRIPT

I had been interested in the philosophy of science and scientific methodology since my graduate school days. I knew a few members of the Vienna Circle, among them Herbert Feigl when he was a colleague at the University of Minnesota. I felt that scientific methodology tended to be a reconstruction of what scientists did, rather than a factual report, and an opportunity to demonstrate the point came when the American Psychological Association commissioned an elaborate series of books, under the editorship of Sigmund Koch, the contributors to which would report how they conducted psychological research. We were asked to follow a rather elaborate guideline, but I ignored it because it forced one into reconstruction rather than narration.

If there is any prevailing theme in the paper, it is the role of accident—the very essence of nonplanning. Pasteur had said that chance favors the prepared mind. I should not have put it quite that way, but one must be alert to take advantage of accidents, and I could give many examples.

I wrote the paper while on sabbatical leave in Putney, Vermont. The pictures of apparatus and rough copies of experimental results were drawn from memory, and in a rather primitive style. There was more humor in the paper than I usually permitted myself to display. I even reprinted the cartoon from the Columbia *Jester,* but only because there was an important point behind it: I believe that my behavior is as orderly as that of the organisms I study and that my rats and pigeons have taught me far more than I have taught them.

I summarized the point of the paper and dismissed much of scientific methodology in this way: "I never faced a Problem which was more than the eternal problem of finding order. I never attacked a problem by constructing a Hypothesis. I never deduced Theorems or submitted them to Experimental Check. So far as I can see, I had no preconceived Model of behavior—certainly not a physiological or mentalistic one and, I believe, not a conceptual one."

C H A P T E R 3

"Superstition" in the Pigeon

EDITOR'S NOTE

The article was written while Skinner served as chairman of the
psychology department at Indiana University, was first published in the
Journal of Experimental Psychology (1948, *38,* 168-172), and has been
reprinted in *Cumulative Record,* as well as many other books. It is
without doubt his best-known experimental paper. Operant conditioning
takes place because of the temporal relation between a response and
reinforcer; therefore, if a potential reinforcer, such as food for a hungry
organism, closely follows a response, it should strengthen the response
even if it only accidentally follows it. In a simple experiment to
demonstrate the phenomenon, Skinner placed a food-deprived pigeon
into an experimental chamber and, with a timing device and automatic
feeder, presented food every 15 seconds, independently of the bird's
behavior. Operant conditioning clearly took place in six of the eight birds
he studied: One made repeated turns about the cage, another repeatedly
thrust its head toward a corner of the cage, two developed a "pendulum
motion of the head and body," and so forth. Conditioning occurred
because some movement, followed by food presentation, was likely to be
repeated and hence likely to be occurring in some form when food was
presented 15 seconds later. The resulting behavior may be called
"superstitious" because, like superstitious behaviors in humans (for
example, rituals for changing one's luck at cards), the behavior is
maintained even though there is no dependency between the behavior
and its reinforcement; it is only a coincidence that reinforcement
sometimes follows the behavior. (Skinner elaborated upon this point
many years later; see "The Force of Coincidence" [1977].) Because of the
lack of dependency, variation in the behavior may result in a "drift" in its
form until it is substantially different; later researchers were greatly
concerned with the drift phenomenon (e.g., Staddon, J.E.R., & Simmelhag,
V.L. *Psychological Review,* 1971, *78,* 3-43).

When reinforcement was withheld for one bird, the superstitious
response occurred more than 10,000 times before its rate declined

significantly, and it was subsequently "reconditioned" with only response-independent reinforcement. Skinner noted that discriminative stimuli may have such superstitious effects. A "second type" of superstition was described in a later paper (1957, with W.H. Morse).

To say that a reinforcement is contingent upon a response may mean nothing more than that it follows the response. It may follow because of some mechanical connection or because of the mediation of another organism; but conditioning takes place presumably because of the temporal relation only, expressed in terms of the order and proximity of response and reinforcement. Whenever we present a state of affairs which is known to be reinforcing at a given level of deprivation, we must suppose that conditioning takes place even though we have paid no attention to the behavior of the organism in making the presentation. A simple experiment demonstrates this to be the case.

A pigeon is reduced to 75 percent of its weight when well fed. It is put into an experimental cage for a few minutes each day. A food hopper attached to the cage may be swung into place so that the pigeon can eat from it. A solenoid and a timing relay hold the hopper in place for 5 seconds at each presentation.

If a clock is now arranged to present the food hopper at regular intervals *with no reference whatsoever to the bird's behavior,* operant conditioning usually takes place. In six out of eight cases the resulting responses were so clearly defined that two observers could agree perfectly in counting instances. One bird was conditioned to turn counter-clockwise about the cage, making two or three turns between reinforcements. Another repeatedly thrust its head into one of the upper corners of the cage. A third developed a "tossing" response, as if placing its head beneath an invisible bar and lifting it repeatedly. Two birds developed a pendulum motion of the head and body, in which the head was extended forward and swung from right to left with a sharp movement followed by a somewhat slower return. The body generally followed the movement and a few steps might be taken when it was extensive. Another bird was conditioned to make incomplete pecking or brushing movements directed toward but not touching the floor. None of these responses appeared in any noticeable strength during adaptation to the cage or until the food hopper was periodically presented. In the remaining two cases, conditioned responses were not clearly marked.

The conditioning process is usually obvious. The bird happens to be executing some response as the hopper appears; as a result it tends to repeat this response. If the interval before the next presentation is not so great that extinction takes place, a second "contingency" is probable. This strengthens the response still further and subsequent reinforcement becomes more probable. It is true that some responses go unreinforced and some reinforcements appear when the response has not just been made, but the net result is the development of a considerable state of strength.

With the exception of the counter-clockwise turn, each response was almost always repeated in the same part of the cage, and it generally involved an orientation toward some feature of the cage. The effect of the reinforcement was to condition the bird to respond to some aspect of the environment rather than merely to execute a series of movements. All responses came to be repeated rapidly between reinforcements—typically five or six times in 15 seconds.

The effect appears to depend upon the rate of reinforcement. In general, we should expect that the shorter the intervening interval, the speedier and more marked the conditioning. One reason is that the pigeon's behavior becomes more diverse as time passes after reinforcement. A hundred photographs, each taken 2 seconds after withdrawal of the hopper, would show fairly uniform behavior. The bird would be in the same part of the cage, near the hopper, and probably oriented toward the wall where the hopper has disappeared or turning to one side or the other. A hundred photographs taken after 10 seconds, on the other hand, would find the bird in various parts of the cage responding to many different aspects of the environment. The sooner a second reinforcement appears, therefore, the more likely it is that the second reinforced response will be similar to the first, and also that they will both have one of a few standard forms. In the limiting case of a very brief interval the behavior to be expected would be holding the head toward the opening through which the magazine has disappeared.

Another reason for the greater effectiveness of short intervals is that the longer the interval, the greater the number of intervening responses emitted without reinforcement. The resulting extinction cancels the effect of an occasional reinforcement.

According to this interpretation the effective interval will depend upon the rate of conditioning and the rate of extinction, and will therefore vary with the deprivation and also presumably between species. Fifteen seconds is a very effective interval at the level of deprivation indicated above. One minute is much less so. When a response has once been set up, however, the interval can be lengthened. In one case it was extended to 2 minutes, and a high rate of responding was maintained with no sign of weakening. In another case, many hours of responding were observed with an interval of 1 minute between reinforcements.

In the latter case, the response showed a noticeable drift in topography. It began as a sharp movement of the head from the middle position to the left. This movement became more energetic, and eventually the whole body of the bird turned in the same direction, and a step or two would be taken.

After many hours, the stepping response became the predominant feature. The bird made a well-defined hopping step from the right to the left foot, meanwhile turning its head and body to the left as before.

When the stepping response became strong, it was possible to obtain a mechanical record by putting the bird on a large tambour directly connected with a small tambour which made a delicate electric contact each time stepping took place. By watching the bird and listening to the sound of the recorder it was possible to confirm the fact that a fairly authentic record was being made. It was possible for the bird to hear the recorder at each step, but this was, of course, in no way correlated with feeding. The record obtained when the magazine was presented once per minute resembles in every respect the characteristic curve for the pigeon under fixed-interval reinforcement of a standard selected response. A well-marked temporal discrimination develops. The bird does not respond immediately after eating, but when 10 or 15 or even 20 seconds have elapsed, it begins to respond rapidly and continues until the reinforcement is received.

In this case it was possible to record the "extinction" of the response when the clock was turned off and the magazine was no longer presented at any time. The bird continued to respond with its characteristic side to side hop. More than 10,000 responses were recorded before "extinction" had reached the point at which few if any responses were made during a 10 or 15 minute interval. When the clock was again started, the periodic presentation of the magazine (still without any connection whatsoever with the bird's behavior) brought out a typical curve for reconditioning after fixed-interval reinforcement, shown in Figure 1. The record has been essentially horizontal for 20 minutes prior to the beginning of this curve. The first reinforcement had some slight effect and the second a greater effect. There is a smooth positive acceleration in rate as the bird returns to the rate of responding which prevailed when it was reinforced every minute.

When the response was again extinguished and the periodic presentation of food then resumed, a different response was picked up. This consisted of a progressive walking response in which the bird moved about the cage. The response of hopping from side to side never reappeared and could not, of course, be obtained deliberately without making the reinforcement contingent upon the behavior.

The experiment might be said to demonstrate a sort of superst' on. The bird behaves as if there were a causal relation between its behavior and the presentation of food, although such a relation is lacking. There are many analogies in human behavior. Rituals for changing one's luck at cards are good examples. A few accidental connections between a ritual and favorable consequences suffice to set up and maintain the behavior in spite of many unreinforced instances. The bowler who has released a ball down the alley but continues to behave as if controlling it by twisting and turning arm and

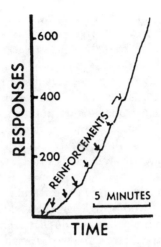

Figure 1 "Reconditioning" of a superstitious response after extinction. The response of hopping from right to left had been thoroughly extinguished just before the record was taken. The arrows indicate the automatic presentation of food at 1-minute intervals without reference to the pigeon's behavior.

shoulder is another case in point. These behaviors have, of course, no real effect upon one's luck or upon a ball halfway down an alley, just as in the present case the food would appear as often if the pigeon did nothing—or, strictly speaking, did something else.

It is perhaps not quite correct to say that conditioned behavior has been set up without any previously determined contingency whatsoever. We have appealed to a uniform sequence of responses in the behavior of the pigeon to obtain an overall net contingency. When we arrange a clock to present food every 15 seconds, we are in effect basing our reinforcement upon a limited set of responses which frequently occur 15 seconds after reinforcement. When a response has been strengthened (and this may result from one reinforcement), the setting of the clock implies an even more restricted contingency. Something of the same sort is true of the bowler. It is not quite correct to say that there is no connection between the twisting and turning and the course taken by the ball at the far end of the alley. The connection was established before the ball left the bowler's hand, but since both the path of the ball and the behavior of the bowler are determined, some relation survives. The subsequent behavior of the bowler may have no effect upon the ball, but the behavior of the ball has an effect upon the bowler. The contingency, though not perfect, is enough to maintain the behavior in strength. The particular form of the behavior adopted by the bowler is due to induction from responses in which there is actual contact with the ball. It is clearly a movement appropriate to changing the ball's direction. But this does not invalidate the comparison, since we are not concerned with what response is selected but with why it persists in strength. In rituals for changing luck the inductive strengthening of a particular form of behavior is generally absent. The behavior of the pigeon in this experiment is of the latter sort, as the variety of responses obtained from different pigeons indicates. Whether there is any unconditioned behavior in the pigeon appropriate to a given effect upon the environment is under investigation.

The results throw some light on incidental behavior observed in experiments in which a discriminative stimulus is frequently presented. Such a stimulus has reinforcing value and can set up superstitious behavior. A pigeon will often develop some response such as turning, twisting, pecking near the locus of the discriminative stimulus, flapping its wings, and so on. In much of the work to date in this field the interval between presentations of the discriminative stimulus has been 1 minute and many of these superstitious responses are short-lived. Their appearance as the result of accidental correlations with the presentation of the stimulus is unmistakable.

POSTSCRIPT

The experiment makes a good lecture demonstration. Put a hungry pigeon in an enclosure in which it can be easily seen. Let the audience watch it for a few moments. Then install a food dispenser with a timer that operates every 20 seconds, and after two or three measures of food have been received and eaten, enclose the whole thing in cardboard walls. Half an hour later, uncover. Almost invariably a clearly defined superstition will be obvious. The pigeon will be doing something "to make the food dispenser work."

Since the contingencies are not responsible for the topography of the behavior, it can change if the intermittent delivery of food is continued. It is likely to drift toward more clearly defined forms because the accidental contingencies are then more effective. Some such process may explain the superstition of a rain dance; if rain eventually follows, the more elaborate the ceremony the more obvious the "connection."

C H A P T E R 4

Symbolic Communication Between Two Pigeons (*Columba livia domestica*)

EDITOR'S NOTE

The article was published in *Science* (1980, *207* (4430), 543-545, with myself and Robert P. Lanza). It is a satire on recent research with chimpanzees and is one of several related papers Professor Skinner and I have written as part of the "Columban Simulation Project." In the experiment described, two pigeons, dubbed Jack and Jill, communicate with each other using arbitrary symbols. Similar accomplishments by chimps and, for that matter, children, are often unnecessarily attributed to intentions and cognitions; environmental histories (in the case of chimps, months or years of intensive training) are often ignored as explanations. This makes some behavior seem more mysterious than it really is. We make the point by jokingly attributing the behaviors of our pigeons to information, cognitions, and intentions, and then offering a simpler environmental account.

We have dealt in a similar manner with "self-awareness," "insight," "morality," and other cognitive constructs. In each case, our goal has been to show how some complex human behavior, usually attributed to mental processes, may be accounted for in terms of observable events.

Jack and Jill later learned each other's roles and achieved additional language-like performances (e.g., see "The Spontaneous Use of Memoranda by Pigeons" [1981]).

In a recent report, Savage-Rumbaugh et al.[1] described the first successful demonstration of symbolic communication between two nonhuman primates. They showed that chimpanzees' nonverbal communication ability could be enhanced through learning. Specifically, the chimpanzees exchanged information about food through the use of geometric symbols. They were first taught to name a number of foods by pressing buttons on which corresponding symbols were marked. Then they were taught to request hidden food by using its symbolic name. Finally, in a test of how well information about a given food could be transmitted from one chimpanzee to the other, one chimpanzee watched while some food was hidden and, in the presence of the second chimpanzee, was asked by the experimenter to indicate the symbolic name for that food. If the second chimpanzee then correctly asked for that food by using its symbolic name, both subjects were rewarded with the food. Also briefly described was a situation in which the chimpanzees spontaneously used symbols to request food from each other. Evidently, communication through the use of symbols is not an activity that is necessarily unique to man. The question naturally arises as to whether it is unique to primates.

This report presents, to our knowledge, the first instance of such symbolic communication between nonprimates—two White Carneaux pigeons *(Columba livia domestica)*. Pigeons are known to communicate under natural conditions by using coos, short grunts, and wing claps.[2] We present here data showing that their natural inclination to communicate can be enhanced through learning and, in particular, that they are able to transmit information to one another by using symbols.

The communication system was similar to that of Savage-Rumbaugh et al. The pigeons expressed words or short phrases by depressing keys embossed with English letters or letters arranged to form words. Depressing a key illuminated it, affording both birds a clear view of the chosen symbol. The keys were arranged on adjoining keyboards (Figure 1) in a two-bird chamber 49 centimeters wide by 30 centimeters deep by 29 centimeters high. The front, top, and sides of the chamber were Plexiglas, and a Plexiglas partition in the center gave each bird a clear view of the other bird and its keyboard. Electromechanical feeders at the base of each of the side walls could be operated separately to give each bird access to mixed grain. A white noise source in one corner of the chamber partially masked extraneous sounds, but no other precautions were taken to shield the subjects from the visual and auditory distractions of the laboratory room. Events in the experiment were controlled and recorded by electromechanical equipment.

The subjects were two moderately hungry adult pigeons named Jack and Jill.[3] Each had had previous experience as a laboratory subject, but neither had been used before in procedures related to language or communication. Jack was the observer throughout the study, and Jill the informer. Each was trained separately for 5 weeks in daily sessions 1 to 3 hours in length before their communication ability was tested.

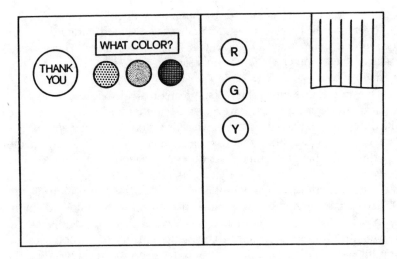

Figure 1   Adjoining keyboards for the two pigeons. Jack's is on the left and Jill's is on the right. Jack needs information about the color recessed 5 centimeters behind the curtain in the upper right-hand corner of Jill's keyboard. The R, G, and Y on Jill's keyboard are black on white. The three keys below the WHAT COLOR? key on Jack's keyboard are yellow, red, and green from left to right.

The animals were first taught to relate symbolic names to colors. Jill was taught to name three colors in response to the keyboard-imposed question "What color?" Jack was taught, conversely, to select the color corresponding to a designated name. When the pigeons were correct, they were rewarded with grain; when incorrect, all chamber lights were extinguished for several seconds. Both subjects learned to relate the colors and symbolic names with greater than 90 percent accuracy during the first 3 weeks of training.

After Jill, the informer, had reached this level of accuracy, she was taught to search for a color that was hidden from view. This was accomplished first by moving the colored lights progressively deeper into a recess in the upper righthand corner of her keyboard (Figure 1) until they were 5 centimeters behind the surface. Jill learned to look at a color by inserting her head into the recess. The recess was then gradually covered by a curtain of gray, opaque vinyl until the colors were entirely hidden. (These precautions were taken to prevent Jack, the observer, from seeing the colors.) Jill learned to thrust her head through slits in the curtain to look at the hidden colors. She continued to name the colors with nearly 100 percent accuracy during this period.

After Jack had demonstrated his competence in decoding symbols into colors, he was taught to ask for symbols by depressing the WHAT COLOR? key. Finally, he was taught that after having been given a symbol, he should reward the informer with food before attempting to decode the symbol. He accomplished this by depressing the THANK YOU key, thus illuminating the key and operating Jill's feeder. Decoding accuracy declined during this stage but reached better than 90 percent in 5 days of training. The subjects practiced their individual assignments for several sessions before the first interanimal test.

During the first interanimal test, greater-than-chance symbolic communication was achieved.[4] However, since neither bird had ever worked with the other before, each was somewhat distracted by the other's presence. To remedy this, we housed the subjects together continuously in the experimental chamber. After 5 days, both pigeons were responding accurately and efficiently on more than 90 percent of the trials.

The final performance was a sustained and natural conversation (Figure 2). Jack initiated it by asking Jill for information about the hidden color. In response, Jill looked at the color behind the curtain and then depressed the key with the symbolic name for that color, illuminating the symbol. Having seen Jill accomplish this, Jack depressed the THANK YOU key, rewarding Jill with food. Then Jack looked closely at the illuminated symbol, decoded it, and selected the appropriate color on his panel, after which the equipment automatically rewarded him with food. Typically without hesitation, Jack then requested another color name.[5] Errors were infrequent, and both subjects were highly attentive and cooperative. If one delayed in depressing a key, the other often vigorously pecked at the restraining partition.

To guarantee that the communication depended on the symbols, a control session was conducted in which the symbol keys on Jill's keyboard were covered. She proved unable to convey to Jack information about the hidden colors through any gestures or sounds. Jack's accuracy in selecting colors dropped to 30 percent for the 135 trials in this session.

There are a number of procedural differences between this study and that of Savage-Rumbaugh et al. First, taking into account the fact that the brain of the pigeon is smaller than that of the chimpanzee, and not wishing to tax the relatively limited information-processing capacity of our subjects, we used 3 rather than 11 stimulus objects. Second, we did not attempt to reverse the informer and observer roles. (We believe that this can be done but is not essential to the demonstration of interanimal communication.) Third, we used colors rather than foods as the stimulus objects to avoid the possibility that our subjects would fail to "distinguish between the use of a food name as its name and the use of that name as a request for food."[6] Fourth, events in all interanimal test sessions in our experiment were controlled by electromechanical equipment, eliminating possible experimenter cuing effects and the need for "experimenter-blind" conditions. Fifth, our observer could not simply duplicate the symbol provided by the informer but instead had to decode the symbol into its referent. Sixth, we did not vary the position of our symbols. (Position was no doubt significant to our subjects, just as the position of letters and figures in mathematical notation is significant to mathematicians.) Seventh, every conversation in our experiment was initiated by the observer's spontaneous request for information. Finally, the observer sustained the informer's cooperation by thanking her with a food reward for supplying information.

We have thus demonstrated that pigeons can learn to engage in a sustained and natural conversation without human intervention, and that one pigeon can transmit information to another entirely through the use of symbols.

It has not escaped our notice that an alternative account of this exchange may be given in terms of the prevailing contingencies of reinforcement. Jack "initiated the conversation" by pecking the WHAT COLOR? key because a peck

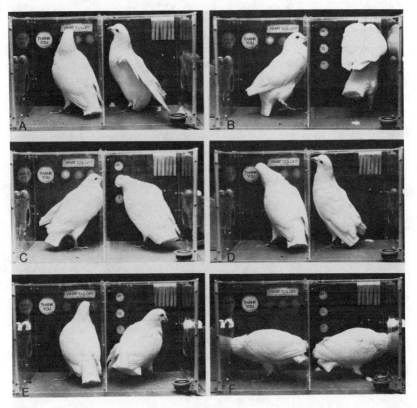

Figure 2   Typical communication sequence. (A) Jack (left) asks Jill (right) for a color name by depressing the WHAT COLOR? key. (B) Jill looks through the curtain at the hidden color. (C) Jill selects the symbolic name for the color while Jack watches. (D) Jack rewards Jill with food by depressing the THANK YOU key. (E) Jack selects the correct color as Jill moves towards her reward. (F) Jack is rewarded with food.

at that key had illuminated it and because this illumination had been reliably followed by the illumination of one of the symbol keys. This was, in turn, the occasion upon which a peck at the THANK YOU key, followed by a peck at a corresponding color key, had produced reinforcement. Jill responded to Jack's "request for information" because the illumination of the WHAT COLOR? key was the occasion upon which looking at the hidden color and then pecking a corresponding symbol key had been reinforced. The performances were established through standard fading, shaping, chaining, and discrimination procedures.[7,8,9,10] A similar account may be given of the Rumbaugh procedure,[11] as well as of comparable human language.[12]

REFERENCES AND NOTES

[1]Savage-Rumbaugh, E.S., Rumbaugh, D.M., & Boysen, S. Symbolic communication between two chimpanzees *(Pan troglodytes). Science,* 1978, *201,* 641-644.

[2]Levi, W.M. *The pigeon.* Sumter, S.C.: Levi, 1957.

[3]The pigeons were both male, but we named them Jack and Jill in tribute to Leonard Bloomfield, who in *Language* (New York: Holt, 1931) represented communication behaviorally by describing an episode in which Jill asked Jack to get her an apple.

[4]If the birds had responded at random to the symbol and color keys, they would have been correct on only about 11 percent of the trials. They responded correctly on more than 50 percent of the trials of the first interanimal test.

[5]The hidden colors were changed in a pseudo-random sequence from trial to trial throughout the experiment.

[6]Savage-Rumbaugh et al., op. cit., p. 642.

[7]Skinner. B.F. *The behavior of organisms: An experimental analysis.* New York: Appleton-Century, 1938.

[8]Skinner, B.F. *Science and human behavior.* New York: Macmillan, 1953.

[9]Catania, A.C. *Learning.* Englewood Cliffs, N.J.: Prentice-Hall, 1979.

[10]Honig, W.K. (Ed.). *Operant behavior: Areas of research and application.* Englewood Cliffs, N.J.: Prentice-Hall, 1966.

[11]Similar accounts may also be given of other recent work with nonhuman primates. See, for example, critiques by H. Rachlin (*The Behavioral and Brain Sciences,* 1978, *1,* 593) and H.S. Terrace (*Journal of the Experimental Analysis of Behavior,* 1979, *31,* 161-175). Other achievements with nonprimates are also relevant; consider, for example, R.O. Straub, M.S. Seidenberg, T.G. Bever, & H.S. Terrace, *Journal of the Experimental Analysis of Behavior,* 1979, *32,* 137-148.

[12]Skinner, B.F. *Verbal behavior.* New York: Appleton-Century-Crofts, 1957.

POSTSCRIPT

Very few people are aware of what can be done by arranging contingencies of reinforcement. Quite simple contingencies are the rule, for example, in "behavior modification." There are two ways in which a more adequate understanding can be used: Complex behavior usually attributed to mental or cognitive processes can be set up, or complex behavior in the world at large can be *interpreted*. The present experiment is an example of the first; my book, *Verbal Behavior,* is an example of the second. The book interprets a field of behavior usually treated in a very different manner by linguists, psycholinguists, and philosophers.

PART TWO

Theory

C H A P T E R   5

Behaviorism at Fifty

EDITOR'S NOTE

This article was first published in *Science* (1963, *140*(3570), 951-958) and later in *Behaviorism and Phenomenology: Contrasting Bases for Modern Psychology,* edited by T.W. Wann (Chicago: University of Chicago Press, 1964, pp. 79-97). An abbreviated version appears as Chapter 8 in Skinner's *Contingencies of Reinforcement* (1969, pp. 221-242). The latter also includes extensive addenda (pp. 242-268) in the form of 11 titled "Notes" on topics such as private stimuli, awareness, and feelings. The title commemorates Watson's seminal paper on behaviorism, "Psychology as the Behaviorist Views It," published in 1913.

Skinner contrasts behaviorism with traditional mentalistic views of humankind. Traits and states of mind, argues Skinner, "offer no real explanation" of human behavior and "stand in the way of a more effective analysis." Though the traditional point of view still receives strong support, an effective science of behavior has now emerged, thanks to the efforts of Darwin, Lloyd Morgan, E.L. Thorndike, John B. Watson, and others. Even Freud "contributed to the behavioristic argument by showing that mental activity did not, at least, *require* consciousness." Some forms of behaviorism, Skinner notes, dealt with the problem of mind by simply ruling it out of the realm of scientific study. His own version, *radical behaviorism,* does not. Private events, argues Skinner, can be considered part of behavior itself and can be interpreted in terms of what we know about public events in behavior. Certain contingencies of reinforcement allow us to respond discriminatively with respect to the world around us; they also allow us to respond discriminatively with respect to events inside of us, though the discriminations are necessarily less precise. "Conscious content," usually considered some sort of copy of the world, may also be considered behavior—the behavior of seeing in the absence of the object seen, hearing in the absence of the object heard, and so on.

Mental "way stations," such as cognitions and expectancies, may also be interpreted in behavioral terms.

Private events are further discussed in "Why I Am Not a Cognitive Psychologist" (1977; Chapter 8 of this book), in Chapters 16 and 17 of *Science and Human Behavior,* extensively in *About Behaviorism* (1974), in Chapter 19 of *Verbal Behavior* (1957), in a classic paper, "The Operational Analysis of Psychological Terms" (1945), in "The Problem of Consciousness—A Debate" (1967, with B. Blanshard), and elsewhere.

Behaviorism, with an accent on the last syllable, is not the scientific study of behavior but a philosophy of science concerned with the subject matter and methods of psychology. If psychology is a science of mental life—of the mind, of conscious experience—then it must develop and defend a special methodology, which it has not yet done successfully. If it is, on the other hand, a science of the behavior of organisms, human or otherwise, then it is part of biology, a natural science for which tested and highly successful methods are available. The basic issue is not the nature of the stuff of which the world is made or whether it is made of one stuff or two but rather the dimensions of the things studied by psychology and the methods relevant to them.

Mentalistic or psychic explanations of human behavior almost certainly originated in primitive animism. When people dreamed of being at distant places in spite of incontrovertible evidence that they had stayed in their beds, it was easy to conclude that some parts of them had actually left their bodies. A particularly vivid memory or a hallucination could be explained in the same way. The theory of an invisible, detachable self eventually proved useful for other purposes. It seemed to explain unexpected or abnormal episodes, even to the people behaving in an exceptional way because they were thus "possessed." It also served to explain the inexplicable. The human organism is so complex that it often seems to behave capriciously. It is tempting to attribute the visible behavior to another organism inside—to a little man or homunculus. The wishes of the little man become the acts of the person observed by others. The inner idea is put into outer words. Inner feelings find outward expression. The explanation is successful, of course, only so long as the behavior of the homunculus can be neglected.

Primitive origins are not necessarily to be held against an explanatory principle, but the little man is still with us in relatively primitive form. He was recently the hero of a television program called "Gateways to the Mind," one of a series of educational films sponsored by the Bell Telephone Laboratories and written with the help of a distinguished panel of scientists. The viewer learned, from animated cartoons, that when a person's finger is pricked, electrical impulses resembling flashes of lightning run up the afferent nerves and appear on a television screen in the brain. The little man wakes up, sees the flashing screen, reaches out, and pulls a lever. More flashes of lightning go down the nerves to the muscles, which then contract, as the finger is pulled away from the threatening stimulus. The behavior of the homunculus was, of course, not explained. An explanation would presumably require another film. And it, in turn, another.

The same pattern of explanation is invoked when we are told that the behavior of a delinquent is the result of a disordered personality or that the vagaries of a patient under analysis are due to conflicts among the superego, ego, and id. Nor can we escape from the primitive features by breaking the little man into pieces and dealing with his wishes, cognitions, motives, and so on, bit by bit. The objection is not that these things are mental but that they offer no real explanation and stand in the way of a more effective analysis.

It has been about 50 years since the behavioristic objection to this practice was first clearly stated, and it has been about 30 years since it has been very much discussed. A whole generation of psychologists has grown up without really coming into contact with the issue. Almost all current textbooks compromise: Rather than risk a loss of adoptions, they define psychology as the science of behavior *and* mental life. Meanwhile the older view has continued to receive strong support from areas in which there has been no comparable attempt at methodological reform. During this period, however, an effective experimental science of behavior has emerged. Much of what it has discovered bears on the basic issue. A restatement of radical behaviorism would therefore seem to be in order.

A rough history of the idea is not hard to trace. An occasional phrase in classic Greek writings which seemed to foreshadow the point of view need not be taken seriously. We may also pass over the early bravado of a La Mettrie who could shock the philosophical bourgeoisie by asserting that Man was only a machine. Nor were those who simply preferred, for practical reasons, to deal with behavior rather than with less accessible, but nevertheless acknowledged, mental activities close to what is meant by behaviorism today.[1]

The entering wedge appears to have been Darwin's preoccupation with the continuity of species. In supporting the theory of evolution, it was important to show that Man was not essentially different from the lower animals—that every human characteristic, including consciousness and reasoning powers, could be found in other species. Naturalists like Romanes began to collect stories which seemed to show that dogs, cats, elephants, and many other species were conscious and showed signs of reasoning. It was Lloyd Morgan, of course, who questioned this evidence with his Canon of Parsimony. Were there not other ways of accounting for what looked like signs of consciousness or rational powers? Thorndike's experiments at the end of the 19th century were in this vein. He showed that the behavior of a cat in escaping from a puzzle-box might seem to show reasoning but could be explained instead as the result of simpler processes. Thorndike remained a mentalist, but he greatly advanced the objective study of behavior which had been attributed to mental processes.

The next step was inevitable: If evidence of consciousness and reasoning could be explained in other ways in animals, why not also in Man? And if this was the case, what became of psychology as a science of mental life? It was John B. Watson who made the first clear, if rather noisy, proposal that psychology should be regarded simply as a science of behavior. He was not in a very good position to defend it. He had little scientific material to use in his reconstruction. He was forced to pad his textbook with discussions of the physiology of receptor systems and muscles and with physiological theories which were at the time no more susceptible to proof than the mentalistic theories they were intended to replace. A need for "mediators" of behavior which might serve as objective alternatives to thought processes led him to emphasize subaudible speech. The notion was intriguing, because one can usually observe oneself thinking in this way, but it was by no means an adequate or comprehensive explanation. He tangled with introspective psychologists by denying the existence of images. He may well have been acting in good faith, for it has been said that he himself did not have visual imagery; but his arguments caused unnecessary trouble. The relative importance of a genetic endowment in explaining behavior proved to be another disturbing digression.

All this made it easy to lose sight of the central argument—that behavior which seemed to be the product of mental activity could be explained in other ways. Moreover, the introspectionists were prepared to challenge it. As late as 1883 Francis Galton[2] could write: "Many persons, especially women and intelligent children, take pleasure in introspection, and strive their very best to explain their mental processes" (p. 87). But introspection was already being taken seriously. The concept of a science of mind in which mental events obeyed mental laws had led to the development of psychophysical methods and to the accumulation of facts which seemed to bar the extension of the principle of parsimony. What might hold for animals did not hold for people because people could see their mental processes.

Curiously enough, part of the answer was supplied by the psychoanalysts, who insisted that, although we might be able to see some of our mental life, we could not see all of it. The kind of thoughts Freud called "unconscious" took place without the knowledge of the thinker. From an association, verbal slip, or dream it could be shown that a man must have responded to a passing stimulus, although he could not tell you that he had done so. More complex thought processes, including problem solving and verbal play, could also go on without the thinker's knowledge. Freud had devised, and never abandoned faith in, one of the most elaborate mental apparatuses of all time. He nevertheless contributed to the behavioristic argument by showing that mental activity did not, at least, *require* consciousness. His proofs that thinking had occurred without introspective recognition were, indeed, clearly in the spirit of Lloyd Morgan. They were operational analyses of mental life—even though, for Freud, only the unconscious part of it. Experimental evidence pointing in the same direction soon began to accumulate.

But that was not the whole answer. What about the part of mental life which one can see? It is a difficult question, no matter what one's point of view, partly because it raises the question of what seeing means and partly because the events seen are private. The fact of privacy cannot, of course, be questioned. Each person is in special contact with a small part of the universe enclosed within the skin. To take a noncontroversial example, each person is uniquely subject to certain kinds of proprioceptive and interoceptive stimulation. Though two people may in some sense be said to see the same light or hear the same sound, they cannot feel the same distention of a bile duct or the same bruised muscle. (When privacy is invaded with scientific instruments, the form of stimulation is changed; the scales read by the scientists are not the private events themselves.)

Mentalistic psychologists insist that there are other kinds of events which are uniquely accessible to the owner of the skin within which they occur but which lack the physical dimensions of proprioceptive or interoceptive stimuli. They are as different from physical events as colors are from wave lengths of light. There are even better reasons, therefore, why two people cannot suffer each other's toothaches, recall each other's memories, or share each other's happinesses. The importance assigned to this kind of world varies. For some, it is the only world there is. For others, it is the only part of the world which can be directly known. For still others, it is a special part of what can be known. In any case, the problem of how one knows about the subjective world of another must be faced. Apart from the question of what "knowing" means, the problem is one of accessibility.

PUBLIC AND PRIVATE EVENTS

One solution, often regarded as behavioristic, is to grant the distinction between public and private events and rule the latter out of scientific consideration. This is a congenial solution for those to whom scientific truth is a matter of convention or agreement among observers. It is essentially the line taken by logical positivism and physical operationism. Hogben[3] has recently redefined "behaviorist" in this spirit. A subtitle of his *Statistical Theory* is "an examination of the contemporary crises in statistical theory from a behaviourist viewpoint," and this is amplified in the following way:

The behaviourist, as I here use the term, does not deny the convenience of classifying *processes* as mental or material. He recognises the distinction between personality and corpse: but he has not yet had the privilege of attending an identity parade in which human minds without bodies are by common recognition distinguishable from living human bodies without minds. Till then, he is content to discuss probability in the vocabulary of *events,* including audible or visibly recorded assertions of human beings as such. (p. 9)

The behavioristic position, so defined, is simply that of the publicist and "has no concern with structure and mechanism" (p. 7).

The point of view is often called operational, and it is significant that P.W. Bridgman's physical operationism could not save him from an extreme solipsism even within physical science itself. Though he insisted that he was not a solipsist, he was never able to reconcile seemingly public physical knowledge with the private world of the scientist.[4,5] Applied to psychological problems, operationism has been no more successful. We may recognize the restrictions imposed by the operations through which we can know of the existence of properties of subjective events, but the operations cannot be identified with the events themselves. S.S. Stevens has applied Bridgman's principle to psychology, not to decide whether subjective events exist, but to determine the extent to which we can deal with them scientifically.[6]

Behaviorists have, from time to time, examined the problem of privacy, and some of them have excluded so-called sensations, images, thought processes, and so on, from their deliberations. When they have done so not because such things do not exist but because they are out of reach of their methods, the charge is justified that they have neglected the facts of consciousness. The strategy is, however, quite unwise. It is particularly important that a science of behavior face the problem of privacy. It may do so without abandoning the basic position of behaviorism. Science often talks about things it cannot see or measure. When you toss a penny into the air, it must be assumed that you toss the earth beneath you downward. It is quite out of the question to see or measure the effect on the earth, but the effect must be assumed for the sake of a consistent account. An adequate science of behavior must consider events taking place within the skin of the organism, not as physiological mediators of behavior, but as part of behavior itself. It can deal with these events without assuming that they have any special nature or must be known in any special way. The skin is not that important as a boundary. Private and public events have the same kinds of physical dimensions.

In the 50 years since a behavioristic philosophy was first stated, facts and principles bearing on the basic issues have steadily accumulated. For one thing, a scientific analysis of behavior has yielded a sort of empirical epistemology. The subject matter of a science of behavior includes the behavior of scientists and other knowers. The techniques available to such a science give an empirical theory of knowledge certain advantages over theories derived from philosophy and logic. The problem of privacy may be approached in a fresh direction by starting with behavior rather than with immediate experience. The strategy is certainly no more arbitrary or circular than the earlier practice, and it has a surprising result. Instead of concluding that we can know only our subjective experiences—that we are bound forever to our private world and that the external world is only a construct—a behavioral theory of knowledge suggests that it is the private world which, if not entirely unknowable, is at least not likely to be known well. The relations between organism and environment involved in knowing are of such a sort that the privacy of the world within the skin imposes more serious limitations on personal knowledge than on the accessibility of that world to the scientist.

An organism learns to react discriminatively to the world around it under certain contingencies of reinforcement. Thus, a child learns to name a color correctly when a given response is reinforced in the presence of the color and extinguished in its absence. The verbal community may make the reinforcement of an extensive repertoire of responses contingent on subtle properties of colored stimuli. We have reason to believe that the child will not discriminate among colors—will not see two colors as different—until exposed to such contingencies. So far as we know, the same process of differential reinforcement is required if a child is to distinguish among events occurring inside the skin.

Many contingencies involving private stimuli need not be arranged by a verbal community, for they follow from simple mechanical relations among stimuli, responses, and reinforcing consequences. The various motions which comprise turning a handspring, for example, are under the control of external and internal stimuli and subject to external and internal reinforcing consequences. But the performer is not necessarily "aware" of the stimuli controlling the behavior, no matter how appropriate and skillful it may be. "Knowing" or "being aware of" what is happening in turning a handspring involves discriminative responses, such as naming or describing, which arise from contingencies necessarily arranged by a verbal environment. Such environments are common. The community is generally interested in what we are doing, have done, or are planning to do and why, and it arranges contingencies which generate verbal responses which name and describe the external and internal stimuli associated with these events. It challenges us by asking "How do you know?" and we answer, if at all, by describing some of the variables of which our verbal behavior was a function. The "awareness" resulting from all this is a social product.

In attempting to set up such a repertoire, however, the verbal community works under a severe handicap. It cannot always arrange the contingencies required for subtle discriminations. It cannot teach a child to call one pattern of private stimuli "diffidence" and another "embarrassment" as effectively as it teaches him or her to call one stimulus "red" and another "orange," for it cannot be sure of the presence or absence of the private patterns of stimuli appropriate to reinforcement or lack of reinforcement. Privacy thus causes trouble, first of all, *for the verbal community.* The individual suffers in turn. Because the community cannot reinforce self-descriptive responses consistently, a person cannot describe or otherwise "know" events occurring within the skin as subtly and precisely as events in the world at large.[7]

There are, of course, differences between external and internal stimuli which are not mere differences in location. Proprioceptive and interoceptive stimuli have a certain intimacy. They are likely to be especially familiar. They are very much with us; we cannot escape from a toothache as easily as from a deafening noise. They may well be of a special kind; the stimuli we feel in pride or sorrow may not closely resemble those we feel in sandpaper or satin. But this does not mean that they differ in physical status. In particular, it does not mean that they can be more easily or more directly known. What is particularly clear and familiar to the potential knower may be strange and distant to the verbal community responsible for the knowledge.

CONSCIOUS CONTENT

What *are* the private events to which, at least in a limited way, a person may come to respond in ways we call "perceiving" or "knowing"? Let us begin with the oldest, and in many ways the most difficult, kind represented by "the stubborn fact of consciousness." What is happening when people observe the conscious contents of their minds, when they "look at their sensations or images"? Western philosophy and science have been handicapped in answering these questions by an unfortunate metaphor. The Greeks could not explain how people could have knowledge of something with which they were not in immediate contact. How could they know an object on the other side of the room, for example? Did they reach out and touch it with some sort of invisible probe? Or did they never actually come in contact with the object at all but only with a copy of it inside their bodies? Plato supported the copy theory with his metaphor of the cave. Perhaps, he said, we never see the real world at all but only shadows of it on the wall of the cave in which each of us is imprisoned. Copies of the real world projected into the body could compose the experience which we directly know. A similar theory could also explain how one can see objects which are "not really there," as in hallucinations, afterimages, and memories. Neither explanation is, of course, satisfactory. How a copy may arise at a distance is at least as puzzling as how one may know an object at a distance. Seeing things which are not really there is no harder to explain than the occurrence of copies of things not there to be copied.

The search for copies of the world within the body, particularly in the nervous system, still goes on, but with discouraging results. If the retina could suddenly be developed, like a photographic plate, it would yield a poor picture. The nerve impulses in the optic tract must have an even more tenuous resemblance to "what is seen." The patterns of vibrations which strike our ear when we listen to music are quickly lost in transmission. The bodily reactions to substances tasted, smelled, and touched would scarcely qualify as faithful reproductions. These facts are discouraging for those who are looking for copies of the real world within the body, but they are fortunate for psychophysiology as a whole. At some point the organism must do more than create duplicates. It must see, hear, smell, and so on, as forms of *action* rather than of *reproduction. It must do some of the things it is differentially reinforced for doing when it learns to respond discriminatively.* The sooner the pattern of the external world disappears after impinging on the organism, the sooner the organism may get on with these other functions.

The need for something beyond, and quite different from, copying is not widely understood. Suppose someone were to coat the occipital lobes of the brain with a special photographic emulsion which, when developed, yielded a reasonable copy of a current visual stimulus. In many quarters this would be regarded as a triumph in the physiology of vision. Yet nothing could be more disastrous, for we should have to start all over again and ask how the organism sees a picture in its occipital cortex, and we should now have much less of the brain available in which to seek an answer. It adds nothing to an explanation of how an organism reacts to a stimulus to trace the pattern of the stimulus into the body. It is most convenient, for both organism and psychophysiologist, if the external world is never copied—if the world we know is simply the world around us. The same may be said of theories according to which the brain interprets signals sent to it and in some sense reconstructs external stimuli. If the real world is, indeed, scrambled in transmission but later reconstructed in the brain, we must then start all over again and explain how the organism sees the reconstruction.

An adequate treatment of this point would require a thorough analysis of the behavior of seeing and of the conditions under which we see (to continue with vision as a convenient modality). It would be unwise to exaggerate our success to date. Discriminative visual behavior arises from contingencies involving external stimuli and overt responses, but possible private accompaniments must not be overlooked. Some of the consequences of such contingencies seem well established. It is usually easiest for us to see a friend when we are looking at him, because visual stimuli similar to those present when the behavior was acquired exert maximal control over the response. But mere visual stimulation is not enough; even after having been exposed to the necessary reinforcement, we may not see a friend who is present unless we have reason to do so. On the other hand, if the reasons are strong enough, we may see him in someone bearing only a superficial resemblance or when no one like him is present at all. If conditions favor seeing something else, we may behave accordingly. If, on a hunting trip, it is important to see a deer, we may glance toward our friend at a distance, see him as a deer, and shoot.

It is not, however, seeing our friend which raises the question of conscious content but "seeing that we are seeing him." There are no natural contingencies for such behavior. We learn to see that we are seeing only because a verbal community arranges for us to do so. We usually acquire the behavior when we are under appropriate visual stimulation, but it does not follow that the thing seen must be present when we see that we are seeing it. The contingencies arranged by the verbal environment may set up self-descriptive responses describing the *behavior* of seeing even when the thing seen is not present.

If seeing does not require the presence of things seen, we need not be concerned about certain mental processes said to be involved in the construction of such things—images, memories, and dreams, for example. We may regard a dream, not as a display of things seen by the dreamer, but simply as the behavior of seeing. At no time during a daydream, for example, should we expect to find within the organism anything which corresponds to the external stimuli present when the dreamer first acquired the behavior now being exhibited. In simple recall we need not suppose that we wander through some storehouse of memory until we find an object which we then contemplate. Instead of assuming that we begin with a tendency to *recognize* such an object once it is found, it is simpler to assume that we begin with a tendency to *see* it. Techniques of self-management which facilitate recall—for example, the use of mnemonic devices—can be formulated as ways of strengthening behavior rather than of creating objects to be seen. Freud dramatized the issue with respect to dreaming when asleep in his concept of dreamwork—an activity in which some part of the dreamer played the role of a theatrical producer while another part sat in the audience. If a dream is, indeed, something seen, then we must suppose that it is wrought as such; but if it is simply the behavior of seeing, the dreamwork may be dropped from the analysis. It took a long time to understand that when one dreamed of a wolf, no wolf was actually there. It has taken much longer to understand that not even a representation of a wolf is there.

Eye movements which appear to be associated with dreaming are in accord with this interpretation, since it is not likely that the dreamer is actually watching a dream on the undersides of the eyelids. When memories are aroused by electrical stimulation of the brain, as in the work of Wilder

Penfield, it is also simpler to assume that it is the behavior of seeing, hearing, and so on which is aroused rather than some copy of early environmental events which the subject then looks at or listens to. Behavior similar to the responses to the original events must be assumed in both cases—the subject sees or hears—but the reproduction of the events seen or heard is a needless complication. The familiar process of response chaining is available to account for the serial character of the behavior of remembering, but the serial linkage of stored experiences (suggesting engrams in the form of sound films) demands a new mechanism.

The heart of the behavioristic position on conscious experience may be summed up in this way: Seeing does not imply something seen. We acquire the behavior of seeing under stimulation from actual objects, but it may occur in the absence of these objects under the control of other variables. (So far as the world within the skin is concerned, it always occurs in the absence of such objects.) We also acquire the behavior of seeing-that-we-are-seeing when we are seeing actual objects, but it may also occur in their absence.

To question the reality or the nature of the things seen in conscious experience is not to question the value of introspective psychology or its methods. Current problems in sensation are mainly concerned with the physiological function of receptors and associated neural mechanisms. Problems in perception are, at the moment, less intimately related to specific mechanisms, but the trend appears to be in the same direction. So far as behavior is concerned, both sensation and perception may be analyzed as forms of stimulus control. The subject need not be regarded as observing or evaluating conscious experiences. Apparent anomalies of stimulus control, which are now explained by appealing to a psychophysical relation or to the laws of perception, may be studied in their own right. It is, after all, no real solution to attribute them to the slippage inherent in converting a physical stimulus into a subjective experience.

The experimental analysis of behavior has a little more to say on this subject. Its techniques have recently been extended to what might be called the psychophysics of lower organisms. Blough's adaptation of the Békésy technique—for example, in determining the spectral sensitivity of pigeons and monkeys—yields sensory data comparable with the reports of a trained observer.[8,9] Herrnstein and van Sommers have recently developed a procedure in which pigeons "bisect sensory intervals."[10] It is tempting to describe these procedures by saying that investigators have found ways to get nonverbal organisms to describe their sensations. The fact is that a form of stimulus control has been investigated without using a repertoire of self-observation or, rather, by constructing a special repertoire, the nature and origin of which are clearly understood. Rather than describe such experiments with the terminology of introspection, we may formulate them in their proper place in an experimental analysis. The behavior of the observer in the traditional psychophysical experiment may then be reinterpreted accordingly.

MENTAL WAY STATIONS

So much for "conscious content," the classical problem in mentalistic philosophies. There are other mental states or processes to be taken into account. Moods, cognitions, and expectancies, for example, are also examined introspectively, and descriptions are used in psychological formulations. The conditions under which descriptive repertoires are set up are much less successfully controlled. Terms describing sensations and images are taught by manipulating discriminative stimuli—a relatively amenable class of variables. The remaining mental events are related to such operations as deprivation and satiation, emotional stimulation, and various schedules of reinforcement. The difficulties they present to the verbal community are suggested by the fact that there is no psychophysics of mental states of this sort. That fact has not inhibited the use of such states in explanatory systems.

In an experimental analysis, the relation between a property of behavior and an operation performed upon the organism is studied directly. Traditional mentalistic formulations, however, emphasize certain way stations. Where an experimental analysis might examine the effect of punishment on behavior, a mentalistic psychology will be concerned first with the effect of punishment in generating feelings of anxiety and then with the effect of anxiety on behavior. The mental state seems to bridge the gap between dependent and independent variables and is particularly attractive when these are separated by long periods of time—when, for example, the punishment occurs in childhood and the effect appears in the behavior of the adult.

The practice is widespread. In a demonstration experiment, a hungry pigeon was conditioned to turn around in a clockwise direction. A final, smoothly executed pattern of behavior was shaped by reinforcing successive approximations with food. Students who had watched the demonstration were asked to write an account of what they had seen. Their responses included the following: (1) The pigeon was conditioned to *expect* reinforcement for the right kind of behavior; (2) the pigeon walked around, *hoping* that something would bring the food back again; (3) the pigeon *observed* that a certain behavior seemed to produce a particular result; (4) the pigeon *felt* that food would be given it because of its action; and (5) the pigeon came to *associate* its action with the click of the food-dispenser. The observed facts could be stated respectively as follows: (1) Reinforcement was delivered *when* the pigeon emitted a given kind of behavior; (2) the pigeon walked around *until* the food container again appeared; (3) a certain behavior *produced* a particular result; (4) food was given to the pigeon *when* it acted in a given way; and (5) the click of the food-dispenser *was temporally related* to the pigeon's action. These statements describe the contingencies of reinforcement. The expressions "expect," "hope," "observe," "feel," and "associate" go beyond them to identify effects on the pigeon. The effect actually observed was clear enough: The pigeon turned more skillfully and more frequently; but that was not the effect reported by the students. (If pressed, they would doubtless have said that the pigeon turned more skillfully and more frequently *because* it expected, hoped, and felt that if it did so food would appear.)

The events reported by the students were observed, if at all, in their own behavior. They were describing what they would have expected, felt, and hoped for under similar circumstances. But they were able to do so only because a verbal community had brought relevant terms under the control of certain stimuli, and this was done *when the community had access only to the kinds of public information available to the students in the demonstration.* Whatever the students knew about themselves which permitted them to infer comparable events in the pigeon must have been learned from a verbal community which saw no more of their behavior than they had seen of the pigeon's. Private stimuli may have entered into the control of their self-descriptive repertoires, but the readiness with which they applied them to the pigeon indicates that external stimuli had remained important. The extraordinary strength of a mentalistic interpretation is really a sort of proof that in describing a private way station one is, to a considerable extent, making use of public information. (The speed and facility with which the mental life of a pigeon or person is reported are suspicious. Nothing is easier than to say that people do things "because they like to do them" or that they do one thing rather than another "because they have made a choice." But have we the knowledge about private lives which statements of that sort imply, or at least ought to imply? It is much more likely that we are employing a standard set of explanations which have no more validity—and in the long run are no more useful—than a standard set of metaphors.)

The mental way station is often accepted as a terminal datum, however. When a man must be trained to discriminate between different planes, ships, and so on, it is tempting to stop at the point at which he can be said to *identify* such objects. It is implied that if he can identify an object, he can name it, label it, describe it, or act appropriately in some other way. In the training process he always behaves in one of these ways; no way station called "identification" appears in practice or need appear in theory. (Any discussion of the discriminative behavior generated by the verbal environment to permit a man to examine his conscious content must be qualified accordingly.)

Cognitive theories stop at way stations where the mental action is usually somewhat more complex than identification. For example, subjects are said to *know* who and where they are, what something is, or what has happened or is going to happen—regardless of the forms of behavior through which this knowledge was set up or which may now testify to its existence. Similarly, in accounting for verbal behavior, a listener or reader is said to understand the *meaning* of a passage, although the actual changes brought about by listening to, or reading, the passage are not specified. In the same way, schedules of reinforcement are sometimes studied simply for their effects on the *expectations* of the organism exposed to them, without discussing the implied relation between expectation and action. Recall, inference, and reasoning may be formulated only to the point at which *an experience is remembered or a conclusion reached,* behavioral manifestations being ignored. In practice, the investigator always carries through to some response, if only a response of self-description.

On the other hand, mental states are often studied as causes of action. A speaker thinks of something to say before saying it, and this explains what is said, although the source of the thought is not examined. An unusual act is called "impulsive," without inquiring further into the origin of the unusual impulse. A behavioral maladjustment shows anxiety, the source of which is neglected. One salivates upon seeing a lemon because it reminds one of a sour taste, but why it does so is not specified. The formulation leads directly to a technology based on the manipulation of mental states. To change voting behavior, we "change opinions"; to induce action, we "strengthen belief"; to make a baby eat, we make it feel hungry; to prevent wars, we reduce "warlike tensions in the minds of men"; to effect psychotherapy, we alter troublesome "mental states." In practice, all these ways of changing minds reduce to manipulating environments, verbal or otherwise.

In many cases we can reconstruct a complete causal chain by identifying the mental state which is the effect of an environmental variable with the mental state which is the cause of action. But this is not always enough. In traditional mentalistic philosophies various things happen at the way station which alter the relation between the terminal events. The psychophysical functions and the perceptual laws which distort the physical stimulus before it reaches the way station have already been mentioned. Once the station is reached, other effects are said to occur. Mental states alter one another. A painful memory may never affect behavior, or may affect it in a different way, if another mental state succeeds in repressing it. Conflicting variables may be reconciled before reaching behavior if we engage in the mental action called "making a decision." Dissonant cognitions generated by conflicting conditions of reinforcement will not be reflected in our behavior if we can "persuade ourselves" that one condition was actually of a different magnitude or kind. These disturbances in simple causal linkages between environment and behavior can be formulated and studied experimentally as interactions among variables; but the possibility has not been fully exploited, and the effects still provide a formidable stronghold for mentalistic theories designed to bridge the gap between dependent and independent variables in the analysis of behavior.

METHODOLOGICAL OBJECTIONS

The behavioristic argument is nevertheless still valid. We may object, first, to the predilection for unfinished causal sequences. A disturbance in behavior is not explained by relating it to felt anxiety until the anxiety has in turn been explained. An action is not explained by attributing it to expectations until the expectations have in turn been accounted for. Complete causal sequences might, of course, include references to way stations, but the fact is that the way station generally interrupts the account in one direction or the other. For example, there must be thousands of instances in the psycho-analytic literature in which a thought or memory is said to have been relegated to the unconscious because it was painful or intolerable, but the percentage of those offering even the most casual suggestion as to why it was painful or intolerable must be very small. Perhaps explanations could have been offered, but the practice has discouraged the completion of the causal sequence.

A second objection is that a preoccupation with mental way stations burdens a science of behavior with all the problems raised by the limitations and inaccuracies of self-descriptive repertoires. We need not take the extreme position that mediating events or any data about them obtained through introspection must be ruled out of consideration, but we should certainly welcome other ways of treating the data more satisfactorily. Independent variables change the behaving organism, often in ways which survive for many years, and such changes affect subsequent behavior. The subject may be able to describe some of these intervening states in useful ways, either before or after they have affected behavior. On the other hand, behavior may be extensively modified by variables of which, and of the effect of which, the subject is never aware. So far as we know, self-descriptive responses do not alter controlling relationships. If a severe punishment is less effective than a mild one, it is not because it cannot be "kept in mind." (Certain behaviors involved in self-management, such as reviewing a history of punishment, may alter behavior; but they do so by introducing other variables rather than by changing a given relation.)

Perhaps the most serious objection concerns the order of events. Observation of one's own behavior necessarily follows the behavior. Responses which seem to be describing intervening states alone may embrace behavioral effects. "I am hungry" may describe, in part, the strength of the speaker's on-going ingestive behavior. "I was hungrier than I thought" seems particularly to describe behavior rather than an intervening, possibly causal, state. More serious examples of a possibly mistaken order are to be found in theories of psychotherapy. Before asserting that the release of a repressed wish has a therapeutic effect on behavior, or that one who undertands a neurotic illness will recover, we should consider the plausible alternative that a change in behavior resulting from therapy has made it possible for the subject to recall a repressed wish or to understand the illness.

The importance of behaviorism as a philosophy of science naturally declines as a scientific analysis becomes more powerful, because there is then less need to use data in the form of self-description. The mentalism that survives in the fields of sensation and perception will disappear as alternative techniques are proved valuable in analyzing stimulus control, and similar changes may be anticipated elsewhere. Cognitive psychologists and others still try to circumvent the explicit control of variables by describing contingencies of reinforcement to their subjects in "instructions." They also try to dispense with recording behavior in a form from which probability of response can be estimated by asking their subjects to evaluate their tendencies to respond. But people rarely respond to descriptions of contingencies as they would under direct exposure to them, nor can they accurately predict their rates of responding, particularly the course of the subtle changes in rate which are a commonplace in the experimental analysis of behavior. These attempts to short-circuit an experimental analysis can no longer be justified on grounds of expedience, and there are many reasons for abandoning them. Much remains to be done, however, before the facts to which they are currently applied can be said to be adequately understood.

BEHAVIORISM AND BIOLOGY

Elsewhere, the scientific study of Man has scarcely recognized the need for reform. The biologists, for example, begin with a certain advantage in studying the behaving organism, for the structures they analyze have an evident physical status. The nervous system is somehow earthier than the behavior for which it is largely responsible. Philosophers and psychologists alike have, from time to time, sought escape from mentalism in physiology. When we see red, we may be seeing the physiological effect of a red stimulus; when we merely imagine red, we may be seeing the same effect re-aroused. Psychophysical and perceptual distortions may be wrought by physiological processes. What we feel as anxiety may be autonomic reactions to threatening stimuli. And so on. This may solve the minor problem of the nature of subjective experience, but it does not solve any of the methodological problems with which behaviorism is most seriously concerned. A physiological translation of mentalistic terms may reassure those who want to avoid dualism, but inadequacies in the formulation survive translation.

When writing about the behavior of organisms, biologists tend to be more mentalistic than psychologists. Adrian could not understand how a nerve impulse could cause a thought. A recent article on the visual space sense in *Science*[11] asserts that "the final event in the chain from the retina to the brain is a psychic experience" (p. 763). Another investigator reports research on "the brain and its contained mind." Pharmacologists study the "psychotropic" drugs. Psychosomatic medicine insists on the influence of mind over matter. And psychologists join their physiological colleagues in looking for feelings, emotions, drives, and pleasurable aspects of positive reinforcement in the brain.

The facts uncovered in such research are important, both for their own sake and for their bearing on behavior. Physiologists study structures and processes without which behavior could not occur. They are in a position to supply a "reductionist" explanation beyond the reach of an analysis which confines itself to terminal variables. They cannot do this well, however, so long as they accept traditional mentalistic formulations. Only an experimental analysis of behavior will define their task in optimal terms. The point is demonstrated by recent research in psychopharmacology. When the behavioral drugs first began to attract attention, they were studied with impromptu techniques based on self-observation, usually designed to quantify subjective reports. Eventually the methods of an experimental analysis proved their value in generating reproducible segments of behavior upon which effects of drugs could be observed and in terms of which they could be effectively defined and classified. For the same reasons, brain physiology will move forward more rapidly when it recognizes that its role is to account for the mediation of behavior rather than of mind.

BEHAVIORISM IN THE SOCIAL SCIENCES

There is also still a need for behaviorism in the social sciences, where psychology has long been used for explanatory purposes. Economics has had its Economic Man. Political science has considered Man as a Political Animal. Parts of anthropology and sociology have found a place for psychoanalysis. The relevance of psychology to linguistics has been debated for more than half a century. Studies of scientific method have oscillated between logical and empirical analyses. In all these fields, "psychologizing" has often had disappointing results and has frequently been rejected by turning to an extreme formalism emphasizing objective facts. Economics confines itself to its own abundant data. Political scientists limit themselves to whatever may be studied with a few empirical tools and techniques and confine themselves, when they deal with theory, to formalistic analyses of political structures. A strong structuralist movement is evident in sociology. Linguistics emphasizes formal analyses of semantics and grammar.

Strait-laced commitments to pure description and formal analysis appear to leave no place for explanatory principles, and the shortcoming is often blamed on the exclusion of mental activities. For example, a recent symposium on "The Limits of Behavioralism in Political Science"[12] complains of a neglect of subjective experience, ideas, motives, feelings, attitudes, values, and so on. This is reminiscent of attacks on behaviorism. In any case, it shows the same misunderstanding of the scope of a behavioral analysis. In its extension to the social sciences, as in psychology proper, behaviorism means more than a commitment to objective measurement. No entity or process which has any useful explanatory force is to be rejected on the ground that it is subjective or mental. The data which have made it important must, however, be studied and formulated in effective ways. The assignment is well within the scope of an experimental analysis of behavior, which thus offers a promising alternative to a commitment to pure description on the one hand and an appeal to mentalistic theories on the other. To extend behaviorism as a philosophy of science to the study of political and economic behavior, of the behavior of people in groups, of people speaking and listening, teaching and learning—this is not "psychologizing" in the traditional sense. It is simply the application of a tested formulation to important parts of the field of human behavior.

REFERENCES AND NOTES

[1]The doctrine of parallelism may have prepared the ground with its acknowledgment that the physical aspects of behavior might be accounted for without referring to mental aspects.

[2]Galton, F. *Inquiries into human faculty and its development.* New York: Macmillan, 1883.

[3]Hogben, L. *Statistical theory.* London: George Allen and Unwin, 1957.

[4]Bridgman, P. *The nature of some of our physical concepts.* New York: Philosophical Library, 1952.

[5]Bridgman, P. *The way things are.* Cambridge: Harvard University Press, 1959.

[6]Stevens, S.S. The operational basis of psychology. *American Journal of Psychology,* 1935, *47,* 323-330.

[7]For an analysis of the ways in which the verbal community may partly resolve its problem, see "The Operational Analysis of Psychological Terms" (1945). Although the private world is defined anatomically as "within the skin," the boundaries are the limits beyond which the reinforcing community cannot maintain effective contingencies.

[8]Blough, D.S., & Schrier, A.M. Scotopic spectral sensitivity in the monkey. *Science,* 1963, *139,* 493-494.

[9]Blough, D.S. Dark adaptation in the pigeon. *Journal of Comparative and Physiological Psychology*, 1956, *49*, 425-430.

[10]Herrnstein, R.J., & van Sommers, P. Method for sensory scaling with animals. *Science*, 1962, *135*, 40-41.

[11]Ogle, K.N. The visual space sense. *Science*, 1962, *135*, 763-771.

[12]Charlesworth, J.C. (Ed.). *The limits of behavioralism in political science*. Philadelphia: American Academy of Political and Social Sciences, 1962.

POSTSCRIPT

All modern languages—but perhaps English most of all—are heavily mentalistic. It is almost impossible to discuss a simple exchange between two people without invoking minds, thoughts, feelings, intentions, and so on. Almost all scholarly treatments of human behavior—philosophy, theology, logistics, political science, economics, and so on—use terms which imply that a person is a creative, initiating agent. For certain purposes the terms work well enough, just as our everyday physical vocabulary works well enough even though it is at variance with physics as a science. It is therefore not surprising that when the first revolutionary wave of behavioristic thought receded in the thirties and forties, psychology should return to its old ways. As a result the central argument of behaviorism began to be overlooked and misunderstood. Textbook accounts became more and more simplified, and were illustrated by stereotyped reports of old experiments, such as Pavlov's conditioned reflex.

Those who remained behavioral scientists reported their experiments for their behavioral colleagues without relating them to the philosophical issues. Philosophers—such as Gilbert Ryle, A.J. Ayer, and those associated with the Vienna Circle—came close to behaviorism but offered no experimental support for their theories. When I was invited to give a paper at a symposium on "Behaviorism and Phenomenology" at Rice University I took the opportunity to restate what seemed to me to be the central theme of radical behaviorism, and I wrote the present paper.

C H A P T E R 6

Freedom and the Control of Men

EDITOR'S NOTE

The article was first published in the *American Scholar* (Winter 1955-56, *25*, 47-65) and has been republished in all editions of *Cumulative Record* and elsewhere. Freedom and control have been major concerns in Skinner's writings for more than 3 decades. They were discussed at length in his utopian novel, *Walden Two* (1948), in *Science and Human Behavior* (1953), in a series of papers—"The Control of Human Behavior" (1955), the current paper, "Some Issues Concerning the Control of Human Behavior" (1956, with Carl Rogers), "The Design of Cultures" (1961), "Contingencies of Reinforcement in the Design of a Culture" (1966), "Visions of Utopia" (1967), "Utopia Through the Control of Human Behavior" (1967), "The Design of Experimental Communities" (1968), "Freedom and Dignity Revisited" (1972), "Walden Two Revisited" (1976), "Between Freedom and Despotism" (1977)—and most extensively in his 1971 best seller, *Beyond Freedom and Dignity*. The papers have been reprinted in *Contingencies of Reinforcement, Cumulative Record,* and *Reflections on Behaviorism and Society* (some with new titles).

In "Freedom and the Control of Men" Skinner argues that a science of behavior may be put to use in cultural design to produce "happy, informed, skillful, well behaved, and productive" people. Many objections to such a program have been made: Human nature is unchangeable, the necessary techniques of change are not available, we would not know what changes to make even if we had the techniques. But change is in fact possible and the techniques are available. The assertion that we don't know what changes to make is "one of the great hoaxes of the century": We can agree, for example, that "health is better than illness, wisdom better than ignorance, love better than hate, and productive energy better

---

This article originally appeared in *American Scholar,* Winter 1955-1956, *25*, 47-65. Reprinted by permission of the publisher.

than neurotic sloth." The scientifically guided community would be run as an experiment; and, as in any experiment, the original design would be constantly modified as new data became available.

The scientific view of humankind has not been widely accepted because, for one thing, it opposes the democratic conception. We commonly characterize people as creative and self-determining, but for the scientist, "caprice is only another name for behavior for which we have not yet found a cause." The democratic view served its purpose in spurring revolution and freeing people from aversive forms of control, but it has outlived its usefulness. "We are all controlled by the world in which we live....The question is this: Are we to be controlled by accident, by tyrants, or by ourselves in effective cultural design?"

Other objections to the scientific utopia are discussed: the apparently important role of accident in the unplanned community, the fear of uniformity, Krutch's claim that the planned community is "lacking in dignity." Skinner argues that "having to be good" is an "expendable honorific." A culture in which people acquire an education and behave well without effort is preferable to the current one, even if it means revising our concepts of credit and dignity. As we move toward a world in which fewer people suffer from a lack of education and basic necessities and in which peace replaces war, we shall be able to dispense with the praise we now give for achievements and the blame we now give for failures: "We may mourn the passing of heroes but not the conditions which make for heroism."

The growth of a science of behavior, concludes Skinner, "is a consistent and probably inevitable part" of Western democracy. It would be a "defeat" for our way of life if, instead of benefiting from it ourselves, it fell into the hands of "despots" or to "those of good will in other political communities" (presumably communists). We would thus "leave to others the next step in the long struggle to control nature and ourselves."

The second half of the 20th century may be remembered for its solution of a curious problem. Although Western democracy created the conditions responsible for the rise of modern science, it is now evident that it may never fully profit from that achievement. The so-called "democratic philosophy" of human behavior to which it also gave rise is increasingly in conflict with the application of the methods of science to human affairs. Unless this conflict is somehow resolved, the ultimate goals of democracy may be long deferred.

I

Just as biographers and critics look for external influences to account for the traits and achievements of those they study, so science ultimately explains behavior in terms of "causes" or conditions which lie beyond the individual. As more and more causal relations are demonstrated, a practical corollary becomes difficult to resist: It should be possible to *produce* behavior according to plan simply by arranging the proper conditions. Now, among the specifications which might reasonably be submitted to a behavioral technology are these: Let people be happy, informed, skillful, well behaved, and productive.

This immediate practical implication of a science of behavior has a familiar ring, for it recalls the doctrine of human perfectibility of 18th- and 19th-century humanism. A science of the human organism shares the optimism of that philosophy and supplies striking support for the working faith that people can build a better world and, through it, better people. The support comes just in time, for there has been little optimism of late among those who speak from the traditional point of view. Democracy has become "realistic," and it is only with some embarrassment that one admits today to perfectionistic or utopian thinking.

The earlier temper is worth considering, however. History records many foolish and unworkable schemes for human betterment, but almost all the great changes in our culture which we now regard as worthwhile can be traced to perfectionistic philosophies. Governmental, religious, educational, economic, and social reforms follow a common pattern. Someone believes that a change in a cultural practice—for example, in the rules of evidence in a court of law, in the characterization of one's relation to God, in the way children are taught to read and write, in permitted rates of interest, or in minimal housing standards—will improve the human condition: by promoting justice, permitting people to seek salvation more effectively, increasing the literacy of a people, checking an inflationary trend, or improving public health and family relations, respectively. The underlying hypothesis is always the same: that a different physical or cultural environment will make a different and better person.

The scientific study of behavior not only justifies the general pattern of such proposals; it promises new and better hypotheses. The earliest cultural practices must have originated in sheer accidents. Those which strengthened the group survived with the group in a sort of natural selection. As soon as people began to propose and carry out changes in practice for the sake of possible consequences, the evolutionary process must have accelerated. The simple practice of making changes must have had survival value. A further acceleration is now to be expected. As laws of behavior are more precisely stated, the changes in the environment required to bring about a given effect may be more clearly specified. Conditions which have been neglected because their effects were slight or unlooked for may be shown to be relevant. New conditions may actually be created, as in the discovery and synthesis of drugs which affect behavior.

This is no time, then, to abandon notions of progress, improvement, or, indeed, human perfectibility. The simple fact is that we are able, and now as never before, to lift ourselves by our own bootstraps. In achieving control of the world of which we are a part, we may learn at last to control ourselves.

II

Timeworn objections to the planned improvement of cultural practices are already losing much of their force. Marcus Aurelius was probably right in advising his readers to be content with a haphazard amelioration of mankind. "Never hope to realize Plato's republic," he sighed, "...for who can change the opinions of men? And without a change of sentiments what can you make but reluctant slaves and hypocrites?" He was thinking, no doubt, of contemporary patterns of control based upon punishment or the threat of punishment which, as he correctly observed, breed only reluctant slaves of those who submit and hypocrites of those who discover modes of evasion. But we need not share his pessimism, for opinions can be changed. The techniques of indoctrination which were being devised by the early Christian Church at the very time Marcus Aurelius was writing are relevant, as are some of the techniques of psychotherapy and of advertising and public relations. Other methods suggested by recent scientific analyses leave little doubt of the matter.

The study of human behavior also answers the cynical complaint that there is a plain "cussedness" which will always thwart efforts to improve people. We are often told that people do not want to be changed, even for the better. Try to help them, and they will outwit you and remain happily wretched. Dostoevsky claimed to see some plan in it. "Out of sheer ingratitude," he complained, or possibly boasted, "man will play you a dirty trick, just to prove that men are still men and not the keys of a piano....And even if you could prove that a man is only a piano key, he would still do something out of sheer perversity—he would create destruction and chaos—just to gain his point....And if all this could in turn be analyzed and prevented by predicting that it would occur, then man would deliberately go mad to prove his point." This is a conceivable neurotic reaction to inept control. A few people may have shown it, and many have enjoyed Dostoevsky's statement because they tend to show it. But that such perversity is a fundamental reaction of the human organism to controlling conditions is sheer nonsense.

So is the objection that we have no way of knowing what changes to make even though we have the necessary techniques. That is one of the great hoaxes of the century—a sort of booby trap left behind in the retreat before the advancing front of science. Scientists themselves have unsuspectingly agreed that there are two kinds of useful propositions about nature—facts and value judgments—and that science must confine itself to "what is," leaving "what ought to be" to others. But with what special sort of wisdom is the nonscientist endowed? Science is only effective knowing, no matter who engages in it. Verbal behavior proves upon analysis to be composed of many different types of utterances, from poetry and exhortation to logic and factual description, but these are not all equally useful in talking about cultural practices. We may classify useful propositions according to the degrees of confidence with which they may be asserted. Sentences about nature range from highly probable "facts" to sheer guesses. In general, future events are less likely to be correctly described than past. When scientists talk about a projected experiment, for example, they must often resort to statements having only a moderate likelihood of being correct; they call them hypotheses.

Designing a new cultural pattern is in many ways like designing an experiment. In drawing up a new constitution, outlining a new educational program, modifying a religious doctrine, or setting up a new fiscal policy, many statements must be quite tentative. We cannot be sure that the practices we specify will have the consequences we predict, or that the consequences will reward our efforts. This is in the nature of such proposals. They are not value judgments—they are guesses. To confuse and delay the improvement of cultural practices by quibbling about the word *improve* is itself not a useful practice. Let us agree, to start with, that health is better than illness, wisdom better than ignorance, love better than hate, and productive energy better than neurotic sloth.

Another familiar objection is the "political problem." Though we know what changes to make and how to make them, we still need to control certain relevant conditions, but these have long since fallen into the hands of selfish people who are not going to relinquish them for such purposes. Possibly we shall be permitted to develop areas which at the moment seem unimportant, but at the first signs of success the strong will move in. This, it is said, has happened to Christianity, democracy, and communism. There will always be those who are fundamentally selfish and evil, and in the long run innocent goodness cannot have its way. The only evidence here is historical, and it may be misleading. Because of the way in which physical science developed, history could until very recently have "proved" that the unleashing of the energy of the atom was quite unlikely, if not impossible. Similarly, because of the order in which processes in human behavior have become available for purposes of control, history may seem to prove that power will probably be appropriated for selfish purposes. The first techniques to be discovered fell almost always to strong, selfish men. History led Lord Acton to believe that power corrupts, but he had probably never encountered absolute power, certainly not in all its forms, and had no way of predicting its effect.

An optimistic historian could defend a different conclusion. The principle that if there is not enough good will in the world the first step is to create more seems to be gaining recognition. The Marshall Plan (as originally conceived), Point Four, the offer of atomic materials to power-starved countries—these may or may not be wholly new in the history of international relations, but they suggest an increasing awareness of the power of governmental good will. They are proposals to make certain changes in the human environment for the sake of consequences which should be rewarding for all concerned. They do not exemplify a disinterested generosity, but an interest which is the interest of everyone. We have not yet seen Plato's philosopher-king, and may not want to, but the gap between real and utopian government is closing.

III

But we are not yet in the clear, for a new and unexpected obstacle has arisen. With a world of our own making almost within reach, we have been seized with distaste for our achievement. We have uneasily rejected opportunities to apply the techniques and findings of science in the service of people, and as the import of effective cultural design has come to be understood, many of us have voiced an outright refusal to have any part in it. Science has been challenged before when it has encroached upon institutions already engaged in the control of human behavior; but what are we to make of benevolent people, with no special interests of their own to defend, who nevertheless turn against the very means of reaching long-dreamed-of goals?

What is being rejected, of course, is the scientific conception of the human organism and its place in nature. So long as the findings and methods of science are applied to human affairs only in a sort of remedial patchwork, we may continue to hold any view of human nature we like. But as the use of science increases, we are forced to accept the theoretical structure with which science represents its facts. The difficulty is that this structure is clearly at odds with the traditional democratic conception of Man. Every discovery of an event which has a part in shaping our behavior seems to leave so much the less to our credit, and as such explanations become more and more comprehensive, the contribution which we may claim for ourselves appears to approach zero. Our creative powers, our original accomplishments in art, science, and morals, our capacity to choose and the right to hold us responsible for the consequences of our choice—none of these is conspicuous in this new self-portrait. We once believed that we were free to express ourselves in art, music, and literature, to inquire into nature, to seek salvation in our own way. We could initiate action and make spontaneous and capricious changes of course. Under the most extreme duress some sort of choice remained to us. We could resist any effort to control us, though it might cost us our lives. But science insists that action is initiated by forces impinging upon the individual, and that caprice is only another name for behavior for which we have not yet found a cause.

In attempting to reconcile these views it is important to note that the traditional democratic conception was not designed as a description in the scientific sense but as a philosophy to be used in setting up and maintaining a governmental process. It arose under historical circumstances and served political purposes apart from which it cannot be properly understood. In rallying people against tyranny it was necessary that individuals be strengthened, that they be taught that they had rights and could govern themselves. To give them a new conception of their worth, their dignity, and their power to save themselves, both here and hereafter, was often the only resource of the revolutionist. When democratic principles were put into practice, the same doctrines were used as a working formula. This is exemplified by the notion of personal responsibility in Anglo-American law. All governments make certain forms of punishment contingent upon certain kinds of acts. In democratic countries these contingencies are expressed by the notion of responsible choice. But the notion may have no meaning under governmental practices formulated in other ways and would certainly have no place in systems which did not use punishment.

The democratic philosophy of human nature is determined by certain political exigencies and techniques, not by the goals of democracy. But exigencies and techniques change; and a conception which is not supported for its accuracy as a likeness—is not, indeed, rooted in fact at all—may be expected to change too. No matter how effective we judge current democratic practices to be, how highly we value them or how long we expect them to survive, they are almost certainly not the *final* form of government. The philosophy of human nature which has been useful in implementing them is also almost certainly not the last word. The ultimate achievement of democracy may be long deferred unless we emphasize the real aims rather than the verbal devices of democratic thinking. A philosophy which has been appropriate to one set of political exigencies will defeat its purpose if, under other circumstances, it prevents us from applying to human affairs the science of Man which probably nothing but democracy itself could have produced.

IV

Perhaps the most crucial part of our democratic philosophy to be reconsidered is our attitude toward freedom—or its reciprocal, the control of human behavior. We do not oppose all forms of control because it is "human nature" to do so. The reaction is not characteristic of all people under all conditions of life. It is an attitude which has been carefully engineered, in large part by what we call the "literature" of democracy. With respect to some methods of control (for example, the threat of force), very little engineering is needed, for the techniques or their immediate consequences are objectionable. Society has suppressed these methods by branding them "wrong," "illegal," or "sinful." But to encourage these attitudes toward objectionable forms of control, it has been necessary to disguise the real nature of certain indispensable techniques, the commonest examples of which are education, moral discourse, and persuasion. The actual procedures appear harmless enough. They consist of supplying information, presenting opportunities for action, pointing out logical relationships, appealing to reason or "enlightened understanding," and so on. Through a masterful piece of misrepresentation, the illusion is fostered that these procedures do not involve the control of behavior; at most, they are simply ways of "changing minds." But analysis not only reveals the presence of well-defined behavioral processes, it demonstrates a kind of control no less inexorable, though in some ways more acceptable, than the bully's threat of force.

Let us suppose that people in whom we are interested are acting unwisely—they are careless in the way they deal with friends, they drive too fast, or they hold their golf clubs the wrong way. We could probably help them by issuing a series of commands: Don't nag, don't drive over 60, don't hold your club that way. Much less objectionable would be "an appeal to reason." We could show them how people are affected by their treatment of them, how accident rates rise sharply at higher speeds, how a particular grip on the club alters the way the ball is struck and corrects a slice. In doing so we resort to verbal mediating devices which emphasize and support certain "contingencies of reinforcement"—that is, certain relations between behavior and its consequences—which strengthen the behavior we wish to set up. The same consequences would possibly set up the behavior without our help, and they eventually take control no matter which form of help we give. The appeal to reason has certain advantages over the authoritative command. A threat of punishment, no matter how subtle, generates emotional reactions and tendencies to escape or revolt. Perhaps controllees merely "feel resentment" at being made to act in a given way, but even that is to be avoided. When we "appeal to reason," they "feel freer to do as they please." The fact is that we have exerted *less* control than in using a threat; since other conditions may contribute to the result, the effect may be delayed or, possibly in a given instance, lacking. But if we have worked a change in behavior at all, it is because we have altered relevant environmental conditions, and the processes we have set in motion are just as real and just as inexorable, if not as comprehensive, as in the most authoritative coercion.

"Arranging an opportunity for action" is another example of disguised control. The power of the negative form has already been exposed in the analysis of censorship. Restriction of opportunity is recognized as far from harmless. As Ralph Barton Perry said in an article which appeared in the Spring, 1953, *Pacific Spectator,* "Whoever determines what alternatives shall be made known to man controls what that man shall choose *from.* He is deprived of freedom in proportion as he is denied access to *any* ideas, or is confined to any range of ideas short of the totality of relevant possibilities." But there is a positive side as well. When we present a relevant state of affairs, we increase the likelihood that a given form of behavior will be emitted. To the extent that the probability of action has changed, we have made a definite contribution. Teachers of history control their students' behavior (or, if the reader prefers, "deprives them of freedom") just as much in *presenting* historical facts as in suppressing them. Other conditions will no doubt affect the students, but the contribution made to their behavior by the presentation of material is fixed and, within its range, irresistible.

The methods of education, moral discourse, and persuasion are acceptable not because they recognize the freedom of the individual or the right to dissent, but because they make only *partial* contributions to the control of behavior. The freedom they recognize is freedom from a more coercive form of control. The dissent which they tolerate is the possible effect of other determiners of action. Since these sanctioned methods are frequently ineffective, we have been able to convince ourselves that they do not represent control at all. When they show too much strength to permit disguise, we give them other names and suppress them as energetically as we suppress the use of force. Education grown too powerful is rejected as propaganda or "brain-washing," while really effective persuasion is described as "undue influence," "demagoguery," "seduction," and so on.

If we are not to rely solely upon accident for the innovations which give rise to cultural evolution, we must accept the fact that some kind of control of human behavior is inevitable. We cannot use good sense in human affairs unless someone engages in the design and construction of environmental conditions which affect human behavior. Environmental changes have always been the condition for the improvement of cultural patterns, and we can hardly use the more effective methods of science without making changes on a grander scale. We are all controlled by the world in which we live, and part of that world has been and will be constructed by us. The question is this: Are we to be controlled by accident, by tyrants, or by ourselves in effective cultural design?

The danger of the misuse of power is possibly greater than ever. It is not allayed by disguising the facts. We cannot make wise decisions if we continue to pretend that human behavior is not controlled, or if we refuse to engage in control when valuable results might be forthcoming. Such

44

FREEDOM AND CONTROL

measures weaken only ourselves, leaving the strength of science to others. The first step in a defense against tyranny is the fullest possible exposure of controlling techniques. A second step has already been taken successfully in restricting the use of physical force. Slowly, and as yet imperfectly, we have worked out an ethical and governmental design in which the strong are not allowed to use the power deriving from their strength to control others. They are restrained by a superior force created for that purpose—the ethical pressure of the group, or more explicit religious and governmental measures. We tend to distrust superior forces, as we currently hesitate to relinquish sovereignty in order to set up an international police force. But it is only through such counter-control that we have achieved what we call peace—a condition in which individuals are not permitted to control each other through force. In other words, control itself must be controlled.

Science has turned up dangerous processes and materials before. To use the facts and techniques of a science of the human organism to the fullest extent without making some monstrous mistake will be difficult and obviously perilous. It is no time for self-deception, emotional indulgence, or the assumption of attitudes which are no longer useful. We are facing a difficult test. We must keep our heads now, or start again—a long way back.

V

Those who reject the scientific conception of the human organism must, to be logical, oppose the methods of science as well. The position is often supported by predicting a series of dire consequences which are to follow if science is not checked. A recent book by Joseph Wood Krutch,[1] *The Measure of Man,* is in this vein. Mr. Krutch sees in the growing science of human behavior the threat of an unexampled tyranny over the mind. If science is permitted to have its way, he insists, "we may never be able really to think again." A controlled culture will, for example, lack some virtue inherent in disorder. We have emerged from chaos through a series of happy accidents, but in an engineered culture it will be "impossible for the unplanned to erupt again." But there is no virtue in the accidental character of an accident, and the diversity which arises from disorder can not only be duplicated by design but vastly extended. The experimental method is superior to simple observation just because it multiplies "accidents" in a systematic coverage of the possibilities. Technology offers many familiar examples. We no longer wait for immunity to disease to develop from a series of accidental exposures, nor do we wait for natural mutations in sheep and cotton to produce better fibers; but we continue to make use of such accidents when they occur, and we certainly do not prevent them. Many of the things we value have emerged from the clash of ignorant armies on darkling plains, but it is not therefore wise to encourage ignorance and darkness.

It is not always disorder itself which we are told we shall miss but certain admirable human qualities which flourish only in the presence of disorder. A person rises above an unpropitious childhood to a position of eminence, and since we cannot give a plausible account of the action of so complex an environment, we attribute the achievement to some admirable personal faculty. But such "faculties" are suspiciously like the explanatory fictions against which the history of science warns us. We admire Lincoln for rising above a deficient school system, but it was not necessarily something *in him* which permitted him to become an educated man in spite of it. His educational environment was certainly unplanned, but it could nevertheless have made a full contribution to his mature behavior. He was a rare man, but the circumstances of his childhood were rare too. We do not give Franklin Delano Roosevelt the same credit for becoming an educated man with the help of Groton and Harvard, although the same behavioral processes may have been involved. The founding of Groton and Harvard somewhat reduced the possibility that fortuitous combinations of circumstances would erupt to produce other Lincolns. Yet the founders can hardly be condemned for attacking an admirable human quality.

Another predicted consequence of a science of human behavior is an excessive uniformity. We are told that effective control—whether governmental, religious, educational, economic, or social—will produce a race whose members differ from each other only through relatively refractory genetic differences. That would probably be bad design, but we must admit that we are not now pursuing another course from choice. In a modern school, for example, there is usually a syllabus which specifies what every student is to learn by the end of each year. This would be flagrant regimentation if anyone expected every student to comply. But some will be poor in particular subjects, others will not study, others will not remember what they have been taught, and diversity is assured. Suppose, however, that we someday possess such effective educational techniques that every student will in fact be put in possession of all the behavior specified in a syllabus. At the end of the year, all students will correctly answer all questions on the final examination and "must all have prizes." Should we reject such a system on the grounds that in making all students excellent it has made them all alike? Advocates of the theory of a special faculty might contend that an important advantage of the present system is that the good student learns *in spite of* a system which is so defective that it is currently producing bad students as well. But if really effective techniques are available, we cannot avoid the problem of design simply by preferring the status quo. At what point should education be made deliberately inefficient?

Such predictions of the havoc to be wreaked by the application of science to human affairs are usually made with surprising confidence. They not only show a faith in the orderliness of human behavior; they presuppose an established body of knowledge with the help of which it can be positively asserted that the changes which scientists propose to make will have quite specific results—albeit not the results they foresee. But the predictions made by the critics of science must be held to be equally fallible and subject also to empirical test. We may be sure that many steps in the scientific design of cultural patterns will produce unforeseen consequences. But there is only one way to find out. And the test must be made, for if we cannot advance in the design of cultural patterns with absolute certainty, neither can we rest completely confident of the superiority of the status quo.

VI

Apart from their possibly objectionable consequences, scientific methods seem to make no provision for certain admirable qualities and faculties which seem to have flourished in less explicitly planned cultures; hence they are called "degrading" or "lacking in dignity." (Mr. Krutch has called the author's *Walden Two* an "ignoble Utopia.") The conditioned reflex is the current whipping boy. Because conditioned reflexes may be demonstrated in animals, they are spoken of as though they were exclusively subhuman. It is implied, as we have seen, that no behavioral processes are involved in education and moral discourse or, at least, that the processes are exclusively human. But people do show conditioned reflexes (for example, when they are frightened by all instances of the control of human behavior because some instances engender fear), and animals do show processes similar to the human behavior involved in instruction and moral discourse. When Mr. Krutch[2] asserts that "'conditioning' is achieved by methods which by-pass or, as it were, short-circuit those very reasoning faculties which education proposes to cultivate and exercise" (pp. 68-69), he is making a technical statement which needs a definition of terms and a great deal of supporting evidence.

If such methods are called "ignoble" simply because they leave no room for certain admirable attributes, then perhaps the practice of admiration needs to be examined. We might say that children whose education has been skillfully planned have been deprived of the right to intellectual heroism. Nothing has been left to be admired in the way they acquire an education. Similarly, we can conceive of moral training which is so adequate to the demands of the culture that people will be good practically automatically, but to that extent they will be deprived of the right to moral heroism, since we seldom admire automatic goodness. Yet if we consider the end of morals rather than certain virtuous means, is not "automatic goodness" a desirable state of affairs? Is it not, for example, the avowed goal of religious education? T.H. Huxley answered the question unambiguously:[3] "If some great power would agree to make me always think what is true and do what is right, on condition of being turned into a sort of clock and wound up every morning before I got out of bed, I should instantly close with the offer" (pp. 192-193). Yet Mr. Krutch quotes this as the scarcely credible point of view of a "proto-modern" and seems himself to share T.S. Eliot's contempt for "...systems so perfect/That no one will need to be good."

"Having to be good" is an excellent example of an expendable honorific. It is inseparable from a particular form of ethical and moral control. We distinguish between the things we *have* to do to avoid punishment and those we *want* to do for rewarding consequences. In a culture which did not resort to punishment we should never "have" to do anything except with respect to the punishing contingencies which arise directly in the physical environment. And we are moving toward such a culture, because the neurotic, not to say psychotic, by-products of control through punishment have long since led compassionate people to seek alternative techniques. Recent research has explained some of the objectionable results of punishment and has revealed resources of at least equal power in "positive reinforcement." It is reasonable to look forward to a time when people will seldom "have" to do anything, although they may show interest, energy, imagination, and productivity far beyond the level seen under the present system (except for rare eruptions of the unplanned).

What we have to do we do with *effort*. We call it "work." There is no other way to distinguish between exhausting labor and the possibly equally energetic but rewarding activity of play. It is presumably good cultural design to replace the former with the latter. But an adjustment in attitudes is needed. We are much more practiced in admiring the heroic labor of a Hercules than the activity of one who works without having to. In a truly effective educational system the student might not "have to work" at all, but that possibility is likely to be received by the contemporary teacher with an emotion little short of rage.

We cannot reconcile traditional and scientific views by agreeing upon *what* is to be admired or condemned. The question is whether anything is to be so treated. Praise and blame are cultural practices which have been adjuncts of the prevailing system of control in Western democracy. All peoples do not engage in them for the same purposes or to the same extent, nor, of course, are the same behaviors always classified in the same way as subject to praise or blame. In admiring intellectual and moral heroism and unrewarding labor, and in rejecting a world in which these would be uncommon, we are simply demonstrating our own cultural conditioning. By promoting certain tendencies to admire and censure, the group of which we are a part has arranged for the social reinforcement and punishment needed to assure a high level of intellectual and moral industry. Under other and possibly better controlling systems, the behavior which we now admire would occur, but not under those conditions which make it admirable, and we should have no reason to admire it because the culture would have arranged for its maintenance in other ways.

To those who are stimulated by the glamorous heroism of the battlefield, a peaceful world may not be a better world. Others may reject a world without sorrow, longing, or a sense of guilt because the relevance of deeply moving works of art would be lost. To many who have devoted their lives to the struggle to be wise and good, a world without confusion and evil might be an empty thing. A nostalgic concern for the decline of moral heroism has been a dominanting theme in the work of Aldous Huxley. In *Brave New World* he could see in the application of science to human affairs only a travesty on the notion of the Good (just as George Orwell, in *1984,* could foresee nothing but horror). Writing in *Esquire* (August, 1955), Huxley has expressed the point this way: "We have had religious revolutions, we have had political, industrial, economic and nationalistic revolutions. All of them, as our descendants will discover, were but ripples in an ocean of conservatism—trivial by comparison with the psychological revolution toward which we are so rapidly moving. *That* will really be a revolution. When it is over, the human race will give no further trouble." (Footnote for the reader of the future: This was not meant as a happy ending. Up to 1956 people had been admired, if at all, either for causing trouble or alleviating it. Therefore—)

It will be a long time before the world can dispense with heroes and hence with the cultural practice of admiring heroism, but we move in that direction whenever we act to prevent war, famine, pestilence, and disaster. It will be a long time before we shall never need to submit to punishing environments or engage in exhausting labor, but we move in that direction whenever we make food, shelter, clothing, and labor-saving devices more readily available. We may mourn the passing of heroes but not the conditions which make for heroism. We can spare the self-made saint or sage as we spare the laundress on the river's bank struggling against fearful odds to achieve cleanliness.

VII

The two great dangers in modern democratic thinking are illustrated in a paper by former Secretary of State Dean Acheson.[4] "For a long time now," writes Mr. Acheson, "we have gone along with some well-tested principles of conduct: That it was better to tell the truth than falsehoods;…that duties were older than and as fundamental as rights; that, as Justice Holmes put it, the mode by which the inevitable came to pass was effort; that to perpetuate a harm was wrong no matter how many joined in it…and so on….Our institutions are founded on the assumption that most people follow these principles most of the time because they want to, and the institutions work pretty well when this assumption is true. More recently, however, bright people have been fooling with the machinery in the human head and they have discovered quite a lot....Hitler introduced new refinements [as the result of which] a whole people have been utterly confused and corrupted. Unhappily neither the possession of this knowledge nor the desire to use it was confined to Hitler....Others dip from this same devil's cauldron" (pp. 14-15).

The first dangerous notion in this passage is that most people follow democratic principles of conduct "because they want to." This does not account for democracy or any other form of government if we have not explained why people *want* to behave in given ways. Although it is tempting to assume that it is human nature to believe in democratic principles, we must not overlook the "cultural engineering" which produced and continues to maintain democratic practices. If we neglect the conditions which produce democratic *behavior,* it is useless to try to maintain a democratic *form* of government. And we cannot expect to export a democratic form of government successfully if we do not also provide for the cultural practices which will sustain it. Our forebears did not discover the essence of human nature; they evolved a pattern of behavior which worked remarkably well under the circumstances. The "set of principles" expressed in that pattern is not the only true set or necessarily the best. Mr. Acheson has presumably listed the most unassailable items; some of them are probably beyond question, but others—concerning duty and effort—may need revision as the world changes.

The second—and greater—threat to the democracy which Mr. Acheson is defending is his assumption that knowledge is necessarily on the side of evil. All the admirable things he mentions are attributed to the innate goodness of man, all the detestable to "fooling with the machinery in the human head." This is reminiscent of the position, taken by other institutions engaged in control, that certain forms of knowledge are in themselves evil. But how out of place in a democratic philosophy! Have we come this far only to conclude that well-intentioned people cannot study human behavior without becoming tyrants or that informed people cannot show good will? Let us for once have strength and good will on the same side.

VIII

Far from being a threat to the tradition of Western democracy, the growth of a science of human behavior is a consistent and probably inevitable part of it. In turning to the external conditions which shape and maintain behavior, while questioning the reality of inner qualities and faculties to which human achievements were once attributed, we turn from the ill-defined and remote to the observable and manipulable. Though it is a painful step, it has far-reaching consequences, for it not only sets higher standards of human welfare but shows us how to meet them. A change in a theory of human nature cannot change the facts. Our achievements in science, art, literature, music, and morals will survive any interpretation we place upon them. The uniqueness of the individual is unchallenged in the scientific view. Man, in short, will remain Man. (There will be much to admire for those who are so inclined. Possibly the noblest achievement to which we can aspire, even according to present standards, is to accept ourselves for what we are, as that is revealed to us by the methods which we have devised and tested on a part of the world in which we have only a small personal stake.)

If Western democracy does not lose sight of the aims of humanitarian action, it will welcome the almost fabulous support of its own science of Man and will strengthen itself and play an important role in building a better world for everyone. But if it cannot put its "democratic philosophy" into proper historical perspective—if, under the control of attitudes and emotions which it generated for other purposes, it now rejects the help of science—then it must be prepared for defeat. For if we continue to insist that science has nothing to offer but a new and more horrible form of tyranny, we may produce just such a result by allowing the strength of science to fall into the hands of despots. And if, with luck, it were to fall instead to those of good will in other political communities, it would be perhaps a more ignominious defeat; for we should then, through a miscarriage of democratic principles, be forced to leave to others the next step in the long struggle to control nature and ourselves.

REFERENCES AND NOTES

[1]Krutch, J.W. *The measure of man.* Indianapolis: Bobbs-Merrill, 1953.
[2]Ibid.
[3]Huxley, T.H. *Method and results: Essays.* New York: D. Appleton, 1897.
[4]Acheson, D. *The pattern of responsibility* (M. Bundy, Ed.). Boston: Houghton Mifflin, 1952.

POSTSCRIPT

The editor of the *New York Times' Sunday Book Review* (John Hutchens, an old friend) had put *Walden Two* on a list of "Should-Be Best Sellers." The public paid no attention. In 1951, the last 86 copies of the first printing were sold and the type distributed. (Those early copies now bring a high premium.) A small college edition was then cheaply printed, but it was not until the early sixties that a quality paperback edition began to sell.

The book had continued to attract attention, however. In 1954, Joseph Wood Krutch published *The Measure of Man,* much of which was about *Walden Two.* I had met Krutch several years before when he and I had participated in a conversation recorded and reprinted in *The American Scholar.* He had subsequently read *Walden Two* and now launched a rather bitter attack. Like other negative critics, I thought he showed a misunderstanding of the implications of an experimental analysis of behavior, for which I had made a case in *Science and Human Behavior.* When the editor of the *American Scholar* asked for another article, I was happy to take the opportunity to answer Krutch and review the implications.

I wrote the preceding article during the summer of 1955 on Monhegan, an island off the coast of Maine, where we had a summer cottage. (Had I written it today, I would probably have called it simply "Freedom and Control." "Men" was used generically in the language of the day.)

C H A P T E R   7

The Phylogeny and Ontogeny
of Behavior

EDITOR'S NOTE

The article was first published in *Science* (1966, *153*(3741), 1205-1213)
and appears as Chapter 7 in *Contingencies of Reinforcement* (1969, pp.
172-198), along with a series of related notes (pp. 199-217). It remains
Skinner's most extensive statement on innate behavior, though he has
dealt with the subject elsewhere: "What Is Psychotic Behavior?" (1956;
Chapter 11 in this text), "Conditioned and Unconditioned Aggression in
Pigeons" (1963, with G.S. Reynolds and A.C. Catania), Chapter 3 in *About
Behaviorism* (1974), "The Shaping of Phylogenic Behavior" (1975),
"Herrnstein and the Evolution of Behaviorism" (1977), and "Selection by
Consequences" (1981), as well as some early papers. Though he has
studied only environmental determinants of behavior, he has never
denied the genetic contribution. Here he makes his views explicit:
Behavior may have its origins either in the lifetime of an individual
("ontogenic" behavior) or in the history of a species ("phylogenic"
behavior). In each case a bit of behavior survives because of its
consequences: Reinforcement during the lifetime of an organism
strengthens only some behavior; the process is called "operant
conditioning." Natural selection favors individuals who behave in some
ways but not others; the potential for certain behavior is thus preserved in
the genetic code. "Ontogenic contingencies" are the contingencies of
reinforcement which operate during the life of an organism to select
behavior; "phylogenic contingencies" are the contingencies of survival
which operate in evolution to select individuals. Changing environments
can select increasingly complex repertoires of behavior at both levels.

In the section called "The Provenance [Origin] of Behavior," Skinner
describes a number of parallels between selection at the two levels. For
example, "adventitious contingencies" will produce superstitious

behaviors at the ontogenic level and useless structures at the phylogenic level.

Ethologists try to explain various unlearned behaviors by speculating about a species' evolutionary history. Such an account, argues Skinner, is difficult to test. Ontogenic contingencies, in contrast, lend themselves to experimental study. The remoteness of phylogenic contingencies leads people to appeal to concepts such as "instinct," "drive," "emotion," "trait," and "need," all of which can be more effectively analyzed in terms of the contingencies that produced the behavior from which the inner states were inferred.

It is often difficult to determine the origins of behavior. Skinner analyzes a number of cases. In imprinting, for example, it is not the behavior of following that is inherited but "a susceptibility to reinforcement by proximity to the mother or mother surrogate"—that is, to certain ontogenic contingencies. Identifying the provenance of behavior is important, says Skinner, "because it tells us something about how behavior can be supported or changed. Most of the controversy concerning heredity and environment has arisen in connection with the practical control of behavior through the manipulation of relevant variables."

Skinner defends the laboratory analysis of behavior as a means of learning about basic behavioral processes. Species differences are minimized and the data show "an extraordinary uniformity over a wide range of species....Although species differences exist and should be studied, an exhaustive analysis of the behavior of a single species is as easily justified as the study of the chemistry or microanatomy of nerve tissue in one species." The laboratory environment is often criticized as "artificial," but "behavior in a natural habitat would have no special claim to genuineness."

Concepts such as "purpose," "adaptation," "imitation," "aggression," and "territoriality" often mask the origins of the behavior in question. A warning cry is taken up and passed along through a flock of birds presumably because of phylogenic contingencies, but "quite apart from any instinct...we learn to do what others are doing because we are then likely to receive the reinforcement they are receiving." Behaviors that contribute to certain social structures or that are said to indicate "communication" can also have both phylogenic and ontogenic origins.

Parts of the behavior of an organism concerned with the internal economy, as in respiration or digestion, have always been accepted as "inherited," and there is no reason why some responses to the external environment should not also come ready-made in the same sense. It is widely believed that many students of behavior disagree. The classical reference is to John B. Watson:[1]

> I should like to go one step further now and say, "Give me a dozen healthy infants, well-formed, and my own specified world to bring them up in and I'll guarantee to take any one at random and train him to become any type of specialist I might select—doctor, lawyer, artist, merchant-chief and, yes, even beggar-man and thief, regardless of his talents, penchants, tendencies, abilities, vocations, and race of his ancestors." I am going beyond my facts and I admit it, but so have the advocates of the contrary and they have been doing it for many thousands of years. (p. 82)

Watson was not denying that a substantial part of behavior is inherited. His challenge appears in the first of four chapters describing "how man is equipped to behave at birth." As an enthusiastic specialist in the psychology of learning he went beyond his facts to emphasize what could be done in spite of genetic limitations. He was actually, as Gray[2] has pointed out, "one of the earliest and one of the most careful workers in the area of animal ethology" (p. 333). Yet he is probably responsible for the persistent myth of what has been called "behaviorism's counterfactual dogma" (p. 1436).[3] And it is a myth. No reputable student of animal behavior has ever taken the position "that the animal comes to the laboratory as a virtual *tabula rasa,* that species differences are insignificant, and that all responses are about equally conditionable to all stimuli" (p. 684).[4]

But what does it mean to say that behavior is inherited? Lorenz[5] has noted that ethologists are not agreed on "the concept of 'what we formerly called innate'" (p. 3). Insofar as the behavior of an organism is simply the physiology of an anatomy, the inheritance of behavior is the inheritance of certain bodily features, and there should be no problem concerning the meaning of "innate" that is not raised by any genetic trait. Perhaps we must qualify the statement that a person inherits a visual reflex, but we must also qualify a similar statement about eye color.

If the anatomical features underlying behavior were as conspicuous as the wings of *Drosophila,* we should describe them directly and deal with their inheritance in the same way, but at the moment we must be content with so-called behavioral manifestations. We describe the behaving organism in terms of its gross anatomy, and we shall no doubt eventually describe the behavior of its finer structures in much the same way, but until then we analyze behavior without referring to fine structures and are constrained to do so even when we wish to make inferences about them.

What features of behavior will eventually yield a satisfactory genetic account? Some kind of inheritance is implied by such concepts as "racial memory" or "death instinct," but a sharper specification is obviously needed. The behavior observed in mazes and similar apparatuses may be "objective," but it is not described in dimensions which yield a meaningful genetic picture. Tropisms and taxes are somewhat more readily quantified, but not all behavior can be thus formulated, and organisms selected for breeding according to tropistic or taxic performances may still differ in other ways.[6]

The probability that an organism will behave in a given way is a more promising datum, but very little has been done in studying its genetics. Modes of inheritance are not, however, the only issues.

THE PROVENANCE OF BEHAVIOR

Upon a given occasion we observe that an animal displays a certain kind of behavior—learned or unlearned. We describe its topography and evaluate its probability. We discover variables, genetic or environmental, of which the probability is a function. We then undertake to predict or control the behavior. All this concerns a current state of the organism. We have still to ask where the behavior (or the structures which thus behave) came from. What we may call the ontogeny of behavior can be traced to contingencies of reinforcement, and in a famous passage Pascal suggested that ontogeny and phylogeny have something in common. "Habit," he said, "is a second nature which destroys the first. But what is this nature? Why is habit not natural? I am very much afraid that nature is itself only first habit as habit is second nature."

The provenance of "first habit" has an important place in theories of the evolution of behavior. A given response is in a sense strengthened by consequences which have to do with the survival of the individual and the species. A given form of behavior leads not to reinforcement but to procreation. (Sheer reproductive activity does not, of course, always contribute to the survival of a species, as the problems of overpopulation remind us. A few well-fed breeders presumably enjoy an advantage over a larger but impoverished population. The advantage may also be selective. It has recently been suggested[7] that some forms of behavior such as the defense of a territory have an important effect in restricting breeding.) Several practical problems raised by what may be called contingencies of selection are remarkably similar to problems which have already been approached experimentally with respect to contingencies of reinforcement.

An Identifiable Unit

A behavioral process, as a change in frequency of response, can be followed only if it is possible to count responses. The topography of an operant need not be completely fixed, but some defining property must be available to identify instances. An emphasis upon the occurrence of a repeatable unit distinguishes an experimental analysis of behavior from historical or anecdotal accounts. A similar requirement is recognized in ethology. As

Julian Huxley[8] has said, "This concept—of unit releasers which act as specific key stimuli unlocking genetically determined… unit behavior patterns—is probably the most important single contribution of Lorenzian ethology to the science of behavior" (p. 423).

The Action of Stimuli

Operant reinforcement not only strengthens a given response; it brings the response under the control of a stimulus. But the stimulus does not elicit the response as in a reflex; it merely sets the occasion upon which the response is more likely to occur. The ethologists' "releaser" also simply sets an occasion. Like the discriminative stimulus, it increases the probability of occurrence of a unit of behavior but does not force it. The principal difference between a reflex and an instinct is not in the complexity of the response but in, respectively, the eliciting and releasing actions of the stimulus.

Origins of Variations

Ontogenic contingencies remain ineffective until a response has occurred. The rat must press the lever at least once "for other reasons" before it presses it "for food." There is a similar limitation in phylogenic contingencies. An animal must emit a cry at least once for other reasons before the cry can be selected as a warning because of the advantage to the species. It follows that the entire repertoire of an individual or species must exist prior to ontogenic or phylogenic selection, but only in the form of minimal units. Both phylogenic and ontogenic contingencies "shape" complex forms of behavior from relatively undifferentiated material. Both processes are favored if the organism shows an extensive, undifferentiated repertoire.

Programmed Contingencies

It is usually not practical to condition a complex operant by waiting for an instance to occur and then reinforcing it. A terminal performance must be reached through intermediate contingencies (programmed instruction). In a demonstration experiment[9] a rat pulled a chain to obtain a marble from a rack, picked up the marble with its forepaws, carried it to a tube projecting 2 inches above the floor of its cage, lifted it to the top of the tube, and dropped it inside. "Every step in the process had to be worked out through a series of approximations, since the component responses were not in the original repertoire of the rat" (p. 340). The "program" was as follows. The rat was reinforced for any movement which caused a marble to roll over any edge of the floor of its cage, then only over the edge on one side of the cage, then over only a small section of the edge, then over only that section slightly raised, and so on. The raised edge became a tube of gradually diminishing diameter and increasing height. The earlier member of the chain, release of the marble from the rack, was added later. Other kinds of programming have been used to establish subtle stimulus control to sustain behavior in spite of infrequent reinforcement, and so on.[10]

A similar programming of complex phylogenic contingencies is familiar in evolutionary theory. The environment may change, demanding that behavior which contributes to survival for a given reason become more complex. Quite different advantages may be responsible for different stages. To take a familiar example, the electric organ of the eel could have become useful in stunning prey only after developing something like its present power. Must we attribute the completed organ to a single complex mutation, or were intermediate stages developed because of other advantages? Much weaker currents, for example, may have permitted the eel to detect the nature of objects with which it was in contact. The same question may be asked about behavior. Pascal's "first habit" must often have been the product of "programmed instruction." Many of the complex phylogenic contingencies which now seem to sustain behavior must have been reached through intermediate stages in which less complex forms had lesser but still effective consequences.

The need for programming is a special case of a more general principle. We do not explain any system of behavior simply by demonstrating that it works to the advantage of, or has "net utility" for, the individual or species. It is necessary to show that a given advantage is contingent upon behavior in such a way as to alter its probability.

Adventitious Contingencies

It is not true, as Lorenz[11] has asserted, that "adaptiveness is always the irrefutable proof that this process [of adaptation] has taken place" (p. 3). Behavior may have advantages which have played no role in its selection. The converse is also true. Events which follow behavior but are not necessarily produced by it may have a selective effect. A hungry pigeon placed in an apparatus in which a food dispenser operates every twenty seconds regardless of what the pigeon is doing acquires a stereotyped response which is shaped and sustained by wholly coincidental reinforcement. The behavior is often "ritualistic"; we call it superstitious.[12] There is presumably a phylogenic parallel. All current characteristics of an organism do not necessarily contribute to its survival and procreation, yet they are all nevertheless "selected." Useless structures with associated useless functions are as inevitable as superstitious behavior. Both become more likely as organisms become more sensitive to contingencies. It should occasion no surprise that behavior has not perfectly adjusted to either ontogenic or phylogenic contingencies.

Unstable and Intermittent Contingencies

Both phylogenic and ontogenic contingencies are effective even though intermittent. Different schedules of reinforcement generate different patterns of changing probabilities. If there is a phylogenic parallel, it is obscure. A form of behavior generated by intermittent selective contingencies is presumably likely to survive a protracted period in which the contingencies are not in force, because it has already proved powerful enough to survive briefer periods, but this is only roughly parallel with the explanation of the greater resistance to extinction of intermittently reinforced operants.

Changing Contingencies

Contingencies also change, and the behaviors for which they are responsible then change too. When ontogenic contingencies specifying topography of response are relaxed, the topography usually deteriorates; and when reinforcements are no longer forthcoming, the operant undergoes extinction. Darwin discussed phylogenic parallels in *The Expression of Emotions in Man and Animals.* His "serviceable associated habits" were apparently both learned and unlearned, and he seems to have assumed that ontogenic contingencies contribute to the inheritance of behavior, at least in generating responses which may then have phylogenic consequences. The behavior of the domestic dog in turning around before lying down on a smooth surface may have been selected by contingencies under which the behavior made a useful bed in grass or brush. If dogs now show this behavior less frequently, it is presumably because a sort of phylogenic extinction has set in. The domestic cat shows a complex response of covering feces which must once have had survival value with respect to predation or disease. The dog has been more responsive to the relaxed contingencies arising from domestication or some other change in predation or disease, and shows the behavior in vestigial form.

Multiple Contingencies

An operant may be affected by more than one kind of reinforcement, and a given form of behavior may be traced to more than one advantage to the individual or the species. Two phylogenic or ontogenic consequences may work together or oppose each other in the development of a given response and presumably show "algebraic summation" when opposed.

Social Contingencies

The contingencies responsible for social behavior raise special problems in both phylogeny and ontogeny. In the development of a language the behavior of a speaker can become more elaborate only as listeners become sensitive to elaborated speech. A similarly coordinated development must be assumed in the phylogeny of social behavior. The dance of the bee returning from a successful foray can have advantageous effects for the species only when other bees behave appropriately with respect to it, but they cannot develop the behavior until the dance appears. The terminal system must have required a kind of subtle programming in which the behaviors of both "speaker" and "listener" passed through increasingly complex stages. A bee returning from a successful foray may behave in a special way because it is excited or fatigued, and it may show phototropic responses related to recent visual stimulation. If the strength of the behavior varies with the quantity or quality of food the bee has discovered and with the distance and direction it has flown, then the behavior may serve as an important stimulus to other bees, even though its characteristics have not yet been affected by such consequences. If different bees behave in different ways, then more effective versions should be selected. If the behavior of a successful bee evokes behavior on the part of listeners which is reinforcing to the speaker, then the speaker's behavior should be ontogenically intensified. The phylogenic development of responsive behavior in the listener should contribute to the final system by providing for immediate reinforcement of conspicuous forms of the dance.

The speaker's behavior may become less elaborate if the listener continues to respond to less elaborate forms. We stop a man who is approaching us by pressing our palm against his chest, but he eventually learns to stop upon seeing our outstretched palm. The practical response becomes a gesture. A similar shift in phylogenic contingencies may account for the "intentional movements" of the ethologists.

Behavior may be intensified or elaborated under differential reinforcement involving the stimulation either of the behaving organism or of others. The more conspicuous a superstitious response, for example, the more effective the adventitious contingencies. Behavior is especially likely to become more conspicuous when reinforcement is contingent on the response of another organism. Some ontogenic instances, called "ritualization," are easily demonstrated. Many elaborate rituals of primarily phylogenic origin have been described by ethologists.

SOME PROBLEMS RAISED BY PHYLOGENIC CONTINGENCIES

Lorenz[13] has recently argued that "our absolute ignorance of the physiological mechanisms underlying learning makes our knowledge of the causation of phyletic adaptation seem quite considerable by comparison" (p. 10). But genetic and behavioral processes are studied and formulated in a rigorous way without reference to the underlying biochemistry. With respect to the provenance of behavior we know much more about ontogenic contingencies than phylogenic. Moreover, phylogenic contingencies raise some very difficult problems which have no ontogenic parallels.

The contingencies responsible for unlearned behavior acted a very long time ago. The natural selection of a given form of behavior, no matter how plausibly argued, remains an inference. We can set up phylogenic contingencies under which a given property of behavior arbitrarily selects individuals for breeding, and thus demonstrate modes of behavioral inheritance, but the experimenter who makes the selection is performing a function of the natural environment which also needs to be studied. Just as the reinforcements arranged in an experimental analysis must be shown to have parallels in "real life" if the results of the analysis are to be significant or useful, so the contingencies which select a given behavioral trait in a genetic experiment must be shown to play a plausible role in natural selection.

Although ontogenic contingencies are easily subjected to an experimental analysis, phylogenic contingencies are not. When the experimenter has shaped a complex response, such as dropping a marble into a tube, the provenance of the behavior raises no problem. The performance may puzzle anyone seeing it for the first time, but it is easily traced to recent, possibly recorded, events. No comparable history can be invoked when a spider is observed to spin a web. We have not seen the phylogenic contingencies at work. All we know is that spiders of a given kind build more or less the same kind of web. Our ignorance often adds a touch of mystery. We are likely to view inherited behavior with a kind of awe not inspired by acquired behavior of similar complexity.

The remoteness of phylogenic contingencies affects our scientific methods, both experimental and conceptual. Until we have identified the variables of which an event is a function, we tend to invent causes. Learned behavior was once commonly attributed to "habit," but an analysis of contingencies of reinforcement has made the term unnecessary. "Instinct," as a hypothetical cause of phylogenic behavior, has had a longer life. We no longer say that our rat possesses a marble-dropping habit, but we are still likely to say that our spider has a web-spinning instinct. The concept of instinct has been severely criticized and is now used with caution or altogether avoided, but explanatory entities serving a similar function still survive in the writings of many ethologists.

A "mental apparatus," for example, no longer finds a useful place in the experimental analysis of behavior, but it survives in discussions of phylogenic contingencies. Here are a few sentences from the writings of prominent ethologists which refer to consciousness or awareness: "The young gosling…gets imprinted upon its mind the image of the first moving object that it sees";[14] "the infant expresses the inner state of contentment by smiling"; [15] "[herring gulls show a] lack of insight into the ends served by their activities";[16] "[chimpanzees were unable] to communicate to others the unseen things in their minds."[17]

In some mental activities awareness may not be critical, but other cognitive activities are invoked. Thorpe[18] speaks of a disposition "which leads the animal to pay particular attention to objects of a certain kind" (p. 3). What we observe is simply that objects of a certain kind are especially effective stimuli. The ontogenic contingencies which generate the behavior called "paying attention" presumably have phylogenic parallels. Other mental activities frequently mentioned by ethologists include "organizing experience" and "discovering relations." Expressions of all these sorts show that we have not yet accounted for the behavior in terms of contingencies, phylogenic or ontogenic. Unable to show how the organism can behave effectively under complex circumstances, we endow it with a special cognitive ability which permits it to do so.

Other concepts replaced by a more effective analysis include "need" or "drive" and "emotion." In ontogenic behavior we no longer say that a given set of environmental conditions first gives rise to an inner state which the organism then expresses or resolves by behaving in a given way. We no longer represent relations among emotional and motivational variables as relations among such states, as in saying that hunger overcomes fear. We no longer use dynamic analogies or metaphors, as in explaining sudden action as the overflow or bursting out of dammed-up needs or drives. If these are common practices in ethology, it is evidently because the functional relations they attempt to formulate are not clearly understood.

Another kind of innate endowment, particularly likely to appear in explanations of human behavior, takes the form of "traits" or abilities." Though often measured quantitatively, their dimensions are meaningful only in placing the individual with respect to a population. The behavior measured is almost always obviously learned. To say that intelligence is inherited is not to say that specific forms of behavior are inherited. Phylogenic contingencies conceivably responsible for "the selection of intelligence" do not specify responses. What has been selected appears to be a susceptibility to ontogenic contingencies, leading particularly to a greater speed of conditioning and the capacity to maintain a larger repertoire without confusion.

It is often said that an analysis of behavior in terms of ontogenic contingencies "leaves something out of account," and this is true. It leaves out of account habits, ideas, cognitive processes, needs, drives, traits, and so on. But it does not neglect the facts upon which these concepts are based. It seeks a more effective formulation of the very contingencies to which those who use such concepts must eventually turn to explain their explanations.

The strategy has been highly successful at the ontogenic level, where the contingencies are relatively clear. As the nature and mode of operation of phylogenic contingencies come to be better understood, a similar strategy should yield comparable advantages.

IDENTIFYING PHYLOGENIC AND ONTOGENIC VARIABLES

The significance of ontogenic variables may be assessed by holding genetic conditions as constant as possible—for example, by studying "pure" strains or identical twins. The technique has a long history. According to Plutarch *(De Puerorum Educatione)*, Licurgus, a Spartan, demonstrated the importance of environment by raising two puppies from the same litter so that one became a good hunter while the other preferred food from a plate. On the other hand, genetic variables may be assessed either by studying organisms upon which the environment has had little opportunity to act (because they are newborn or have been reared in a controlled environment) or by comparing groups subject to extensive, but on the average probably similar, environmental histories. Behavior exhibited by most of the members of a species is often accepted as inherited if it is unlikely that all the members could have been exposed to relevant ontogenic contingencies.

When contingencies are not obvious, it is perhaps unwise to call any behavior either inherited or acquired. Field observations, in particular, will often not permit a distinction. Friedmann[19] has described the behavior of the African honey guide as follows:

> When the bird is ready to begin guiding, it either comes to a person and starts a repetitive series of churring notes or it stays where it is and begins calling....
> As the person comes to within 15 or 20 feet,...the bird flies off with an initial conspicuous downward dip, and then goes off to another tree, not necessarily in sight of the follower, in fact more often out of sight than not. Then it waits there, churring loudly until the follower again nears it, when the action is repeated. This goes on until the vicinity of the bees' nest is reached. Here the bird suddenly ceases calling and perches quietly in a tree nearby. It waits there for the follower to open the hive, and it usually remains there until the person has departed with his loot of honey-comb, when it comes down to the plundered bees' nest and begins to feed on the bits of comb left strewn about. (p. 55)

The author is quoted as saying that the behavior is "purely instinctive," but it is possible to explain almost all of it in other ways. If we assume that honey guides eat broken bees' nests and cannot eat unbroken nests, that men (not to mention baboons and ratels) break bees' nests, and that birds more easily discover unbroken nests, then only one other assumption is needed to explain the behavior in ontogenic terms. We must assume that the response which produces the churring note is elicited either (1) by any stimulus which frequently precedes the receipt of food (comparable behavior is shown by a hungry dog jumping about when food is being prepared for it) or (2) when food, ordinarily available, is missing (the dog jumps about when food is not being prepared for it on schedule). An unconditioned honey guide occasionally sees men breaking nests. It waits until they have gone, and then eats the remaining scraps. Later it sees men near but not breaking nests, either because they have not yet found the nests or have not yet reached them. The sight of a man near a nest, or the sight of man when the buzzing of bees around a nest can be heard, begins to function in either of the ways just noted to elicit the churring response. The first step in the construction of the final pattern is thus taken by the honey guide. The second step is taken by the man (or baboon or ratel, as the case may be). The churring sound becomes a conditioned stimulus in the presence of which a search for bees' nests is frequently successful. The buzzing of bees would have the same effect if the man could hear it.

The next change occurs in the honey guide. When a man approaches and breaks up a nest, his behavior begins to function as a conditioned reinforcer which, together with the fragments which he leaves behind, reinforces churring, which then becomes more probable under the circumstances and emerges primarily as an operant rather than as an emotional response. When this has happened, the geographical arrangements work themselves out naturally. Men learn to move toward the churring sound, and they break nests more often after walking toward nests than after walking in other directions. Taking a position that induces men to walk toward a nest is therefore differentially reinforced in the honey guide. The contingencies are subtle, but we should remember that the final topography is often far from perfect.

As we have seen, contingencies which involve two or more organisms raise special problems. The churring of the honey guide is useless until men respond to it, but men will not respond in an appropriate way until the churring is related to the location of bees' nests. The conditions just described compose a sort of program which could lead to the terminal performance. It may be that the conditions will not often arise, but another characteristic of social contingencies quickly takes over. When one honey guide and one man have entered into this symbiotic arrangement, conditions prevail under which other honey guides and other men will be much more rapidly conditioned. A second man will more quickly learn to go in the direction of the churring sound because the sound is already spatially related to bees' nests. A second honey guide will more readily learn to churr in the right places because men respond in a way which reinforces that behavior. When a large number of birds have learned to guide and a large number of men have learned to be guided, conditions are highly favorable for maintaining the system. (It is said that, where men no longer bother to break bees' nests, they no longer comprise an occasion for churring, and the honey guide turns to the ratel or baboon. The change in contingencies has occurred too rapidly to work through natural selection. Possibly an instinctive response has been unlearned, but the effect is more plausibly interpreted as the extinction of an operant.)

Imprinting is another phenomenon which shows how hard it is to detect the nature and effect of phylogenic contingencies. In Thomas More's *Utopia,* eggs were incubated. The chicks "are no sooner out of the shell, and able to stir about, but they seem to consider those that feed them as their mothers, and follow them as other chickens do the hen that hatched them." Later accounts of imprinting have been reviewed by Gray.[20] Various facts suggest phylogenic origins: The response of following an imprinted object appears at a certain age; if it cannot appear then, it may not appear at all; and so on. Some experiments by Peterson,[21] however, suggest that what is inherited is not the behavior of following but a susceptibility to reinforcement by proximity to the mother or mother surrogate. A distress call reduces the distance between mother and chick when the mother responds appropriately, and walking toward the mother has the same effect. Both behaviors may therefore be reinforced,[22] but they appear before these ontogenic contingencies come into play and are, therefore, in part at least, phylogenic. In the laboratory, however, other behaviors can be made effective which phylogenic contingencies are not likely to have strengthened. A chick can be conditioned to peck a key, for example, by moving an imprinted object toward it when it pecks or to walk away from the object if, through a mechanical arrangement, this behavior actually brings the object closer. To the extent that chicks follow an imprinted object simply because they thus bring the object closer or prevent it from becoming more distant, the behavior could be said to be "species-specific" in the unusual sense that it is the product of *ontogenic* contingencies which prevail for all members of the species.

Ontogenic and phylogenic behaviors are not distinguished by any essence or character. Form of response seldom if ever yields useful classifications. The verbal response *Fire!* may be a command to a firing squad, a call for help, or an answer to the question *What do you see?* The topography tells us little, but the controlling variables permit us to distinguish three very different verbal operants.[23] The sheer forms of instinctive and learned behaviors also tell us little. Animals court, mate, fight, hunt, and rear their young, and they use the same effectors in much the same way in all sorts of learned behavior. Behavior is behavior whether learned or unlearned; it is only the controlling variables which make a difference. The difference is not always important. We might show that a honey guide is controlled by the buzzing of bees rather than by the sight of a nest, for example, without prejudice to the question of whether the behavior is innate or acquired.

Nevertheless the distinction is important if we are to undertake to predict or control the behavior. Implications for human affairs have often affected the design of research and the conclusions drawn from it. A classical example concerns the practice of exogamy. Popper[24] writes:

> Mill and his psychologistic school of sociology...would try to explain [rules of exogamy] by an appeal to 'human nature,' for instance to some sort of instinctive aversion against incest (developed perhaps through natural selection...); and something like this would also be the naïve or popular explanation. [From Marx's] point of view...however, one could ask whether it is not the other way round, that is to say, whether the apparent instinct is not rather a product of education, the effect rather than the cause of the social rules and traditions demanding exogamy and forbidding incest. It is clear that these two approaches correspond exactly to the very ancient problem whether social laws are "natural" or "conventional." (p. 89)

Much earlier, in his *Supplement to the Voyage of Bougainville*, Diderot[25] considered the question of whether there is a natural basis for sexual modesty or shame *(pudeur)*. Though he was writing nearly 100 years before Darwin, he pointed to a possible basis for natural selection. "The pleasures of love are followed by a weakness which puts one at the mercy of one's enemies. That is the only natural thing about modesty; the rest is convention" (p. 185). Those who are preoccupied with sex are exposed to attack (indeed, may be stimulating attack); hence, those who engage in sexual behavior under cover are more likely to breed successfully. Here are phylogenic contingencies which either make sexual behavior under cover stronger than sexual behavior in the open or reinforce the taking of cover when sexual behavior is strong. Ontogenic contingencies through which organisms seek cover to avoid disturbances during sexual activity are also plausible.

The issue has little to do with the character of incestuous or sexual behavior, or with the way people "feel" about it. The basic distinction is between provenances. And provenance is important because it tells us something about how behavior can be supported or changed. Most of the controversy concerning heredity and environment has arisen in connection with the practical control of behavior through the manipulation of relevant variables.

INTERRELATIONS AMONG PHYLOGENIC AND ONTOGENIC VARIABLES

The ways in which animals behave compose a sort of taxonomy of behavior comparable to other taxonomic parts of biology. Only a very small percentage of existing species has as yet been investigated. (A taxonomy of behavior may indeed be losing ground as new species are discovered.) Moreover, only a small part of the repertoire of any species is ever studied. Nothing approaching a fair sampling of species-specific behavior is therefore ever likely to be made.

Specialists in phylogenic contingencies often complain that those who study learned behavior neglect the genetic limitations of their subjects, as the comparative anatomist might object to conclusions drawn from the intensive study of a single species. Beach,[26] for example, has written: "Many...appear to believe that in studying the rat they are studying all or nearly all that is important in behavior....How else are we to interpret... [a] 457-page opus which is based exclusively upon the performance of rats in bar-pressing situations but is entitled simply *The Behavior of Organisms?*" (p. 119). There are many precedents for concentrating on one species (or at most a very few species) in biological investigations. Mendel discovered the basic laws of genetics—in the garden pea. Morgan worked out the theory of the gene—for the fruitfly. Sherrington investigated the integrative action of the nervous system—in the dog and cat. Pavlov studied the physiological activity of the cerebral cortex—in the dog.

In the experimental analysis of behavior many species differences are minimized. Stimuli are chosen to which the species under investigation can respond and which do not elicit or release disrupting responses: Visual stimuli are not used if the organism is blind, or very bright lights if they evoke evasive action. A response is chosen which may be emitted at a high rate without fatigue and which will operate recording and controlling equipment: We do not reinforce a monkey when it pecks a disk with its nose or a pigeon when it trips a toggle switch—though we might do so if we wished. Reinforcers are chosen which are indeed reinforcing, either positively or negatively. In this way species differences in sensory equipment, in effector systems, in susceptibility to reinforcement, and in possibly disrupting repertoires are minimized. The data then show an extraordinary uniformity over a wide range of species. For example, the processes of extinction, discrimination, and generalization, and the performances generated by various schedules of reinforcement are reassuringly similar. (Those who are interested in fine structure may interpret these practices as minimizing the importance of sensory and motor areas in the cortex and emotional and motivational areas in the brain stem, leaving for study the processes associated with nerve tissue as such, rather than with gross anatomy.) Although species differences exist and should be studied, an exhaustive analysis of the behavior of a single species is as easily justified as the study of the chemistry or microanatomy of nerve tissue in one species.

A rather similar objection has been lodged against the extensive use of domesticated animals in laboratory research.[27] Domesticated animals offer many advantages. They are more easily handled, they thrive and breed in captivity, they are resistant to the infections encountered in association with human beings, and so on. Moreover, we are primarily interested in the most domesticated of all animals—Man. Wild animals are, of course, different— possibly as different from domesticated varieties as some species are from others, but both kinds of differences may be treated in the same way in the study of basic processes.

The behavioral taxonomist may also argue that the contrived environment of the laboratory is defective since it does not evoke characteristic phylogenic behavior. A pigeon in a small enclosed space pecking a disk which operates a mechanical food dispenser is behaving very differently from pigeons at large. But in what sense is this behavior not "natural"? If there is a natural phylogenic environment, it must be the environment in which a given kind of behavior evolved. But the phylogenic contingencies responsible for current behavior lie in the distant past. Within a few thousand years—a period much too short for genetic changes of any great magnitude—all current species have been subjected to drastic changes in climate, predation, food supply, shelter, and so on. Certainly no land mammal is now living in the environment which selected its principal genetic features, behavioral or otherwise. Current environments are almost as "unnatural" as a laboratory. In any case, behavior in a natural habitat would have no special claim to genuineness. What an organism does is a fact about that organism regardless of the conditions under which it does it. A behavioral process is none the less real for being exhibited in an arbitrary setting.

The relative importance of phylogenic and ontogenic contingencies cannot be argued from instances in which unlearned or learned behavior intrudes or dominates. Breland and Breland[28] have used operant conditioning and programming to train performing animals. They conditioned a pig to deposit large wooden coins in a "piggy bank." "The coins were placed several feet from the bank and the pig required to carry them to the bank and deposit them.... At first the pig would eagerly pick up one dollar, carry it to the bank, run back, get another, carry it rapidly and neatly, and so on.... Thereafter, over a period of weeks the behavior would become slower and slower. He might run over eagerly for each dollar, but on the way back, instead of carrying the dollar and depositing it simply and cleanly, he would repeatedly drop it, root it, drop it again, root it along the way, pick it up, toss it up in the air, drop it, root it some more, and so on" (p. 683). They also conditioned a chicken to deliver plastic capsules containing small toys by moving them toward the purchaser with one or two sharp straight pecks. The chickens began to grab at the capsules and "pound them up and down on the floor of the cage" (p. 682), perhaps as if they were breaking seed pods or pieces of food too large to be swallowed. Since other reinforcers were not used, we cannot be sure that these phylogenic forms of food-getting behavior appeared because the objects were manipulated under food-reinforcement. The conclusion is plausible, however, and not disturbing. A shift in controlling variables is often observed. Under reinforcement on a so-called "fixed-interval schedule," competing behavior emerges at predictable points.[29] The intruding behavior may be learned or unlearned. It may disrupt a performance or, as Kelleher[30] has shown, it may not. The facts do not show an inherently greater power of phylogenic contingencies in general. Indeed, the intrusions may occur in the other direction. A hungry pigeon which was being trained to guide missiles[31] received food on a schedule which generated a high rate of pecking at a target projected on a plastic disk. It began to peck at the food as rapidly as at the target. The rate was too high to permit it to take grains into its mouth, and it began to starve. A product of ontogenic contingencies had suppressed one of the most powerful phylogenic activities. The behavior of civilized people shows the extent to which environmental variables may mask an inherited endowment.

MISLEADING SIMILARITIES

Since phylogenic and ontogenic contingencies act at different times and shape and maintain behavior in different ways, it is dangerous to try to arrange their products on a single continuum or to describe them with a single set of terms.

An apparent resemblance concerns intention or purpose. Behavior which is influenced by its consequences seems to be directed toward the future. We say that spiders spin webs in order to catch flies and that people set nets in order to catch fish. The "order" is temporal. No account of either form of behavior would be complete if it did not make some reference to its effects. But flies or fish which have not yet been caught cannot affect behavior. Only past effects are relevant. Spiders which have built effective webs have been more likely to leave offspring, and setting a net in a way that has caught fish has been reinforced. Both forms of behavior are therefore more likely to occur again, but for very different reasons.

The concept of purpose has had an important place in evolutionary theory. It is still sometimes said to be needed to explain the variations upon which natural selection operates. In human behavior a "felt intention" or "sense of purpose" which precedes action is sometimes proposed as a current surrogate for future events. People who set nets "know why they are doing so," and something of the same sort may have produced the spider's web-spinning behavior which then became subject to natural selection. But people behave because of operant reinforcement even though they cannot "state their purpose"; and, when they can, they may simply be describing their behavior and the contingencies responsible for its strength. Self-knowledge is at best a by-product of contingencies; it is not a cause of the behavior generated by them. Even if we could discover a spider's felt intention or sense of purpose, we could not offer it as a cause of the behavior.

Both phylogenic and ontogenic contingencies may seem to "build purpose into" an organism. It has been said that one of the achievements of cybernetics has been to demonstrate that machines may show purpose. But we must look to the construction of the machine, as we look to the phylogeny and ontogeny of behavior, to account for the fact that an ongoing system acts as if it had a purpose.

Another apparent characteristic in common is "adaptation." Both kinds of contingencies change the organism so that it adjusts to its environment in the sense of behaving in it more effectively. With respect to phylogenic contingencies, this is what is meant by natural selection. With respect to ontogeny, it is what is meant by operant conditioning. Successful responses are selected in both cases, and the result is adaptation. But the processes of selection are very different, and we cannot tell from the mere fact that behavior is adaptive which kind of process has been responsible for it.

More specific characteristics of behavior seem to be common products of phylogenic and ontogenic contingencies. Imitation is an example. If we define imitation as behaving in a way which resembles the observed behavior of another organism, the term will describe both phylogenic and ontogenic behavior. But important distinctions need to be made. Phylogenic contingencies are presumably responsible for well-defined responses released by similar behavior (or its products) on the part of others. A warning cry is taken up and passed along by others; one bird in a flock flies off and the others fly off; one member of a herd starts to run and the others start to run. A stimulus acting upon only one member of a group thus quickly affects other members, with plausible phylogenic advantages.

The parrot displays a different kind of imitative behavior. Its vocal repertoire is not composed of inherited responses, each of which, like a warning cry, is released by the sound of a similar response in others. It acquires its imitative behavior ontogenically, but only because of an apparently inherited susceptibility to reinforcement by the familiar sounds it produces. Its responses need not be released by immediately preceding stimuli (the parrot speaks when not spoken to); but an echoic stimulus is often effective, and the response is then a sort of imitation.

A third type of imitative contingency does not presuppose an inherited tendency to be reinforced by behaving as others behave. When other organisms are behaving in a given way, similar behavior is likely to be reinforced, since they would probably not be behaving in that way if it were not. Quite apart from any instinct of imitation, we learn to do what others are doing because we are then likely to receive the reinforcement they are receiving. We must not overlook distinctions of this sort if we are to use or cope with imitation in a technology of behavior.

Aggression is another term which conceals differences in provenance. Inherited repertoires of aggressive responses are elicited or released by specific stimuli. Azrin, for example, has studied the stereotyped, mutually aggressive behavior evoked when two organisms receive brief electric shocks. But he and his associates have also demonstrated that the opportunity to engage in such behavior functions as a reinforcer and, as such, may be used to shape an indefinite number of "aggressive" operants of arbitrary topographies.[32] Evidence of damage to others may be reinforcing for phylogenic reasons because it is associated with competitive survival. Competition in the current environment may make it reinforcing for ontogenic reasons. To deal successfully with any specific aggressive act we must respect its provenance. (Emotional responses, the bodily changes we feel when we are aggressive, like sexual modesty or aversion to incest, may conceivably be the same whether of phylogenic or ontogenic origin; the importance of the distinction is not thereby reduced.) Konrad Lorenz's recent book *On Aggression*[33] could be seriously misleading if it diverts our attention from relevant manipulable variables in the current environment to phylogenic contingencies which, in their sheer remoteness, encourage a nothing-can-be-done-about-it attitude.

The concept of territoriality also often conceals basic differences. Relatively stereotyped behavior displayed in defending a territory, as a special case of phylogenic aggression, has presumably been generated by contingencies involving food supplies, breeding, population density, and so on. But cleared territory, associated with these and other advantages, becomes a conditioned reinforcer and as such generates behavior much more specifically adapted to clearing a given territory. Territorial behavior may also be primarily ontogenic. Whether the territory defended is as small as a spot on a crowded beach or as large as a sphere of influence in international politics, we shall not get far in analyzing the behavior if we recognize nothing more than "a primary passion for a place of one's own"[34] or insist that "animal behavior provides prototypes of the lust for political power."[35]

Several other concepts involving social structure also neglect important distinctions. A hierarchical pecking order is inevitable if the members of a group differ with respect to aggressive behavior in any of the forms just mentioned. There are therefore several kinds of pecking orders, differing in their provenances. Some dominant and submissive behaviors are presumably phylogenic stereotypes; the underdog turns on its back to escape further attack, but it does not follow that the vassal prostrating himself before king or priest is behaving for the same reasons. The ontogenic contingencies which shape the organization of a large company or governmental administration show little in common with the phylogenic contingencies responsible for the hierarchy in the poultry yard. Some forms of human society may resemble the anthill or beehive, but not because they exemplify the same behavioral processes.[36]

Basic differences between phylogenic and ontogenic contingencies are particularly neglected in theories of communication. In the inherited signal systems of animals the behavior of a "speaker" furthers the survival of the species when it affects a "listener." The distress call of a chick evokes appropriate behavior in the hen; mating calls and displays evoke appropriate responses in the opposite sex; and so on. De Laguna[37] has suggested that animal calls could be classified as declarations, commands, predictions, and so on, and Sebeok[38] has recently attempted a similar synthesis in modern linguistic terms, arguing for the importance of a science of zoosemiotics.

The phylogenic and ontogenic contingencies leading, respectively, to instinctive signal systems and to verbal behavior are quite different. One is not an early version of the other. Cries, displays, and other forms of communication arising from phylogenic contingencies are particularly insensitive to operant reinforcement. Like phylogenic repertories in general, they are restricted to situations which elicit or release them and hence lack the variety and flexibility which favor operant conditioning. Vocal responses which at least closely resemble instinctive cries have been conditioned, but much less easily than responses using other parts of the skeletal nervous system. The vocal responses in the human child which are so easily shaped by operant reinforcement are not controlled by specific releasers. It was the development of an undifferentiated vocal repertoire which brought a new and important system of behavior within range of operant reinforcement through the mediation of other organisms.[39]

Many efforts have been made to represent the products of both sets of contingencies in a single formulation. An utterance, gesture, or display, whether phylogenic or ontogenic, is said to have a referent which is its meaning, the referent or meaning being inferred by a listener. Information theory offers a more elaborate version: The communicating organism selects a message from the environment, reads out relevant information from storage, encodes the message, and emits it; the receiving organism decodes the message, relates it to other stored information, and acts upon it effectively. All these activities, together with the storage of material, may be either phylogenic or ontogenic. The principal terms in such analyses (input, output, sign, referent, and so on) are objective enough, but they do not adequately describe the actual behavior of the speaker or the behavior of the listener responding to the speaker. The important differences between phylogenic and ontogenic contingencies must be taken into account in an adequate analysis. It is not true, as Sebeok[40] contends, that "any viable hypothesis about the origin and nature of language will have to incorporate the findings of zoosemiotics" (p. 1013). Just as we can analyze and teach imitative behavior without analyzing the phylogenic contingencies responsible for animal mimicry, or study and construct human social systems without analyzing the phylogenic contingencies which lead to the social life of insects, so we can analyze the verbal behavior of man without taking into account the signal systems of other species.

Purpose, adaptation, imitation, aggression, territoriality, social structure, and communication—concepts of this sort have, at first sight, an engaging generality. They appear to be useful in describing both ontogenic and phylogenic behavior and to identify important common properties. Their very generality limits their usefulness, however. A more specific analysis is needed if we are to deal effectively with the two kinds of contingencies and their products.

REFERENCES AND NOTES

[1]Watson, J.B. *Behaviorism.* New York: Norton, 1925.

[2]Gray, P.H. The descriptive study of imprinting in birds from 1873 to 1953. *Journal of General Psychology,* 1963, *68,* 333-346.

[3]Hirsch, J. Behavior genetics and individuality understood. *Science,* 1963, *142,* 1436-1442.

[4]Breland, K., & Breland, M. The misbehavior of organisms. *American Psychologist,* 1961, *16,* 681-684.

[5]Lorenz, K. *Evolution and modification of behavior.* Chicago: University of Chicago Press, 1965.

[6]Erlenmeyer-Kimling, L., Hirsch, J., & Weiss, J.M. Studies in experimental behavior genetics: III. Selection and hybridization analyses of individual differences in the sign of geotaxis. *Journal of Comparative and Physiological Psychology,* 1962, *55,* 722-731.

[7]Wynne-Edwards, V.C. Self-regulating systems in populations of animals. *Science,* 1965, *147,* 1543-1548.

[8]Huxley, J. Psychometabolism: General and Lorenzian. *Perspectives in Biology and Medicine,* 1964, *7,* 399-432.

[9]Skinner, B.F. *The behavior of organisms: An experimental analysis.* New York: Appleton-Century, 1938.

[10]Skinner, B.F. *The technology of teaching.* New York: Appleton-Century-Crofts, 1968.

[11]Lorenz, op. cit.

[12]See Chapter 3 in this volume.

[13]Lorenz, op. cit.

[14]Thorpe, W.H. The learning abilities of birds. Part 2. *The Ibis,* 1951, *93,* 252-296.

[15]Huxley, op. cit.

[16]Tinbergen, N. *The herring-gull's world.* London: Collins, 1953.

[17]Kortlandt, A., & Frankenberger, Z. *Current Anthropology,* 1965, *6,* 320.

[18]Thorpe, W.H. The learning ablities of birds. Part 1. *The Ibis,* 1951, *93,* 1-52.

[19]Friedmann, H. African honey-guides. *Science,* 1956, *123,* 55.

[20]Gray, op. cit.

[21]Peterson, N. Control of behavior by presentation of an imprinted stimulus. *Science,* 1960, *132,* 1395-1396.

[22]Hoffman, H.S., Schiff, D., Adams, J., & Serle, J.L. Enhanced distress vocalization through selective reinforcement. *Science,* 1966, *151,* 352-354.

[23]Skinner, B.F. *Verbal behavior.* New York: Appleton-Century-Crofts, 1957.

[24]Popper, K.R. *The open society and its enemies* (Vol. 2). London: Routledge and Kegan Paul, 1957.

[25]Diderot, D. *Supplement au voyage de Bougainville.* Paris: Librairie E. Droz, 1935. (Originally published, 1796.)

[26]Beach, F.A. The snark was a boojum. *American Psychologist,* 1950, *5,* 115-124.

[27]Kavanau, J.L. Behavior: Confinement, adaptation, and compulsory regimes in laboratory studies. *Science,* 1964, *143,* 490.

[28]Breland & Breland, op. cit.

[29]Skinner, B.F., & Morse, W.H. Concurrent activity under fixed-interval reinforcement. *Journal of Comparative and Physiological Psychology,* 1957, *50,* 279-281.

[30]Kelleher, R.T. Variables and behavior. *American Psychologist,* 1962, *17,* 659-660.

[31]See Chapter 12 in this volume.

[32]Azrin, N.H., Hutchinson, R.R., & McLaughlin, R. The opportunity for aggression as an operant reinforcer during aversive stimulation. *Journal of the Experimental Analysis of Behavior,* 1965, *8,* 171-180.

[33]Lorenz, K. *On aggression.* New York: Harcourt, Brace & World, 1966. (German ed., 1963.)

[34] Ardrey, R. *African genesis.* New York: Atheneum, 1961.

[35]Dubos, R. Humanistic biology. *American Scientist,* 1965, *53,* 4-19.

[36]Allee, W.C. *Cooperation among animals.* New York: Abelard-Schuman, 1938.

[37]De Laguna, G. *Speech: Its function and development.* New Haven: Yale University Press, 1927.

[38]Sebeok, T. Animal communication. *Science,* 1965, *147,* 1006-1014.

[39]Skinner, B.F. *Verbal behavior.* New York: Appleton-Century-Crofts, 1957.

[40]Sebeok, op. cit.

POSTSCRIPT

Those who explore behavioral processes by constructing various contingencies of reinforcement, like those who propose ways of modifying behavior by changing such contingencies, naturally emphasize the environmental control of behavior. Perhaps it is therefore only natural that those who study innate behavior should feel that their work has been neglected. In any case, there is a stubborn contention among ethologists and other behavioral biologists that behaviorists deny any genetic contribution to behavior. An unfortunate remark by John B. Watson—the claim that he could take a dozen healthy infants and train them to become any type of specialist he might select—no doubt contributed to the misunderstanding; but Watson himself was one of the first ethologists.

A central issue has recently been revived by sociobiologists, who argue, mainly on structural grounds, that genetic principles reach into the most complex kinds of human behavior—that, for example, individuals who sacrifice themselves for their country must possess a gene of altruism. It is possible, however, to distinguish three kinds of contingencies of selection generating altruistic behavior; one is genetic, one individual, and one cultural. Other formal properties such as aggression and territoriality have also been attributed to genes while neglecting the different kinds of contingencies of selection involved.

It seemed to me that the neglect of operant conditioning by ethologists was a more serious issue, and an invitation to speak at a symposium on genetics at the University of Kentucky in 1965 provided the occasion for the present paper.

CHAPTER 8

Why I Am Not
a Cognitive Psychologist

EDITOR'S NOTE

The article was first published in *Behaviorism* (Fall 1977, *5*, 1–10) and has been reprinted in *Reflections on Behaviorism and Society* (1978, pp. 97–112). Skinner argues that the behaviors from which we infer such things as "associations" and "abstractions" are determined by contingencies of reinforcement. Cognitive concepts are often simply internalized surrogates of such contingencies. Terms such as "mind" and "will" are often simply synonyms for "behavior." Skinner analyzes a number of mentalistic statements made by psychologists, biologists, historians, and others. Such statements rarely specify manipulable variables and hence are not very useful in solving problems. A behavioral analysis points to such variables.

"Preference," "choice," "intention," and so on are means by which cognitivists internalize action. But they do not cause action and hence the real causes must still be found.

"Far more damaging to an effective analysis," says Skinner, "is the internalization of the environment." The world is said to be stored in our bodies in the form of "knowledge," but, again, this is an unnecessary and cumbersome way station in the analysis of behavior. Computers have made the storage metaphor more fashionable. "The struggle to make machines that think like people has had the effect of supporting theories in which people think like machines." Behavior is said by cognitivists to be guided by internalized rules. But behavior is often produced by contingencies of reinforcement; rules need not be stored for effective behavior to occur. Language is often said to be rule-governed, but it is more likely a product of contingencies: "We speak because our behavior is shaped and maintained by the practices of a verbal community."

This article originally appeared in *Behaviorism,* Fall 1977, *5*, 1–10. Reprinted by permission of the publisher.

Skinner concludes: Speculations about mental life are relevant neither to an analysis of behavior nor to physiological investigations, and they impede the search for practical ways of changing behavior.

The issues have been explored in many other works (see Chapters 4 and 5 in this volume).

The variables of which human behavior is a function lie in the environment. We distinguish between (1) the selective action of that environment during the evolution of the species, (2) its effect in shaping and maintaining the repertoire of behavior which converts each member of the species into a person, and (3) its role as the occasion upon which behavior occurs. Cognitive psychologists study these relations between organism and environment, but they seldom deal with them directly. Instead they invent internal surrogates which become the subject matter of their science.

Take, for example, the so-called process of association. In Pavlov's experiment a hungry dog hears a bell and is then fed. If this happens many times, the dog begins to salivate when it hears the bell. The standard mentalistic explanation is that the dog "associates" the bell with the food. But it was Pavlov who associated them! "Associate" means to join or unite. The dog merely begins to salivate upon hearing the bell. We have no evidence that it does so because of an internal surrogate of the contingencies.

In the "association of ideas" the ideas are internal replicas of stimuli, to which I shall return. If we have eaten lemons, we may taste lemon upon seeing a lemon or see a lemon upon tasting lemon juice, but we do not do this because *we* associate the flavor with the appearance. They are associated in the lemon. "Word associations" are at least correctly named. If we say "home" when someone says "house," it is not because we associate the two words but because they are associated in daily English usage. Cognitive association is an invention. Even if it were real, it would go no further toward an explanation than the external contingencies upon which it is modeled.

Another example is abstraction. Consider a simple experiment. A hungry pigeon can peck any one of a number of panels bearing the names of colors—"white," "red," "blue," "green"—and the pecks are reinforced with small amounts of food. Any one of a number of objects—blocks, books, flowers, toy animals—can be seen in an adjacent space. The following contingencies are then arranged: Whenever the object is white, no matter what its shape or size, pecking only the panel marked "white" is reinforced; whenever the object is red, pecking only the panel marked "red" is reinforced; and so on. Under these conditions the pigeon eventually pecks the panel marked "white" when the object is white, the panel marked "red" when the object is red, and so on. Children are taught to name colors with similar contingencies, and we all possess comparable repertoires sustained by the reinforcing practices of our verbal environments.

But what is said to be going on in the mind? Karl Popper[1] has put a classical issue this way: "We can say either that (1) the universal term 'white' is a label attached to a set of things, or that (2) we collect the set because they share an intrinsic property of 'whiteness.'" Popper says the distinction is important; natural scientists may take the first position but social scientists must take the second. Must we say, then, that the pigeon is either attaching a universal term to a set of things or collecting a set of things because they share an intrinsic property? Clearly, it is the *experimenter,* not the pigeon, who "attaches" the white key to the white objects displayed and who collects the set of objects on which a single reinforcing event is made contingent. Should we not simply attribute the behavior to the experimental contingencies? And if so, why not for children or ourselves? Behavior comes under the control of stimuli under certain contingencies of reinforcement. Special contingencies maintained by verbal communities produce "abstractions." We do attach physical labels to physical things and we collect physical objects according to labeled properties, but comparable cognitive processes are inventions which, even if real, would be no closer to an explanation than the external contingencies.

Another cognitive account of the same data would assert that a person, if not a pigeon, forms an abstract *idea* or develops a *concept* of color. The development of concepts is an especially popular cognitive field. (The horticultural metaphor minimizes contributions from the environment. We may hasten the growth of the mind but we are no more responsible for its final character than farmers for the character of the fruits and vegetables they so carefully nourish.) Color vision is part of the genetic endowment of most people, and it develops or grows in a physiological sense, possibly to some extent after birth. Nevertheless, most stimuli acquire control because of their place in contingencies of reinforcement. As the contingencies become more complex, they shape and maintain more complex behavior. It is the environment that develops, not a mental or cognitive possession.

A passage from a recent discussion of the development of sexual identity in a child might be translated as follows: "The child forms a concept based upon what it has observed and been told of what it means to be a boy or girl." (A child's behavior is affected by what it has observed and been told about being a boy or girl.) "This concept is oversimplified, exaggerated, and stereotyped." (The contingencies affecting the behavior are simplified and exaggerated and involve stereotyped behavior on the part of parents and others.) "As the child develops cognitively, its concepts, and consequently its activities, become more sophisticated and realistic." (As the child grows older, the contingencies become more subtle and more closely related to the actual sex of the child.) Children do not go around forming concepts of their sexual identity and "consequently" behaving in special ways; they slowly change their behavior as people change the ways in which they treat them because of their sex. Behavior changes because the contingencies change, not because a mental entity called a concept develops.

•   •   •

Many mentalistic or cognitive terms refer not only to contingencies but to the behavior they generate. Terms like "mind," "will," and "thought" are often simply synonyms of "behavior." A historian writes: "What may be called a stagnation of thought prevailed, as though the mind, exhausted after building up the spiritual fabric of the Middle Ages, had sunk into inertia." Exhaustion is a plausible metaphor when a quiet period follows an active one, but it was behavior that became stagnant and inert, presumably because the contingencies changed. Certain social conditions ("the spiritual fabric of the Middle Ages") made people active. A second set of conditions, possibly produced by the very behavior generated by the first, made them much less so. To understand what actually happened we should have to discover why the contingencies changed, not why thought became stagnant or inert.

Behavior is internalized as mental life when it is too slight to be observed by others—when, as we say, it is covert. A writer has pointed out that "the conductor of an orchestra maintains a certain even beat according to an internal rhythm, and he can divide that beat in half again and again with an accuracy rivaling any mechanical instrument." But is there an *internal* rhythm? Beating time is behavior. Parts of the body often serve as pendulums useful in determining speed, as when the amateur musician beats time with a foot or the rock player with the whole body, but other well-timed behavior must be learned. Conductors beat time steadily because they have learned to do so under rather exacting contingencies of reinforcement. The behavior may be reduced in scale until it is no longer visible to others. It is still sensed by the conductor, but it is a sense of behavior, not of time. The history of "man's development of a sense of time" over the centuries is not a matter of cognitive growth but of the invention of clocks, calendars, and ways of keeping records—in other words, of an environment that "keeps time."

When a historian reports that in a given period "a wealthy, brilliant, and traditional governing class lost its will," he is reporting simply that it stopped acting like a wealthy, brilliant, and traditional governing class. Deeper changes are suggested by the term "will" but they are not identified. They could not have been changes in particular people, since the period lasted more than one lifetime. What changed were presumably the conditions affecting the behavior of members of the class. Perhaps they lost their money; perhaps competing classes became more powerful.

Feelings, or the bodily conditions we feel, are commonly taken as the causes of behavior. We go for a walk "because we feel like going." It is surprising how often the futility of such an explanation is not recognized. A distinguished biologist, C.H. Waddington,[2] reviewing a book by Tinbergen, writes as follows:

> It is not clear how far he [Tinbergen] would go along with the argument of one of the most perceptive critical discussions of ethology by Suzanne Langer, who argues that each step in a complex structure of behavior is controlled, not by a hierarchical set of neural centers, but by the immediate feeling of the animal. The animal, she claims, does the next thing in the sequence, not to bring about a useful goal, or even as a move toward an enjoyable consummation, but because he actually feels like doing it at the moment. (p. 3)

Evidently Waddington himself goes along partway with this "perceptive view."

But suppose Langer is right. Suppose animals simply do what they feel like doing. What is the next step in explaining their behavior? Clearly, a science of animal behavior must be replaced or supplemented by a science of animal feelings. It would be as extensive as the science of behavior because there would presumably be a feeling for each act. But feelings are harder to identify and describe than the behavior attributed to them, and we should have abandoned an objective subject matter in favor of one of dubious status, accessible only through necessarily defective channels of introspection. The contingencies would be the same. The feelings and the behavior would have the same causes.

A British statesman recently asserted that the key to crime in the streets was "frustration." Young people mug and rob because they feel frustrated. But why do they feel frustrated? One reason may be that many of them are unemployed, either because they do not have the education needed to get jobs or because jobs are not available. To solve the problem of street crime, therefore, we must change the schools and the economy. But what role is played in all this by frustration? Is it the case that when one cannot get a job one feels frustrated and that when one feels frustrated one mugs and robs, or is it simply the case that when one cannot earn money, one is more likely to steal it—and possibly to experience a bodily condition called frustration?

Since many of the events which must be taken into account in explaining behavior are associated with bodily states that can be felt, what is felt may serve as a clue to the contingencies. But the feelings are not the contingencies and cannot replace them as causes.

·   ·   ·

By its very nature operant behavior encourages the invention of mental or cognitive processes said to initiate action. In a reflex, conditioned or unconditioned, there is a conspicuous prior cause. Something triggers the response. But behavior that has been positively reinforced occurs upon occasions which, though predisposing, are never compelling. The behavior seems to start up suddenly, without advance notice, as if spontaneously generated. Hence the invention of such cognitive entities as intention, purpose, or will. The same issues were debated with respect to the theory of evolution and for the same reason: Selection is a special causal mode not easily observed. Because controlling circumstances which lie in an organism's history of reinforcement are obscure, the mental surrogate gets its chance. Under positive reinforcement we do, as we say, what we are free to do; hence the notion of free will as an initiating condition. (I think it was Jonathan Edwards who said that we believe in free will because we know about our behavior but not about its causes.)

When we do not know why people do one thing rather than another, we say that they "choose" or "make decisions." Choosing originally meant examining, scrutinizing, or testing. Etymologically, deciding means cutting off other possibilities, moving in a direction from which there is no return. Choosing and deciding are thus conspicuous forms of behavior, but cognitive psychologists have nevertheless invented internal surrogates. Anatol Rapoport[3] puts it this way: "A subject in a psychological experiment is offered a choice among alternatives and selects one alternative over others." When this happens, he says, "common sense suggests that he is guided by a preference." Common sense does indeed suggest it, and so do cognitive psychologists, but where and what is a preference? Is it anything more than a tendency to do one thing rather than another? When we cannot tell whence the wind cometh and whither it goeth, we say that it "bloweth where it listeth," and common sense, if not cognitive psychology, thus credits it with a preference. (List, by the way, is an example of a term with a physical referent used to refer to a mental process. It means, of course, to lean—as in the list of a ship. And since things usually fall in the direction in which they are leaning, we say that people lean toward a candidate in an election as a rough way of predicting how they will vote. The same metaphor is found in "inclination"; we are "inclined" to vote for X. But it does not follow that we have internal leanings and inclinations which affect our behavior.)

"Intention" is a rather similar term which once meant stretching. The cognitive version is a critical issue in current linguistics. Must the intention of the speaker be taken into account? In an operant analysis verbal behavior is determined by the consequences which follow in a given verbal environment, and consequences are what cognitive psychologists are really talking about when they speak of intentions. All operant behavior "stretches toward" a future even though the only consequences responsible for its strength have already occurred. I go to a drinking fountain "with the intention of getting a drink of water" in the sense that I go because in the past I have got a drink when I have done so. (I may go for the first time, following directions, but that is not an exception; it is an example of rule-governed behavior, of which more later.)

•   •   •

So much for the cognitive internalization of contingencies of reinforcement and the invention of cognitive causes of behavior. Far more damaging to an effective analysis is the internalization of the environment. The Greeks invented the mind to explain how the real world could be known. For them, to know meant to be acquainted with, to be intimate with. The term cognition itself is related to coitus, as in the biblical sense in which a man is said to know a woman. Having no adequate physics of light and sound nor any chemistry of taste and odor, the Greeks could not understand how a world outside the body, possibly some distance away, could be known. There must be internal copies. Hence cognitive surrogates of the real world.

The distinction between reality and conscious experience has been made so often that it now seems self-evident. Fred Attneave[4] has recently written that "the statement that the world as we know it is a representation is, I think, a truism—there is really no way in which it can be wrong" (p. 493). But there are at least two ways, depending upon the meaning. If the statement means that we can know only representations of the outside world, it is a "truism" only if we are not our bodies but inhabitants located somewhere inside. Our bodies are in contact with the *real* world and can respond to it directly, but if we are tucked away up in the head, we must be content with representations.

Another possible meaning is that knowing is the very process of constructing mental copies of real things, but if that is the case how do we know the copies? Do we make copies of *them?* And is that regress infinite?

Some cognitive psychologists recognize that knowing is action but try to make the point by appealing to another mental surrogate. Knowledge is said to be "a system of propositions." According to one writer, "when we use the word 'see' we refer to a bridge between a pattern of sensory stimulation and knowledge which is propositional." But "propositional" is simply a laundered version of "behavioral," and the "bridge" is between stimuli and behavior and was built when the stimuli were part of the contingencies.

Representational theories of knowledge are modeled on practical behavior. We do make copies of things. We construct representational works of art, because looking at them is reinforced in much the same way as looking at what they represent. We make maps, because our behavior in following them is reinforced when we arrive at our destination in the mapped territory. But are there internal surrogates? When we daydream, do we first construct copies of reinforcing episodes which we then watch, or do we simply see things once again? And when we learn to get about in a given territory, do we construct cognitive maps which we then follow or do we follow the territory? If we follow a cognitive map, must we learn to do so, and will that require a map of the map? There is no evidence of the mental construction of images to be looked at or maps to be followed. The body responds to the world, at the point of contact; making copies would be a waste of time.

•   •   •

Knowledge is a key term in cognitive theory, and it covers a good deal of ground. It is often contrasted with perception. We are said to be able to *see* that there are 3 dots on a card but only to *know* that there are 13 after counting them, even though counting is a form of behavior. After noting that one spiral can be seen to be continuous but that another can be discovered to be so only by tracing, Bela Julesz[5] has said that "any visual task that cannot be performed spontaneously, without effort or deliberation, can be regarded as a cognitive task rather than as a perceptual one" (p. 34), though all the steps in that example are also clearly behavioral.

"Knowing how to do something" is an internal surrogate of behavior in its relation to contingencies. A child learns to ride a bicycle and is then said to possess knowledge of how to ride. The child's behavior has been changed by the contingencies of reinforcement maintained by bicycles; the child has not taken possession of the contingencies.

To speak of knowing *about* things is also to construct an internal surrogate of contingencies. We watch a football game and are then said to possess knowledge of what happened. We read a book and are said to know what it is about. The game and the book are somehow "represented" in our minds: We are "in possession of certain facts." But the evidence is simply that we can describe what happened at the game and report what the book was about. Our behavior has been changed, but there is no evidence that we have acquired knowledge. To be "in possession of the facts" is not to contain the facts within ourselves but to have been affected by them.

Possession of knowledge implies storage, a field in which cognitive psychologists have constructed a great many mental surrogates of behavior. The organism is said to take in and store the environment, possibly in some processed form. Let us suppose that a young girl saw a picture yesterday and when asked to describe it today, does so. What has happened? A traditional answer would run something like this: When she saw the picture yesterday the girl formed a copy in her mind (which, in fact, was really all she saw). She encoded it in a suitable form and stored it in her memory, where it remained until today. When asked to describe the picture today, she searched her memory, retrieved the encoded copy, and converted it into something like the original picture, which she then looked at and described. The account is modeled on the physical storage of memoranda. We make copies and other records, and respond to them. But do we do anything of the sort in our minds?

If anything is "stored," it is behavior. We speak of the "acquisition" of behavior, but in what form is it possessed? Where is behavior when an organism is not behaving? Where at the present moment, and in what form, is the behavior I exhibit when I am listening to music, eating my dinner, talking with a friend, taking an early morning walk, or scratching an itch? A cognitive psychologist has said that verbal behavior is stored as "lexical memories." Verbal behavior often leaves public records which can be stored in files and libraries, and the metaphor of storage is therefore particularly plausible. But is the expression any more helpful than saying that my behavior in eating my dinner is stored as prandial memories, or scratching an itch as a prurient memory? The observed facts are simple enough: I have acquired a repertoire of behavior, parts of which I display upon appropriate occasions. The metaphor of storage and retrieval goes well beyond those facts.

The computer, together with information theory as designed to deal with physical systems, has made the metaphor of input-storage-retrieval-output fashionable. The struggle to make machines that think like people has had the effect of supporting theories in which people think like machines. Mind has recently been defined as "the system of organizations and structures ascribed to an individual that processes inputs...and provides output to the various subsystems and the world." But organizations and structures of what? (The metaphor gains power from the way in which it disposes of troublesome problems. By speaking of input one can forget all the travail of sensory-psychology and physiology; by speaking of output one can forget all the problems of reporting and analyzing action; and by speaking of the storage and retrieval of information one can avoid all the difficult problems of how organisms are indeed changed by contact with their environments and how those changes survive.)

Sensory data are often said to be stored as images, much like the images said to represent the real world. Once inside, they are moved about for cognitive purposes. There is a familiar experiment on color generalization in which a pigeon pecks at a disk of, say, green light, the behavior being reinforced on a variable interval schedule. When a stable rate of responding develops, no further reinforcements are given, and the color of the disk is changed. The pigeon responds to another color at a rate which depends upon how much it differs from the original; rather similar colors evoke fairly high rates, very different colors low rates. A cognitive psychologist might explain the matter in this way: The pigeon takes in a new color (as "input"), retrieves the original color from memory, where it has been stored in some processed form, puts the two colored images side by side so that they may be easily compared, and after evaluating the difference, responds at the appropriate rate. But what advantage is gained by moving from a pigeon that responds to different colors on a disk to an inner pigeon that responds to colored images in its mind? The simple fact is that because of a known history of reinforcement, different colors control different rates.

The cognitive metaphor is based upon behavior in the real world. We store samples of material and retrieve and compare them with other samples. We compare them in the literal sense of putting them side by side to make differences more obvious. And we respond to different things in different ways. But that is all. The whole field of the processing of information can be reformulated as changes in the control exerted by stimuli.

•   •   •

The storage of practical knowledge raises another problem. When I learn, say, to take apart the rings of a puzzle, it seems unlikely that I store my knowledge of how to do so as a copy of the puzzle or of the contingencies the puzzle maintains for those trying to solve it. Instead cognitive theory holds that I store a rule. Rules are widely used as mental surrogates of behavior, in part because they can be memorized and hence "possessed," but there is an important difference between rules and the contingencies they describe. Rules can be internalized in the sense that we can say them to ourselves, but in doing so we do not internalize the contingencies.

I may learn to solve the puzzle in either of two ways. I may move the rings about until I hit upon a response that separates them. The behavior will be strengthened, and if I do the same thing a number of times, I will eventually be able to take the rings apart quickly. My behavior has been shaped and maintained by its effects on the rings. I may, on the other hand, simply follow printed directions supplied with the puzzle. The directions describe behavior that separates the rings, and if I have already learned to follow directions, I can avoid the possibly long process of having my behavior shaped by the contingencies.

Directions are rules. Like advice, warnings, maxims, proverbs, and governmental and scientific laws, they are extremely important parts of a culture, enabling people to profit from the experience of others. Those who have acquired behavior through exposure to contingencies describe the contingencies, and others then circumvent exposure by behaving in the ways described. But cognitive psychologists contend that something of the same sort happens internally when people learn directly from the contingencies. They are said to discover rules which they themselves then follow. But rules are not *in* the contingencies, nor must they be "known" by those who acquire behavior under exposure to them. (We are lucky that this should be so, since rules are verbal products which arose very late in the evolution of the species).

The distinction between rules and contingencies is currently important in the field of verbal behavior. Children learn to speak through contact with verbal communities, possibly without instruction. Some verbal responses are effective and others not, and over a period of time more and more effective behavior is shaped and maintained. The contingencies having this effect can be analyzed. A verbal *response* "means" something in the sense that the speaker is under the control of particular circumstances; a verbal *stimulus* "means" something in the sense that the listener responds to it in particular ways. The verbal community maintains contingencies of such a nature that responses made upon particular occasions serve as useful stimuli to listeners who then behave appropriately to the occasions.

More complex relations among the behaviors of speaker and listener fall within the fields of syntax and grammar. Until the time of the Greeks, no one seems to have known that there were rules of grammar, although people spoke grammatically in the sense that they behaved effectively under the contingencies maintained by verbal communities, as children today learn to talk without being given rules to follow. But cognitive psychologists insist that speakers and listeners must discover rules for themselves. One authority, indeed, has defined speaking as "engaging in a rule-governed form of intentional behavior." But there is no evidence that rules play any part in the behavior of the ordinary speaker. By using a dictionary and a grammar we may compose acceptable sentences in a language we do not otherwise speak, and we may occasionally consult a dictionary or a grammar in speaking our own language, but even so we seldom speak by applying rules. We speak because our behavior is shaped and maintained by the practices of a verbal community.

·   ·   ·

Having moved the environment inside the head in the form of conscious experience and behavior in the form of intention, will, and choice, and having stored the effects of contingencies of reinforcement as knowledge and rules, cognitive psychologists put them all together to compose an internal simulacrum of the organism, a kind of doppelgänger, not unlike the classical homunculus, whose behavior is the subject of what Piaget and others have called "subjective behaviorism." The mental apparatus studied by cognitive psychology is simply a rather crude version of contingencies of reinforcement and their effects.

Every so-called cognitive process has a physical model. We *associate* things by putting them together. We *store* memoranda and retrieve them for later use. We *compare* things by putting them side by side to emphasize differences. We *discriminate* things one from another by separating them and treating them in different ways. We *identify* objects by isolating them from confusing surroundings. We *abstract* sets of items from complex arrays. We describe contingencies of reinforcement in *rules*. These are the actions of real persons. It is only in the fanciful world of an inner person that they become mental processes.

The very speed with which cognitive processes are invented to explain behavior should arouse our suspicions. Molière made a joke of a medical example more than 300 years ago: "I am asked by the learned doctors for the cause and reason why opium puts one to sleep, to which I reply that there is in it a soporific virtue the nature of which is to lull the senses." Molière's candidate could have cited evidence from introspection, invoking a collateral effect of the drug, by saying: "To which I reply that opium makes one feel sleepy." But the soporific virtue itself is a sheer invention, and it is not without current parallels.

A conference was recently held in Europe on the subject of scientific creativity. A report published in *Science*[6] begins by pointing out that more than 90 percent of scientific innovation has been accomplished by fewer than 10 percent of all scientists. The next sentence might be paraphrased in this way: "I am asked by the learned doctors for the cause and reason why this should be so, to which I reply that it is because only a few scientists possess creativity." Similarly, "I am asked by the learned doctors for the cause and reason why children learn to talk with great speed, to which I reply that it is because they possess linguistic competence." Molière's audiences laughed.

•   •   •

Cognitive psychologists have two answers to the charge that the mental apparatus is a metaphor or construct. One is that cognitive processes are known through introspection. Do not all thinking persons know that they think? And if behaviorists say they do not, are they not either confessing a low order of mentality or acting in bad faith for the sake of their position? No one doubts that behavior involves internal processes; the question is how well they can be known through introspection. As I have argued elsewhere, self-knowledge, consciousness, or awareness became possible only when the species acquired verbal behavior, and that was very late in its history. The only nervous systems then available had evolved for other purposes and did not make contact with the more important physiological activities. Those who see themselves thinking see little more than their perceptual and motor behavior, overt and covert. They could be said to observe the results of "cognitive processes" but not the processes themselves—a "stream of consciousness" but not what causes the streaming, the "image of a lemon" but not the act of associating appearance with flavor, their use of an abstract term but not the process of abstraction, a name recalled but not its retrieval from memory, and so on. We do not, through introspection, observe the physiological processes through which behavior is shaped and maintained by contingencies of reinforcement.

But physiologists observe them and cognitive psychologists point to resemblances which suggest that they and the physiologists are talking about the same things. The very fact that cognitive processes are going on inside the organism suggests that the cognitive account is closer to physiology than the contingencies of reinforcement studied by those who analyze behavior. But if cognitive processes are simply modeled upon the environmental contingencies, the fact that they are assigned to space inside the skin does not bring them closer to a physiological account. On the contrary, the fascination with an imagined inner life has led to a neglect of the observed facts. The cognitive constructs give physiologists a misleading account of what they will find inside.

•　　•　　•

In summary, then, I am not a cognitive psychologist for several reasons. I see no evidence of an inner world of mental life relative either to an analysis of behavior as a function of environmental forces or to the physiology of the nervous system. The respective sciences of behavior and physiology will move forward most rapidly if their domains are correctly defined and analyzed.

I am equally concerned with practical consequences. The appeal to cognitive states and processes is a diversion which could well be responsible for much of our failure to solve our problems. We need to change our behavior and we can do so only by changing our physical and social environments. We choose the wrong path at the very start when we suppose that our goal is to change the "minds and hearts of men and women" rather than the world in which they live.

REFERENCES AND NOTES

[1]Popper, K.R. *Poverty of historicism.* London: Routledge and Kegan Paul, 1957.
[2]Waddington, C.H. How to succeed in nature without really trying. *New York Times Book Review,* February 3, 1974, pp. 2–3.
[3]Rapoport, A. *Experimental games and their uses in psychology.* Morristown, N.J.: Silver Burdett Company, General Learning Press, 1973.
[4]Attneave, F. How do you know? *American Psychologist,* 1974, *29,* 493–499.
[5]Julesz, B. Experiments in the visual perception of texture. *Scientific American,* April 1975, pp. 34–43.
[6]Maugh, T.H. II. Creativity: Can it be dissected? Can it be taught? *Science,* 1974, *184,* 1273.

POSTSCRIPT

For many years as I read a paper or a book about human behavior, I would make a running (usually covert) translation of mentalistic terms into behavioral terms. At one time I started to compile a dictionary in which I would give translations of common mentalistic terms, in each case citing the contingencies of reinforcement responsible for the behavior otherwise attributed to the cognitive process.

But more was involved than simple translation. The practices of cognitive psychologists needed to be made clear. The freedom of using mentalistic terms without serious restraint was causing trouble: There was a great loss in rigor in psychological thinking.

The present paper contains examples of "translations" bearing on three special fields: (1) *perception* (reinterpreted as the acquisition of the control of behavior by stimuli, under appropriate contingencies of reinforcement), (2) *action* (the internalization of behavior and the probability of behaving), and (3) *the cognitive processes* said to relate action to perception (the overall contingencies responsible for the behavior of the individual).

In general I reject any appeal to physiology in explaining behavior on the grounds that physiology is still far less advanced than the analysis of behavior and has yet to deal with the processes responsible for the behavior attributed to contingencies of reinforcement; but in this paper I made an appeal to physiology, or rather, anatomy, where the available facts were clear and relevant. The question is this: How much of what is going on in our own bodies as the effect of contingencies of reinforcement can be observed through introspection? If introspection became possible only after the development of a rather sophisticated verbal behavior, providing the contingencies under which people actually observed their own behavior or their own bodily processes, then there would not have been time for the evolution of an appropriate nervous system. The available nervous systems had evolved for other reasons. Hence, we cannot "observe cognitive processes" because we do not have nerves going to the right places in the brain. At most we can observe the contingencies of reinforcement and their effects, and this is all that cognitive psychologists actually do.

C H A P T E R   9

A Lecture on "Having" a Poem

EDITOR'S NOTE

The article was first published in the third edition of *Cumulative Record* (1972, pp. 345-355). An edited version appeared at about the same time in the *Saturday Review* (July 15, 1972, *55*, 32-35). It was given as a lecture at the Poetry Center in New York City on October 13, 1971; the lecture format has been retained. Skinner compares the writing of a poem to the act of giving birth: A woman seems to be creating something when she has a baby, but in fact she is merely passing along genes supplied by her husband and parents; she is a "locus" in which something new grows, but she makes no creative contribution. A poet, too, seems to be creating something when writing a poem, but he or she, too, can be considered a locus through which a unique set of genes and a unique environmental history are expressed. The product is new because of its unique determinants; no act of creation is necessary to explain it. So-called "purposive" and "creative" acts in the lifetime of an organism can be explained by the same mechanisms with which Darwin explained so-called "purposive" and "creative" acts in evolution—variation and selection.

Skinner begins the lecture with some casual remarks about Noam Chomsky, one of his most outspoken critics. These are his most extensive published comments on Chomsky, whose explosive review of Skinner's *Verbal Behavior* persuaded many linguists that the book was not worth reading. It has taken nearly two decades for interest to grow again. According to Skinner, the review (which, to this day, he has not read in its entirety) simply missed the point of his book.

Skinner also recounts an exchange with I.A. Richards, a long-time friend and colleague who had also criticized *Verbal Behavior*. Their dispute culminated in the publication of two poems in *Encounter* magazine in 1962. Skinner reads and interprets all of his own poem and portions of Richards's. Skinner's position is poetically abbreviated: "All's behavior—and the rest is naught."

Related issues are explored in "Creating the Creative Artist,"
published in 1970.

What I am going to say has the curious property of illustrating itself. The
quotation marks in my title are intended to suggest that there is a sense in
which having a poem is like having a baby, and in that sense I am in labor; I
am having a lecture. In it I intend to raise the question of whether I am
responsible for what I am saying, whether I am actually originating anything,
and to what extent I deserve credit or blame. That is one issue in *Beyond
Freedom and Dignity,* but since I am having a verbal baby, the argument
goes back to an earlier book.

In his review of *Beyond Freedom and Dignity* in *The New York Times,*[1]
Christopher Lehmann-Haupt begins with two sentences dear to the hearts of
my publishers, and they have not allowed them to become hidden under a
bushel. But later in the review, unhappy about some of the implications, he
tries to fault me. "Well then," he writes, "what about the most serious (and
best advertised) attack that has been leveled against behaviorism in recent
years—namely, Noam Chomsky's attempts to demonstrate man's innate
linguistic powers, which began with Chomsky's famous review of Skinner's
book *Verbal Behavior.* Skinner says nothing explicit on the matter in *Beyond
Freedom and Dignity.* Indeed, Chomsky's name is never brought up (which
seems disingenuous on Skinner's part). Have we got him there?"

Let me tell you about Chomsky. I published *Verbal Behavior* in 1957. In
1958 I received a 55-page typewritten review by someone I had never heard
of named Noam Chomsky. I read half a dozen pages, saw that it missed the
point of my book, and went no further. In 1959, I received a reprint from the
journal *Language.*[2] It was the review I had already seen, now reduced to 32
pages in type, and again I put it aside. But then, of course, Chomsky's star
began to rise. Generative grammar became the thing—and a very big thing it
seemed to be. Linguists have always managed to make their discoveries
earthshaking. In one decade everything seems to hinge on semantics, in
another decade on the analysis of the phoneme. In the sixties, it was
grammar and syntax, and Chomsky's review began to be widely cited and
reprinted and became, in fact, much better known than my book.

Eventually the question was asked, why had I not answered Chomsky?
My reasons, I am afraid, show a lack of character. In the first place I should
have had to read the review, and I found its tone distasteful. It was not really a
review of my book but of what Chomsky took, erroneously, to be my
position. I should also have had to bone up on generative grammar, which
was not my field, and to do a good job I should have had to go into
structuralism, a theory which Chomsky, like Claude Lévi-Strauss, acquired

from Roman Jakobson. According to the structuralists we are to explain human behavior by discovering its organizing principles, paying little or no attention to the circumstances under which it occurs. If anything beyond structure is needed by way of explanation, it is to be found in a creative mind—Lévi-Strauss's savage mind or Chomsky's innate rules of grammar. (Compare the recent analysis of Shakespeare's sonnet "Th' expence of spirit" by Jakobson and Lawrence Jones[3] with my earlier analysis in *Verbal Behavior*. Where Jakobson and Jones confine themselves to the structure or pattern of the poem as it appears to the reader, I used the same features to illustrate the behavioral processes of formal and thematic strengthening which, to put it roughly, made words available to the poet as he wrote.) No doubt I was shirking a responsibility in not replying to Chomsky, and I am glad an answer has now been supplied by Kenneth MacCorquodale in the *Journal of the Experimental Analysis of Behavior*.[4]

A few years ago *Newsweek* magazine carried the disagreement further, going beyond linguistics and structuralism to the philosophy of the 17th century. I was said to be a modern disciple of John Locke, for whom the mind began as a clean slate or *tabula rasa* and who thought that knowledge was acquired only from experience, while Chomsky was said to represent Descartes, the rationalist, who was not sure he existed until he thought about it. *Newsweek* suggested that the battle was going my way, and the reaction by the generative grammarians was so violent that the magazine found it necessary to publish four pro-Chomsky letters. Each one repeated a common misunderstanding of my position. One implied that I was a stimulus-response psychologist (which I am not) and another that I think people are very much like pigeons (which I do not). One had at least a touch of wit. Going back to our supposed 17th century progenitors, the writer advised *Newsweek* to "Locke up Skinner and give Chomsky Descartes blanche." (But Chomsky cannot use a *carte blanche,* of course; it is too much like a *tabula rasa*.)

Ironically, Chomsky was later invited to give the John Locke Lectures at Oxford. I was at Cambridge University at the time, and the BBC thought it would be interesting if we were to discuss our differences on television. I don't know what excuse Chomsky gave, but I agreed to participate only if the moderator could guarantee equal time. I suggested that we use chess clocks. My clock would be running when I was talking, and Chomsky's when he was talking, and in that way I planned to have the last 15 or 20 minutes to myself. The BBC thought that my suggestion would not make for a very interesting program.

Verbal Behavior was criticized in a different way by an old friend, I.A. Richards, whose interest in the field goes back, of course, to *The Meaning of Meaning*.[5] For nearly 40 years Ivor Richards and I have respected each other while disagreeing rather violently. I have never been able to understand why he feels that the works of Coleridge make an important contribution to our understanding of human behavior, and he has never been able to understand why I feel the same way about pigeons. He has at times been deeply distressed. He once asked me to lecture to his freshman course in General Education. I turned up at the appointed hour, he made a few announcements, and then he said, "I now present the Devil," and sat down. And I had not yet published *Verbal Behavior,* that outrageous invasion of Richards's territory which might indeed have borne the subtitle, *The Meaninglessness of Meaning.*

When my book appeared, and in turn Chomsky's review, Ivor Richards sent me a poem. It was prefaced by two quotations, one from my book and one from the review, and it proceeded to document the extraordinary extent to which each of us believed that he was absolutely right. The poem began:

> Confidence with confidence oppose.
> Knowledge ducks under in between two No's
> So firmly uttered. Look again. You'll see
> Uncertainty beside uncertainty.

Some unacknowledged uncertainties were then cited and analyzed.

A few months later I received a second poem. It was called "Verbal Behaviour" and began as follows:

> No sense in fretting to be off the ground,
> There's never hurry whither we are bound,
> Where all's behaviour—and the rest is naught,
> Not even rest, but void beyond all thought.

It went on to argue that behaviorism will mean the death of the individual, the end of Man's divine image of himself. The behaviorist contends that

> The Angels are a sketch
> *They* made long since to comfort the sore wretch
> Cast out of Paradise he knew not why
> To start his long climb back into the sky.

But he will never reach Paradise again because the behaviorist will tear off his wings, crying, to set him free:

> These gleaming sails are but the flattering means,
> (Theologic gear, Pythagorean beans!)
> Whereby grubs flit and feed and lay their eggs,
> By metaphor, beyond the reach of legs.
> No psyche more! Homunculus-theory, out!
> Verbal behaviour's all it's all about.[6]

It seemed to me that this had gone far enough, and so I replied—in kind—as follows:

For Ivor Richards

Yes, "all's behavior—and the rest is naught."

And thus compressed
Into "the rest
Of all,"
A thought
Is surely neither bad nor wrong.

Or right or good?
No, no.
Define
And thus expunge
The *ought,*
The *should!*
Nothing is so
(See History.)

Let not the strong
Be cozened
By *Is* and *Isn't,*
Was and *Wasn't.*
Truth's to be sought
In *Does* and *Doesn't.*

Decline
To be.

And call
Him neither best
Nor blessed
Who wrought
That silly jest,
The Fall.

(It was a Plunge.)

A few days later Ivor Richards phoned. Why not publish our poems? I had no objection, and so he sent them to an American magazine. The editor agreed that they were interesting but that, since we were both at Harvard, it was a sort of in-house joke which might not appeal to their West Coast readers. Stephen Spender, however, had no West Coast readers to worry about, and our poems were eventually published in *Encounter.*[7]

That is the only poem I have published since college, and it must serve as my only credential in discussing the present topic. I am unwilling to let it stand without comment, and so I offer the following exegesis, as it might be written by some future candidate for a Ph.D. in English literature.

The poet begins with a quotation from his friend's poem, picking up a slight redundancy. If all's behavior, then of course the rest is naught. And it is perhaps just as well, since a thought reduced to nothing can scarcely be bad or wrong. But what about the possibility that it might be right or good? No, logical positivism will take care of that. By defining our values we expunge them.

A new theme then appears, perhaps best stated in the immortal words of Henry Ford, "History is bunk," but here extended to the present as well as the past, as the poet attacks existentialism as well as the uses of history. The theme is broached in the contemptuous lines

> Nothing is so
> (See History.)

but developed more explicitly when we are warned not to be deceived by *Is* and *Isn't* (so much for the Existentialists) or *Was* and *Wasn't* (so much for the Historians). Then follows that stirring behavioristic manifesto:

> Truth's to be sought
> In *Does* and *Doesn't.*

At this point, almost as if exhausted, the poet enters upon a new mood. Behaviorism has squeezed thought to death and with it consciousness and mind. George Kateb made the point later in his review of *Beyond Freedom and Dignity* in the *Atlantic Monthly,*[8] insisting that "Skinner foresees and condones the atrophy of consciousness." But since foreseeing and condoning are conscious acts, the behaviorist is engaged in a kind of intellectual suicide. To use a strangely inept expression, mind is to die by its own hand. The position is stated with stunning economy:

> Decline
> *To be.*

(We note here a certain infelicity. *To be* is a verb, and as such can be conjugated but not declined. But we must remember that an intentional suicide is likely to be distraught and an unintentional one at least careless. One thinks of Ophelia. The semantic blemish therefore simply adds to the tone of the passage.)

The theme of suicide becomes clear when the poet turns to his friend's reference to the fallen Angel and warns us against accepting uncritically "that silly jest, The Fall." (Note in passing that *silly* is cognate with the German *selig,* meaning holy or sacred.) "Fall" is wrong because it suggests chance. (Chance, of course, comes from the Latin *cadere* meaning *to fall*—the fall of a die or penny—and is it entirely irrelevant that "jest" is etymologically related to "cast," as in casting dice?) Make no mistake; the Fall was not an accident. It was a deliberate plunge.

Thus might some beknighted graduate student of the future write in search of partial fulfillment. Whether or not my competence in discussing poetry will be established, I cannot say. If not, I must fall back upon that stock reply of the critic when the playwright who has received a bad review points out that the critic has never written a play, and the critic replies, "Neither have I laid an egg, but I am a better judge of an omelet than any hen." It is a stale and musty joke, and I should not allow it to injure the tone of my lecture if it did not serve the important function of bringing me to my point. I am to compare having a poem with having a baby, and it will do no harm to start with a lower class of living things. Samuel Butler suggested the comparison years ago when he said that a poet writes a poem as a hen lays an egg, and both feel better afterwards.

But there are other points of similarity, and on one of them Butler built a whole philosophy of purposive evolution. The statement was current in early post-Darwinism days that "a hen is only an egg's way of making another egg." It is not, of course, a question of which comes first, though that is not entirely irrelevant. The issue is who *does* what, who *acts* to produce something and therefore deserves credit. Must we give the hen credit for the egg or the egg for the hen? Possibly it does not matter, since no one is seriously interested in defending the rights of hen or egg, but something of the same sort can be said about poets, and then it does matter. Do poets create, originate, initiate the thing called a poem, or is their behavior merely the product of their genetic and environmental histories?

I raised that question a number of years ago with a distinguished poet at a conference at Columbia University. I was just finishing *Verbal Behavior* and could not resist summarizing my position. I thought it was possible to account for verbal behavior in terms of the history of the speaker, without reference to ideas, meanings, propositions, and the like. The poet stopped me at once. He could not agree. "That leaves no place for me as a poet," he said, and he would not discuss the matter further. It was a casual remark which, I am sure, he has long since forgotten, and I should hesitate to identify him if he had not recently published something along the same lines.

When Jerome Weisner was recently inaugurated as president of Massachusetts Institute of Technology, Archibald MacLeish[9] read a poem.* He praised Dr. Weisner as:

> A good man in a time when men are
> scarce, when the intelligent foregather,
> follow each other around like sheep in a fog,
> bleat in the rain, complain

*Excerpted from "A Good Man in a Bad Time," from NEW AND COLLECTED POEMS 1917–1976 by Archibald MacLeish. Copyright © 1976 by Archibald MacLeish. Reprinted by permission of Houghton Mifflin Company.

because Godot never comes; because
all life is a tragic absurdity—Sisyphus
sweating away at his rock and the rock
won't; because freedom and dignity...

Oh, weep, they say, for freedom and dignity!
You're not free: It's your grandfather's itch you're scratching.
You have no dignity: You're not a man,
you're a rat in a vat of rewards and punishments,
you think you've chosen the rewards, you haven't:
The rewards have chosen you.

                                          Aye! Weep!

I am just paranoid enough to believe that he is alluding to *Beyond Freedom and Dignity*. In any case, he sums up the main issue rather effectively: "You think you've chosen the rewards; you haven't. The rewards have chosen you." To put it more broadly, people do not act upon the environment, perceiving it and deciding what to do about it; the environment acts upon them, determining that they will perceive it and act in special ways. George Eliot glimpsed the issue: "Our deeds determine us, as much as we determine our deeds," though she did not understand *how* we are determined by our deeds. Something does seem to be taken away from Keats when his behavior is traced to his genetic and personal histories. Only those who truly initiate their behavior can claim that they are free to do so and that they deserve credit for any achievement. If the environment is the initiating force, they are not free, and the environment must get the credit.

The issue will be clearer if we turn to a biological parallel—moving from the oviparous hen to the viviparous human mother. When we say that a woman "bears" a child, we suggest little by way of creative achievement. The verb refers to carrying the fetus to term. The expression "gives birth" goes little further; a bit of a platonic idea, birth, is captured by the mother and given to the baby, which then becomes born. We usually say simply that a woman "has" a baby where "has" means little more than possess. To have a baby is to come into possession of it. The woman who does so is then a mother, and the child is her child. But what is the nature of her contribution? She is not responsible for the skin color, eye color, strength, size, intelligence, talents, or any other feature of her baby. She gave it half its genes, but she got those from *her* parents. She could, of course, have damaged the baby. She could have aborted it. She could have caught rubella at the wrong time or taken drugs, and as a result the baby would have been defective. *But she made no positive contribution.*

A biologist has no difficulty in describing the role of the mother. She is a place, a locus in which a very important biological process takes place. She supplies protection, warmth, and nourishment, but she does not design the baby who profits from them. The poet is also a locus, a place in which certain genetic and environmental causes come together to have a common effect. Unlike a mother, the poet has access to a poem during gestation and may tinker with it. A poem seldom makes its appearance in a completed form. Bits and pieces *occur* to the poet, who rejects or allows them to stand, and who puts them together to *compose* a poem. But they come from a past history, verbal and otherwise, and the poet has had to learn how to put them together. The act of composition is no more an act of creation than "having" the bits and pieces composed.

But can this interpretation be correct if a poem is unquestionably new? Certainly the plays of Shakespeare did not exist until he wrote them. Possibly all their parts could be traced by an omniscient scholar to Shakespeare's verbal and nonverbal histories, but he must have served some additional function. How otherwise are we to explain the creation of something new?

The answer is again to be found in biology. A little more than 100 years ago the act of creation was debated for a very different reason. The living things on the surface of the earth show a fantastic variety—far beyond the variety in the works of Shakespeare—and they had long been attributed to a creative Mind. The anatomy of the hand, for example, was taken as evidence of a prior design. And just as we are told today that a behavioral analysis cannot explain the "potentially infinite" number of sentences composable by a speaker, so it was argued that no physical or biological process could explain the potentially infinite number of living things on the surface of the earth. (Curiously enough the creative behavior invoked by way of explanation was verbal: "In the beginning was the word...," supplemented no doubt by a *generative* grammar.)

The key term in Darwin's title is Origin. Novelty could be explained without appeal to prior design if random changes in structure were selected by their consequences. It was the contingencies of survival which created new forms. Selection is a special kind of causality, much less conspicuous than the push-pull causality of 19th-century physics, and Darwin's discovery may have appeared so late in the history of human thought for that reason. The selective action of the consequences of behavior was also overlooked for a long time. It was not until the 17th century that any important initiating action by the environment was recognized. People acted upon the world, but the world did not act upon them. The first evidence to the contrary was of the conspicuous push-pull kind. Descartes's (*pace* Chomsky) theoretical anticipation of the reflex and the reflex physiology of the 19th century gave rise to a stimulus-response psychology in which behavior was said to be triggered by the environment. There is no room in such a formulation for a more important function. When people act, the consequences may strengthen their tendency to act in the same way again. The Law of Effect, formulated nearly three-quarters of a century ago by Edward L. Thorndike, owed a great deal to Darwinian theory, and it raised very similar issues. It is not some prior purpose, intention, or act of will which accounts for novel behavior; it is the "contingencies of reinforcement." (Among the behaviors thus explained are techniques of self-management, once attributed to "higher mental processes," which figure in the gestation of new topographies.)

We often know that some part of our history is contributing to the piece we are writing. We may, for example, reject a phrase because we see that we have borrowed it from something we have read. But it is quite impossible for us to be aware of all our history, and it is in this sense that we do not know where our behavior comes from. Having a poem, like having a baby, is in large part a matter of exploration and discovery, and both poet and mother are often surprised by what they produce. And, unaware of the origins of the behavior, the poet is likely to attribute it to a creative mind, an "unconscious" mind, perhaps, or a mind belonging to someone else—to a muse, for example, who has been invoked to come and write the poem.

A person produces a poem and a woman produces a baby, and we call the person a poet and the woman a mother. Both are essential as loci in which vestiges of the past come together in certain combinations. The process is creative in the sense that the products are new. Writing a poem is the sort of thing men and women do as men and women, having a baby is the sort of thing a woman does as a woman, and laying an egg is the sort of thing a hen does as a hen. To deny a creative contribution does not destroy man *qua* man or woman *qua* woman any more than Butler's phrase destroys hen *qua* hen. There is no threat to the essential masculinity of man, the muliebrity of woman, or the gallity of *Gallus gallus*.

What is threatened, of course, is the autonomy of the poet. The autonomous is the uncaused, and the uncaused is miraculous, and the miraculous is God. For the second time in a little more than a century a theory of selection by consequences is threatening a traditional belief in a creative mind. And is it not rather strange that although we have abandoned that belief with respect to the creation of the world, we fight so desperately to preserve it with respect to the creation of a poem?

But is there anything wrong with a supportive myth? Why not continue to believe in our creative powers if the belief gives us satisfaction? The answer lies in the future of poetry. To accept a wrong explanation because it flatters us is to run the risk of missing a right one—one which in the long run may offer more by way of "satisfaction." Poets know all too well how long a sheet of paper remains a *carte blanche*. To wait for genius or a genie is to make a virtue of ignorance. If poetry is a good thing, if we want more of it and better, and if writing poems is a rewarding experience, then we should look afresh at its sources.

Perhaps the future of poetry is not that important, but I have been using a poem simply as an example. I could have developed the same theme in art, music, fiction, scholarship, science, invention—in short, wherever we speak of *original* behavior. We say that we "have" ideas and again in the simple sense of coming into possession of them. An idea "occurs to us" or "comes to mind." And if for idea we read "the behavior said to express an idea," we come no closer to an act of creation. We "have" behavior, as the etymology of the word itself makes clear. It "occurs to us" to act in a particular way, and it is not any prior intention, purpose, or plan which disposes us to do so. By analyzing the genetic and individual histories responsible for our behavior, we may learn how to be more original. The task is not to think of new forms of behavior but to create an environment in which they are likely to occur.

Something of the sort has happened in the evolution of cultures. Over the centuries men and women have built a world in which they behave much more effectively than in a natural environment, but they have not done so by deliberate design. A culture evolves when new practices arise which make it more likely to survive. We have reached a stage in which our culture induces some of its members to be concerned for its survival. A kind of deliberate design is then possible, and a scientific analysis is obviously helpful. We can build a world in which men and women will be better poets, better artists, better composers, better novelists, better scholars, better scientists—in a word, better people. We can, in short, "have" a better world.

And that is why I am not much disturbed by the question with which George Kateb concludes his review of *Beyond Freedom and Dignity.* He is attacking my utopianism, and he asks, "Does Skinner not see that only silly geese lay golden eggs?" The question brings us back to the oviparous again, but it does not matter, for the essential issue is raised by all living things. It is characteristic of the evolution of a species, as it is of the acquisition of behavior and of the evolution of a culture, that ineffective forms give rise to effective. Perhaps a goose is silly if, because she lays a golden egg, she gets the ax; but, silly or not, she has laid a golden egg. And what if that egg hatches a golden goose? There, in an eggshell, is the great promise of evolutionary theory. A silly goose, like Butler's hen, is simply the way in which an egg produces a *better* egg.

And now my labor is over. I have had my lecture. I have no sense of fatherhood. If my genetic and personal histories had been different, I should have come into possesion of a different lecture. If I deserve any credit at all, it is simply for having served as a place in which certain processes could take place. I shall interpret your polite applause in that light.

REFERENCES AND NOTES

[1]Lehmann-Haupt, C. Skinner's design for living. *The New York Times,* September 22, 1971, p. 49.

[2]Chomsky, N. *Verbal behavior*—reviewed. *Language,* 1959, *35,* 26–58.

[3]Jakobson, R., & Jones, L. *Shakespeare's verbal art in "Th' expence of spirit."* The Hague: Mouton, 1970.

[4]MacCorquodale, K. On Chomsky's review of Skinner's *Verbal behavior. Journal of the Experimental Analysis of Behavior,* 1970, *13,* 83–99.

[5]Richards, I.A., & Ogden, C.K. *The meaning of meaning.* New York: Harcourt, Brace & World, 1923.

[6]Both of Ivor Richards's poems are reprinted by permission of Dr. I.A. Richards's Literary Estate. Portions of these poems first appeared in Chapter 1 of a book by I.A. Richards entitled *So Much Nearer* (London: Times Literary Supplement, 1960).

[7]Richards, I.A., & Skinner, B.F. Verbal behaviour. *Encounter,* November 1962, pp. 42–44. Reprinted by permission of the publisher.

[8]Kateb, G. Toward a wordless world. *Atlantic Monthly,* October 1971, pp. 122–125.

[9]The poem appeared in *The Boston Herald Traveler* (October 8, 1971, p. B3) and other papers after Weisner's inauguration. A revised version of MacLeish's poem was published under the title "A Good Man in a Bad Time" in MacLeish's *New and Collected Poems, 1917–1976* (Boston: Houghton Mifflin, 1976, pp. 9–11). The section of the revised version which corresponds to the section Skinner quotes reads:

> A time when men are scarce,
> when fools forgather,
> follow each other around in the fog like
> sheep, bleat in the rain, complain
> that Godot never comes,
> that all life is a tragic absurdity, Sisyphus
> sweating away at his rock and the rock
> won't. "Weep," they say, "for freedom and dignity!
> You're not free: it's your grandfather's itch you're scratching.
> You have no dignity. You're not a man.
> You're a rat in a vat of rewards and punishments.
> The rewards have chosen *you.*" Aye, weep!

POSTSCRIPT

An invitation to give a lecture at the Poetry Center in New York City revived an early interest in literature and brought out a very different style of presentation. Writing and giving the lecture were fun. There is no hint of high seriousness in my remarks about Chomsky (whom I have never been able to take seriously), or scholarly research in English literature, or motherhood.

Yet the lecture has an important central theme. *Beyond Freedom and Dignity* was still on the best-seller list when I gave the lecture, and I was offering a delicate example of its central thesis: A scientific analysis of behavior robs people of the credit which has been given them over the

centuries, particularly for their originality. Juvenile delinquents have
learned how to excuse themselves by blaming their behavior on their
genetic and environmental histories, but poets are unwilling to
acknowledge the same sources of the behavior for which they are
applauded.

PART THREE

Applications

CHAPTER 10

The Science of Learning
and the Art of Teaching

EDITOR'S NOTE

The article first appeared in the *Harvard Educational Review* (1954, *24*, 86–97) and later as Chapter 2 in *The Technology of Teaching* (1968, pp. 9–28). The photographs are from *The Technology of Teaching*. This is Skinner's seminal work on education, though, as he recounts in *The Shaping of a Behaviorist,* he had toyed with a kind of programmed textbook as early as the late 1930s. In this essay Skinner describes the first teaching machine based on principles of behavior established in the laboratory. Within a few years a movement had begun. Advances are described in a number of subsequent publications: "Teaching Machines" (*Science,* 1958), "The Programming of Verbal Knowledge" (1959), "Special Problems in Programming Language Instruction for Teaching Machines" (1960), "The Use of Teaching Machines in College Instruction" (1960, with J.G. Holland), "Teaching Machines" (*The Review of Economics and Statistics,* 1960), "Modern Learning Theory and Some New Approaches to Teaching" (1960), "The Theory Behind Teaching Machines" (1961), "Why We Need Teaching Machines" (1961), "Learning Theory and Future Research" (1961), "Teaching Machines" (*Scientific American,* 1961), "Reflections on a Decade of Teaching Machines" (1963), "L'Avenir des Machines à Enseigner" (1963), "New Methods and New Aims in Teaching" (1964), "The Technology of Teaching" (1965), "Why Teachers Fail" (1965), "Teaching Science in High School—What Is Wrong?" (1968), *Development of Methods of Preparing Materials for Teaching Machines* (an edited booklet of selections from grant reports, 1968), "Contingency Management in the Classroom" (1969), "Some Implications of Making Education More Efficient" (1973), "The Free and Happy Student" (1973), and "Designing Higher Education" (1974). Several of the more important papers were collected, along with some new material, to form the *The Technology of Teaching.* Another book, *The Analysis of Behavior: A Program for Self-Instruction* (1961, with J.G. Holland), was the first programmed textbook.

The teaching machine movement waned by the mid-1960s. American industry was prepared to make the proper investment, but the educational establishment was not. In recent years, as sophisticated computers have become less and less expensive, educators have become increasingly interested in "computer-aided instruction," usually called simply "CAI." Many CAI programs were inspired by those of the old programmed instruction movement.

The article begins with an almost exuberant summary of some of the accomplishments of the experimental analysis of behavior. Reinforcement permits us "to shape the behavior of an organism almost at will," Skinner says. Schedules of reinforcement tell us how behavior is maintained. Complex processes, such as attention, problem-solving, dark-adaptation, and discrimination have been investigated, and "the species of the organism has made surprisingly little difference."

A technology of behavior change based on the "exciting prospect of an advancing science of learning" can be used to supplement ineffective and inefficient methods of conventional teaching, says Skinner. The key is to divide up "[the] whole process of becoming competent in any field" into "a very large number of very small steps" and then to provide reinforcement "upon the accomplishment of each step." It would be difficult for a teacher to do this, but suitable machines can be built. Skinner describes a small mechanical device he invented to teach arithmetic. A problem appears in a window. The student sets an answer by adjusting sliders and then turns a knob. If the answer is correct, a bell rings and the next problem appears; if it is incorrect, the knob will not turn. The machine allows material to be programmed in small steps and provides immediate reinforcement for correct answers. With many such machines in a classroom, each child can progress at his or her own rate. The teacher, meanwhile, is free to spend more time with individual students. A similar device for teaching spelling is briefly described. Educators, concludes Skinner, "must accept the fact that a sweeping revision of educational practices is possible and inevitable."

Some promising advances have recently been made in the field of learning. Special techniques have been designed to arrange what are called contingencies of reinforcement—the relations which prevail between behavior on the one hand and the consequences of that behavior on the other—with the result that a much more effective control of behavior has been achieved. It has long been argued that an organism learns mainly by producing changes in its environment, but it is only recently that these changes have been carefully manipulated. In traditional devices for the study of learning—in the serial maze, for example, or in the T-maze, the problem box, or the familiar discrimination apparatus—the effects produced by the organism's behavior are left to many fluctuating circumstances. There is many a slip between the turn-to-the-right and the food-cup at the end of the alley. It is not surprising that techniques of this sort have yielded only very rough data from which the uniformities demanded by an experimental science can be extracted only by averaging many cases. In none of this work has the behavior of the individual organism been predicted in more than a statistical sense. The learning processes which are the presumed object of such research are reached only through a series of inferences.

Recent improvements in the conditions which control behavior in the field of learning are of two principal sorts. The Law of Effect has been taken seriously; we have made sure that effects *do* occur and that they occur under conditions which are optimal for producing the changes called learning. Once we have arranged the particular type of consequence called a reinforcement, our techniques permit us to shape the behavior of an organism almost at will. It has become a routine exercise to demonstrate this in classes in elementary psychology by conditioning such an organism as a pigeon. Simply by presenting food to a hungry pigeon at the right time, it is possible to shape three or four well-defined responses in a single demonstration period—such responses as turning around, pacing the floor in the pattern of a figure eight, standing still in a corner of the demonstration apparatus, stretching the neck, or stamping the foot. Extremely complex performances may be reached through successive stages in the shaping process, the contingencies of reinforcement being changed progressively in the direction of the required behavior. The results are often quite dramatic. In such a demonstration one can *see* learning take place. A significant change in behavior is often obvious as the result of a single reinforcement.

A second important advance in technique permits us to maintain behavior in given states of strength for long periods of time. Reinforcements continue to be important, of course, long after an organism has learned *how* to do something, long after it has acquired behavior. They are necessary to maintain the behavior in strength. Of special interest is the effect of various schedules of intermittent reinforcement. Most of the basic schedules have been investigated and in general have been reduced to a few principles. On the theoretical side we now have a fairly good idea of why a given schedule produces its appropriate performance. On the practical side we have learned how to maintain any given level of activity for daily periods limited only by the physical endurance of the organism and from day to day without substantial change throughout its life. Many of these effects would be traditionally assigned to the field of motivation, although the principal operation is simply the arrangement of contingencies of reinforcement.

These new methods of shaping behavior and of maintaining it in strength are a great improvement over the traditional practices of profes-sional animal trainers, and it is not surprising that our laboratory results are already being applied to the production of performing animals for commercial purposes. In a more academic environment they have been used for demonstration purposes which extend far beyond an interest in learning as such. For example, it is not too difficult to arrange the complex contingencies which produce many types of social behavior. Competition is exemplified by two pigeons playing a modified game of Ping-Pong.[1] The pigeons drive the ball back and forth across a small table by pecking at it. When the ball gets by one pigeon, the other receives food. The task of constructing such a "social relation" is probably completely out of reach of the traditional animal trainer. It requires a carefully designed program of gradually changing contingencies and the skillful use of schedules to maintain the behavior in strength. Each pigeon is separately prepared for its part in the total performance, and the social relation is then arbitrarily constructed. The events leading up to this stable state are excellent material for the study of the factors important in nonsynthetic social behavior. It is instructive to consider how a similar series of contingencies could arise in the case of the human organism through the evolution of cultural patterns. Cooperation can also be set up, perhaps more easily than competition. Two pigeons have been trained to coordinate their behavior in a cooperative endeavor with a precision which equals that of the most skillful human dancers.[2]

In a more serious vein, these techniques have made it possible to explore the complexities of the individual organism and to analyze some of the serial or coordinate behaviors involved in attention, problem solving, various types of self-control, and the subsidiary systems of responses within a single organism called "personalities." Some of these are exemplified in what are called multiple schedules of reinforcement.[3] In general a given schedule has an effect upon the rate at which a response is emitted. Changes in the rate from moment to moment show a pattern typical of the schedule. The pattern may be as simple as a constant rate of responding at a given value; it may be a gradually accelerating rate between certain extremes; it may be an abrupt change from not responding at all to a given stable high rate. It has been shown that the performance characteristic of a given schedule can be brought under the control of a particular stimulus and that different performances can be brought under the control of different stimuli in the same organism. In one experiment performances appropriate to *nine* different schedules were brought under the control of appropriate stimuli presented at random. When Stimulus 1 was present, the pigeon executed the performance appropriate to Schedule 1. When Stimulus 2 was present, the pigeon executed the performance appropriate to Schedule 2. And so on. This result is important because it makes the extrapolation of our laboratory results to daily life much more plausible. We are all constantly shifting from schedule to schedule as our immediate environment changes.

It is also possible to construct very complex *sequences* of schedules. It is not easy to describe these in a few words, but two or three examples may be mentioned. In one experiment the pigeon generates a performance appropriate to Schedule A where the reinforcement is simply the production of the stimulus characteristic of Schedule B, to which the pigeon then responds appropriately. Under a third stimulus, the bird yields a performance appropriate to Schedule C where the reinforcement in this case is simply the production of the stimulus characteristic of Schedule D, to which the bird then responds appropriately. In a special case, first investigated by L.B. Wyckoff, Jr., the organism responds to one stimulus where the reinforcement consists of the *clarification* of the stimulus controlling another response. The first response becomes, so to speak, an objective form of "paying attention" to the second stimulus. In an important version of this experiment, we could say that the pigeon is telling us whether it is paying attention to the *shape* of a spot of light or to its *color*.

One of the most dramatic applications of these techniques has been made by Floyd Ratliff and Donald S. Blough, who have skillfully used multiple and serial schedules of reinforcement to study complex perceptual processes in the infrahuman organism. They have achieved a sort of psychophysics without verbal instruction. In an experiment by Blough, for example, a pigeon draws a detailed dark-adaptation curve showing the characteristic breaks of rod and cone vision. The curve is recorded continuously in a single experimental period and is quite comparable with the curves of human subjects. The pigeon behaves in a way which, in the human case, we should not hesitate to describe by saying that it adjusts a very faint patch of light until it can just be seen.[4]

In all this work, the species of the organism has made surprisingly little difference. It is true that the organisms studied have all been vertebrates, but they still cover a wide range. Comparable results have been obtained with pigeons, rats, dogs, monkeys, human children, and psychotic subjects. In spite of great phylogenic differences, all these organisms show amazingly similar properties of the learning process. It should be emphasized that this has been achieved by analyzing the effects of reinforcement and by designing techniques which manipulate reinforcement with considerable precision. Only in this way can the behavior of the individual organism be brought under such precise control. It is also important to note that through a gradual advance to complex interrelations among responses, the same degree of rigor is being extended to behavior which would usually be assigned to such fields as perception, thinking, and personality dynamics.

SCHOOLROOM TEACHING

From this exciting prospect of an advancing science of learning, it is a great shock to turn to that branch of technology which is most directly concerned with the learning process—education. Let us consider, for example, the teaching of arithmetic in the lower grades.[5] The school is concerned with imparting to the child a large number of responses of a special sort. The responses are all verbal. They consist of speaking and writing certain words, figures, and signs which, to put it roughly, refer to numbers and to arithmetic operations. The first task is to shape these responses—to get the child to pronounce and to write responses correctly—but the principal task is to bring this behavior under many sorts of stimulus control. This is what happens when the child learns to count, to recite tables, to count while ticking off the items in an assemblage of objects, to respond to spoken or written numbers by saying "odd," "even," or "prime." Over and above this elaborate repertoire of numerical behavior, most of which is often dismissed as the product of rote learning, the teaching of arithmetic looks forward to those complex serial arrangements of responses involved in original mathematical thinking. The child must acquire responses of transposing, clearing fractions, and so on, which modify the order or pattern of the original material so that the response called a solution is eventually made possible.

Now, how is this extremely complicated verbal repertoire set up? In the first place, what reinforcements are used? Fifty years ago the answer would have been clear. At that time educational control was still frankly aversive. The child read numbers, copied numbers, memorized tables, and performed operations upon numbers to escape the threat of the birch rod or cane. Some positive reinforcements were perhaps eventually derived from the increased efficiency of the child in the field of arithmetic and in rare cases some automatic reinforcement may have resulted from the sheer manipulation of the medium—from the solution of problems or the discovery of the intricacies of the number system. But for the immediate purposes of education the child acted to avoid or escape punishment. It was part of the reform movement known as progressive education to make the positive consequences more immediately effective, but anyone who visits the lower grades of the average school today will observe that a change has been made, not from aversive to positive control, but from one form of aversive stimulation to another. The child at a desk, filling in a workbook, is behaving primarily to escape from the threat of a series of minor aversive events—the teacher's displeasure, the criticism or ridicule of classmates, an ignominious showing in a competition, low marks, a trip to the office "to be talked to" by the principal, or a word to the parent, who may still resort to the birch rod. In this welter of aversive consequences, getting the right answer is in itself an insignificant event, any effect of which is lost amid the anxieties, the boredom, and the aggressions which are the inevitable by-products of aversive control.

Secondly, we have to ask how the contingencies of reinforcement are arranged. When is a numerical operation reinforced as "right"? Eventually, of course, the pupil may be able to check the answer and achieve some sort of automatic reinforcement, but in the early stages the reinforcement of being right is usually accorded by the teacher. The contingencies provided are far from optimal. It can easily be demonstrated that, unless explicit mediating behavior has been set up, the lapse of only a few seconds between response and reinforcement destroys most of the effect. In a typical classroom, nevertheless, long periods of time customarily elapse. The teacher may walk up and down the aisle, for example, while the class is working on a sheet of problems, pausing here and there to call an answer right or wrong. Many minutes intervene between the child's response and the teacher's reinforcement. In many cases—for example, when papers are taken home to be corrected—as much as 24 hours may intervene. It is surprising that this system has any effect whatsoever.

A third notable shortcoming is the lack of a skillful program which moves forward through a series of progressive approximations to the final complex behavior desired. A long series of contingencies is necessary to bring the pupil into the possession of mathematical behavior most efficiently. But the teacher is seldom able to reinforce at each step in such a series because it is impossible to deal with the pupil's responses one at a time. It is usually necessary to reinforce the behavior in blocks of responses—as in correcting a worksheet or page from a workbook. The responses within such a block must not be interrelated. The answer to one problem must not depend upon the answer to another. The number of stages through which one may progressively approach a complex pattern of behavior is therefore small, and the task so much the more difficult. Even the most modern workbook in beginning arithmetic is far from exemplifying an efficient *program* for shaping mathematical behavior.

Perhaps the most serious criticism of the current classroom is the relative infrequency of reinforcement. Since pupils are usually dependent upon the teacher for being told that they are right, and since many pupils are usually dependent upon the same teacher, the total number of contingencies which may be arranged during, say, the first 4 years, is on the order of only a few thousand. But a very rough estimate suggests that efficient mathematical behavior at this level requires something on the order of

25,000 contingencies. We may suppose that even in the brighter student a given contingency must be arranged several times to place the behavior well in hand. The responses to be set up are not simply the various items in tables of addition, subtraction, multiplication, and division; we have also to consider the *alternative* forms in which each item may be stated. To the learning of such material we should add hundreds of responses such as those concerned with factoring, identifying primes, memorizing series, using short-cut techniques of calculation, and constructing and using geometric representations or number forms. Over and above all this, the whole mathematical repertoire must be brought under the control of concrete problems of considerable variety. Perhaps 50,000 contingencies is a more conservative estimate. In this frame of reference the daily assignment in arithmetic seems pitifully meagre.

The result of all this is, of course, well known. Even our best schools are under criticism for their inefficiency in the teaching of drill subjects such as arithmetic. The condition in the average school is a matter of widespread national concern. Modern children simply do not learn arithmetic quickly or well. Nor is the result simply incompetence. The very subjects in which modern techniques are weakest are those in which failure is most conspicuous, and in the wake of an ever-growing incompetence come the anxieties, uncertainties, and aggressions which in their turn present other problems to the school. Most pupils soon claim the asylum of not being "ready" for arithmetic at a given level or, eventually, of not having a mathematical mind. Such explanations are readily seized upon by defensive teachers and parents. Few pupils ever reach the stage at which automatic reinforcements follow as the natural consequences of mathematical behavior. On the contrary, the figures and symbols of mathematics have become standard emotional stimuli. The glimpse of a column of figures, not to say an algebraic symbol or an integral sign, is likely to set off, not mathematical behavior, but a reaction of anxiety, guilt, or fear.

Teachers are usually no happier about this than pupils. Denied the opportunity to control via the birch rod, quite at sea as to the mode of operation of the few techniques at their disposal, they spend as little time as possible on drill subjects and eagerly subscribe to philosophies of education which emphasize material of greater inherent interest. A confession of weakness is their extraordinary concern lest children be taught something unnecessary. The repertoire to be imparted is carefully reduced to an essential minimum. In the field of spelling, for example, a great deal of time and energy has gone into discovering just those words which the young child is going to use, as if it were a crime to waste one's educational power in teaching an unnecessary word. Eventually, weakness of technique emerges in the disguise of a reformulation of the aims of education. Skills are minimized in favor of vague achievements— educating for democracy, educating the whole child, educating for life, and so on. And there the matter ends; for, unfortunately, these philosophies do not in turn suggest improvements in techniques. They offer little or no help in the design of better classroom practices.

THE IMPROVEMENT OF TEACHING

There would be no point in urging these objections if improvement were impossible. But the advances which have recently been made in our control of the learning process suggest a thorough revision of classroom practices and, fortunately, they tell us how the revision can be brought about. This is not, of course, the first time that the results of an experimental science have been brought to bear upon the practical problems of education. The modern classroom does not, however, offer much evidence that research in the field of learning has been respected or used. This condition is no doubt partly due to the limitations of earlier research. But it has been encouraged by a too hasty conclusion that the laboratory study of learning is inherently limited because it cannot take into account the realities of the classroom. In the light of our increasing knowledge of the learning process we should, instead, insist upon dealing with those realities and forcing a substantial change in them. Education is perhaps the most important branch of scientific technology. It deeply affects the lives of all of us. We can no longer allow the exigencies of a practical situation to suppress the tremendous improvements which are within reach. The practical situation must be changed.

There are certain questions which have to be answered in turning to the study of any new organism. What behavior is to be set up? What reinforcers are at hand? What responses are available in embarking upon a program of progressive approximation which will lead to the final form of the behavior? How can reinforcements be most efficiently scheduled to maintain the behavior in strength? These questions are all relevant in considering the problem of the child in the lower grades.

In the first place, what reinforcements are available? What does the school have in its possession which will reinforce a child? We may look first to the material to be learned, for it is possible that this will provide considerable automatic reinforcement. Children play for hours with mechanical toys, paints, scissors and paper, noise-makers, puzzles—in short, with almost anything which feeds back significant changes in the environment and is reasonably free of aversive properties. The sheer control of nature is itself reinforcing. This effect is not evident in the modern school because it is masked by the emotional responses generated by aversive control. It is true that automatic reinforcement from the manipulation of the environment is probably only a mild reinforcer and may need to be carefully husbanded, but one of the most striking principles to emerge from recent research is that the *net* amount of reinforcement is of little significance. A very slight reinforcement may be tremendously effective in controlling behavior if it is wisely used.

If the natural reinforcement inherent in the subject matter is not enough, other reinforcers must be employed. Even in school the children are occasionally permitted to do "what they want to do," and access to reinforcements of many sorts may be made contingent upon the more immediate consequences of the behavior to be established. Those who advocate competition as a useful social motive may wish to use the reinforcements which follow from excelling others, although there is the difficulty that in this case the reinforcement of one child is necessarily aversive to another. Next in order we might place the goodwill and affection of the teacher, and only when that has failed need we turn to the use of aversive stimulation.

In the second place, how are these reinforcements to be made contingent upon the desired behavior? There are two considerations here— the gradual elaboration of extremely complex patterns of behavior and the maintenance of the behavior in strength at each stage. The whole process of becoming competent in any field must be divided into a very large number of very small steps, and reinforcement must be contingent upon the accomplishment of each step. This solution to the problem of creating a complex repertoire of behavior also solves the problem of maintaining the behavior in strength. We could, of course, resort to the techniques of scheduling already developed in the study of other organisms, but in the present state of our knowledge of educational practices scheduling appears to be most effectively arranged through the design of the material to be learned. By making each successive step as small as possible, the frequency of reinforcement can be raised to a maximum, while the possibly aversive consequences of being wrong are reduced to a minimum. Other ways of designing material would yield other programs of reinforcement. Any supplementary reinforcement would probably have to be scheduled in the more traditional way.

These requirements are not excessive, but they are probably incompatible with the current realities of the classroom. In the experimental study of learning it has been found that the contingencies of reinforcement which are most efficient in controlling the organism cannot be arranged through the personal mediation of the experimenter. An organism is affected by subtle details of contingencies which are beyond the capacity of the human organism to arrange. Mechanical and electrical devices must be used. Mechanical help is also demanded by the sheer number of contingencies which may be used efficiently in a single experimental session. We have recorded many millions of responses from a single organism during thousands of experimental hours. Personal arrangement of the contin-

gencies and personal observation of the results are c̦
the human organism is, if anything, more sensitive to ̦
than the other organisms we have studied. We have ev̦
therefore, that the most effective control of human lea
instrumental aid. The simple fact is that, as a mere reinfor̦
the teacher is out of date. This would be true even of a
devoting full time to a single child. The inadequacy is multip̦
when a teacher must serve as a reinforcing device to many chil̦   ̦ce.
To take advantage of recent advances in the study of learning, n̦ ̦chanical
devices must be used.

A TEACHING MACHINE

The technical problem of providing the necessary instrumental aid is not particularly difficult. There are many ways in which the necesssary contingencies may be arranged, either mechanically or electrically. An inexpensive device which solves most of the principal problems has already been constructed (Figure 1). It is still in the experimental stage, but it suggests the kind of instrument which seems to be required. The device is a box about the size of a small record player. On the top surface is a window through which a question or problem printed on a paper tape may be seen. The child answers the question by moving one or more sliders upon which the digits 0 through 9 are printed. The answer appears in square holes punched in the paper upon which the question is printed. When the answer has been set, the child turns a knob. The operation is as simple as adjusting a television set. If the answer is right, the knob turns freely and can be made to ring a bell or provide some other conditioned reinforcement. If the answer is wrong, the knob will not turn. A counter may be added to tally wrong answers. The knob must then be reversed slightly and a second attempt at a right answer made. (Unlike the flash card, the device reports a wrong answer without giving the right answer.) When the answer is right, a further turn of the knob engages a clutch which moves the next problem into place in the window. This movement cannot be completed, however, until the sliders have been returned to zero.

The important features of the device are these: Reinforcement for the right answer is immediate. The mere manipulation of the device will probably be reinforcing enough to keep the average pupil at work for a suitable period each day, provided traces of earlier aversive control can be wiped out. A teacher may supervise an entire class at work on such devices at the same time, yet the children may progress at their own rates, completing as many problems as possible within the class period. Those who are forced to be away from school may return to pick up where they left off. Gifted children will advance rapidly, but can be kept from getting too far ahead

Figure 1   An early machine to teach arithmetic. Material, such as an equation to be completed, appears in the square window on a paper tape. Holes are punched in the tape where figures are missing. The boy causes figures to appear in the holes by moving sliders. When the proper sliders have been moved, the equation or other material is complete. The boy then turns a knob on the front of the machine. The machine senses the composed answer, and if it is correct, the knob turns freely and a new frame of material moves into place. If the setting is wrong, the knob will not turn and the positions of the sliders must then be corrected. A counter may be added to tally wrong answers. (This machine was demonstrated at the University of Pittsburgh, March, 1954.)

either by being excused from arithmetic for a time or by being given special sets of problems which take them into some of the interesting bypaths of mathematics.

The device makes it possible to present carefully designed material in which one problem can depend upon the answer to the preceding problem and where, therefore, the most efficient progress to an eventually complex repertoire can be made. Provision has been made for recording the commonest mistakes so that the tapes can be modified as experience dictates. Additional steps can be inserted where pupils tend to have trouble, and ultimately the material will reach a point at which the answers of the average child will almost always be right.

If the material itself proves not to be sufficiently reinforcing, other reinforcers in the possession of the teacher or school may be made contingent upon the operation of the device or upon progress through a series of problems. Supplemental reinforcement would not sacrifice the advantages gained from immediate reinforcement and from the possibility of constructing an optimal series of steps which approach the complex repertoire of mathematical behavior most efficiently.

A similar device in which the sliders carry the letters of the alphabet has been designed to teach spelling (Figure 2). In addition to the advantages which can be gained from precise reinforcement and careful programming, the device will teach reading at the same time. It can also be used to establish the large and important repertoire of verbal relationships encountered in logic and science. In short, it can teach verbal thinking. The device can also be operated as a multiple-choice self-rater.

Some objections to the use of such devices in the classroom can easily be foreseen. The cry will be raised that the child is being treated as a mere

Figure 2   A machine to teach spelling and arithmetic similar to that in Figure 1 except that there are more sliders and letters can be presented as well as figures. Material appears in the rectangular opening with one or more figures or letters missing. When the sliders have been moved to complete the material, the pupil turns a crank as shown. If the setting is correct, a new frame of material moves into place and the sliders return to their home position. If the material is wrong, the sliders return but the frame remains and another setting must be made.

animal and that an essentially human intellectual achievement is being analyzed in unduly mechanistic terms. Mathematical behavior is usually regarded, not as a repertoire of responses involving numbers and numerical operations, but as evidence of mathematical ability or the exercise of the power of reason. It is true that the techniques which are emerging from the experimental study of learning are not designed to "develop the mind" or to further some vague "understanding" of mathematical relationships. They are designed, on the contrary, to establish the very behaviors which are taken to be the evidences of such mental states or processes. This is only a special case of the general change which is under way in the interpretation of human affairs. An advancing science continues to offer more and more convincing alternatives to traditional formulations. The behavior in terms of which human thinking must eventually be defined is worth treating in its own right as the substantial goal of education.

Of course teachers have a more important function than to say right or wrong. The changes proposed should free them for the effective exercise of that function. Marking a set of papers in arithmetic—"Yes, nine and six *are* fifteen; no, nine and seven *are not* eighteen"—is beneath the dignity of any intelligent person. There is more important work to be done—in which the teacher's relations to the pupil cannot be duplicated by a mechanical device. Instrumental help would merely improve these relations. One might say that the main trouble with education in the lower grades today is that the child is obviously not competent and *knows it* and that the teacher is unable to do anything about it and *knows that too.* If the advances which have recently been made in our control of behavior can give the child a genuine competence in reading, writing, spelling, and arithmetic, then teachers may begin to function, not in lieu of a cheap machine, but through intellectual, cultural, and emotional contacts of that distinctive sort which testify to their status as human beings.

Another possible objection is that mechanized instruction will mean technological unemployment. We need not worry about this until there are enough teachers to go around and until the hours and energy demanded of the teacher are comparable to those in other fields of employment. Mechanical devices will eliminate the more tiresome labor of teaching but they will not necessarily shorten the time during which teachers remain in contact with pupils.

A more practical objection: Can we afford to mechanize our schools? The answer is clearly Yes. The devices I have just described could be produced as cheaply as a small radio or phonograph. There would need to be far fewer devices than pupils, for they could be used in rotation. But even if we suppose that the instrument eventually found to be most effective would cost several hundred dollars and that large numbers of them would be required, our economy should be able to stand the strain. Once we have accepted the possibility and the necessity of mechanical help in the classroom, the economic problem can easily be surmounted. There is no reason why the schoolroom should be any less mechanized than, for example, the kitchen. A country which annually produces millions of refrigerators, dishwashers, automatic washing machines, automatic clothes driers, and automatic garbage disposers can certainly afford the equipment necessary to educate its citizens to high standards of competence in the most effective way.

There is a simple job to be done. The task can be stated in concrete terms. The necessary techniques are known. The equipment needed can easily be provided. Nothing stands in the way but cultural inertia. But what is more characteristic of the modern temper than an unwillingness to accept the traditional as inevitable? We are on the threshold of an exciting and revolutionary period, in which the scientific study of the human organism will be put to work in its best interests. Education must play its part. It must accept the fact that a sweeping revision of educational practices is possible and inevitable. When it has done this, we may look forward with confidence to a school system which is aware of the nature of its tasks, secure in its methods, and generously supported by the informed and effective citizens whom education itself will create.

REFERENCES AND NOTES

[1]Skinner, B.F. Two "synthetic social relations." *Journal of the Experimental Analysis of Behavior,* 1962, *5,* 531–533.
[2]Ibid.
[3]Ferster, C.B., & Skinner, B.F. *Schedules of reinforcement.* New York: Appleton-Century-Crofts, 1957.
[4]Blough, D.S. Dark adaptation in the pigeon. *Journal of Comparative and Physiological Psychology,* 1956, *49,* 425–430.
[5]Obviously this is not the "new math," but a similar analysis might be made of any material suitable for the same grades.

POSTSCRIPT

I began to design some early teaching machines shortly after I visited my younger daughter's fourth-grade arithmetic class in November, 1953. Research in operant conditioning and its extension to the interpretation of verbal behavior suggested much more effective instructional practices. A particular example was the well-established principle through which complex forms of behavior are reached by "successive approximation"— that is, by reinforcing a series of simpler forms. Fortunately, I was asked to give a paper at a conference at the University of Pittsburgh which was to deal with the application of psychological principles to various fields, and I asked if I could choose education. This paper was the result.

The contrast between successful techniques in the field of operant research and the self-defeating practices of the classroom was, I thought, shocking. Children were our most valuable natural resource. A technology of behavior should be applied to developing it. As in the operant laboratory, instrumentation was needed, and after my lecture I demonstrated a machine to teach arithmetic. (A professor of educational psychology in the audience was heard to remark to a colleague: "He's kidding!") A few years later, with the help of my colleague, James G. Holland, I set up a self-instruction room in the Harvard Yard and used machines to teach part of the introductory course for which I had written *Science and Human Behavior.*

Within a decade the teaching machine movement exploded. Machines based upon almost every conceivable theory of learning were offered to the public. Thirty years before, Sidney Pressey had published papers on a "teaching machine" which was the basis for some of the newer proposals. The underlying principle of programmed instruction, which Pressey rejected, seemed to me more important than the machine. It had a strong "motivating" effect on the students. A subject matter was broken into a large number of small steps, each step being made as easy as possible. Although the material was new, students were right more than half the time, and the reinforcement associated with success and progress was therefore highly effective.

The achievements of programmed instruction were abundantly demonstrated. In 1960 I visited an eighth-grade class in a Roanoke, Virginia, school in which, under the direction of Allen Calvin, the students covered all of ninth-grade algebra in half the usual time, getting equivalent grades and, in fact, much better grades for retention when measured a year later. In spite of many hundreds of similar successes, my paper still carries the same message: Education *could* be vastly improved if the principles derived from an experimental analysis of behavior were put into effect.

C H A P T E R 11

What Is Psychotic Behavior?

EDITOR'S NOTE

The article first appeared in a book called *Theory and Treatment of the Psychoses: Some Newer Aspects* (St. Louis: Committee on Publications, Washington University, 1956, pp. 77–99) and has been reprinted in all editions of *Cumulative Record.* It was first given as a lecture to a group of psychiatrists; the lecture format has been retained. Related works include: "A Critique of Psychoanalytic Concepts and Theories" (1954), "The Psychological Point of View" (1957; entitled "Psychology in the Understanding of Mental Disease" in *Cumulative Record*), "Animal Research in the Pharmacotherapy of Mental Disease" (1959), "Some Relations Between Behavior Modification and Basic Research" (1972), and "Compassion and Ethics in the Care of the Retardate" (1972). Chapter 24 in *Science and Human Behavior* (1953), entitled "Psychotherapy," is especially relevant, as are various sketches in *Notebooks* (1980). Skinner summarizes his views on Freud early in the Evans interview (*B.F. Skinner: The Man and His Ideas,* Dutton, 1968).

The essay is an early, though extremely rigorous, statement of (a) the behavioristic position in general, and (b) Skinner's objections to mentalistic psychologies (see Chapters 5 and 8). Psychotic behavior is simply behavior, Skinner writes, and can be studied and perhaps ultimately understood using the methodology of the burgeoning science of behavior. Behavior, our dependent variable, is to be explained by appealing to "certain external, generally observable, and possibly controllable hereditary and environmental conditions....We have given. We have only to try and see." Yet the variables that determine behavior are seldom dealt with explicitly but are instead expressed as various inaccessible internal states, such as instincts, drives, memories, personalities, and so on. Changes in behavior are typically characterized

This article originally appeared in *Theory and Treatment of the Psychoses: Some Newer Aspects* (St. Louis: Committee on Publications, Washington University, 1956). Reprinted by permission of the publisher.

as mental activities, such as thinking, learning, and repressing. Skinner depicts in some illuminating diagrams the shift people often make from the outer to the inner world. The shift, Skinner notes, "has the unfortunate effect of a loss of physical status," which makes measurement impossible. "We look inside the organism for a *simpler* system, in which the causes of behavior are less complex than the actual hereditary and environmental events and in which the behavior of a personality is more...orderly than the day-to-day activity of the organism." But the inner state "cannot be any simpler than its causes or its effects." It is a spurious simplicity, doomed to "ultimate failure [as] an explanatory scheme." Hypothesizing an inner state may also impede the search for external controlling variables. This does not mean, says Skinner, that the organism is empty, but only that we must look to the physiologist for the inside story.

We have only crude access to internal states through introspection, Skinner argues. "Psychiatry itself is responsible for the notion that one need not be aware of the feelings, thoughts, and so on, which are said to affect behavior."

Toward the end of the article Skinner briefly describes the first large-scale study of operant conditioning in humans, conducted with psychotic patients at the Metropolitan State Hospital in Waltham, Massachusetts, in the mid-1950s. Patients worked for candies, cigarettes, and so on by pulling plungers on a vending machine. The effects of social contingencies and of various schedules of reinforcement were investigated. The project is further described in published abstracts (e.g., Skinner, B.F., Solomon, H.C., & Lindsley, O.R. A new method for the experimental analysis of the behavior of psychotic patients. *Journal of Nervous and Mental Disease*, 1954, *120*, 403–406), technical reports, and a number of papers by Ogden Lindsley, the man who directed the work (e.g., Free-operant conditioning and psychotherapies. *Current Psychiatric Therapies*, 1963, *3*, 47–56).

Since my field of specialization lies some distance from psychiatry, it may be well to begin with credentials. The first will be negative. In the sense in which my title is most likely to be understood, I am wholly unqualified to discuss the question before us. The number of hours I have spent in the presence of psychotic people (assuming that I am myself sane) is negligible compared with what many of you might claim, and the time I have spent in relevant reading and discussion would suffer equally from the same comparison. I am currently interested in some research on psychotic subjects, to which I shall refer again later, but my association with that program in no way qualifies me as a specialist.

Fortunately, I am not here to answer the question in that sense at all. A more accurate title would have been "What is *behavior?*—with an occasional reference to psychiatry." Here I will list such positive credentials as seem appropriate. I have spent a good share of my professional life in the experimental analysis of the behavior of organisms. Almost all my subjects have been below the human level (most of them rats or pigeons) and all, so far as I know, have been sane. My research has not been designed to test any theory of behavior, and the results cannot be evaluated in terms of the statistical significance of such proofs. The object has been to discover the functional relations which prevail between measurable aspects of behavior and various conditions and events in the life of the organism. The success of such a venture is gauged by the extent to which behavior can, as a result of the relationships discovered, actually be predicted and controlled. Here we have, I think, been fortunate. Within a limited experimental arrangement, my colleagues and I have been able to demonstrate a lawfulness in behavior which seems to us quite remarkable. In more recent research it has been possible to maintain—actually, to sharpen—this degree of lawfulness while slowly increasing the complexity of the behavior studied. The extent of the prediction and control which has been achieved is evident not only in "smoothness of curves" and uniformity of results from individual to individual or even species to species, but in the practical uses which are already being made of the techniques—for example, in providing baselines for the study of pharmacological and neurological variables, or in converting a lower organism into a sensitive psychophysical observer.

Although research designed in this way has an immediate practical usefulness, it is not independent of one sort of theory. A primary concern has been to isolate a useful and expedient measure. Of all the myriad aspects of behavior which present themselves to observation, which are worth watching? Which will prove most useful in establishing functional relations? From time to time many different characteristics of behavior have seemed important. Students of the subject have asked how well organized behavior is, how well adapted it is to the environment, how sensitively it maintains a homeostatic equilibrium, how purposeful it is, or how successfully it solves practical problems or adjusts to daily life. Many have been especially interested in how an individual compares with others of the same species or with members of other species in some arbitrary measure of the scope, complexity, speed, consistency, or other property of behavior. All these aspects may be quantified, at least in a rough way, and any one may serve as a dependent variable in a scientific analysis. But they are not all equally productive. In research which emphasizes prediction and control, the topography of behavior must be carefully specified. Precisely what is the organism doing? The most important aspect of behavior so described is its probability of emission. How likely is it that an organism will engage in behavior of a given sort, and what conditions or events change this likelihood? Although probability of action has only recently been explicitly recognized in behavior theory, it is a key concept to which many classical notions, from reaction tendencies to the Freudian wish, may be reduced. Experimentally we deal with it as the *frequency* with which an organism behaves in a given way under specified circumstances, and our methods are designed to satisfy this requirement. Frequency of response has proved to be a remarkably sensitive variable, and with its aid the exploration of causal factors has been gratifyingly profitable.

One does not engage in work of this sort for the sheer love of rats or pigeons. As the medical sciences illustrate, the study of animals below the human level is dictated mainly by convenience and safety. But the species of primary interest is always Man. Such qualifications as I have to offer in approaching the present question spring about equally from the experimental work just mentioned and from a parallel preoccupation with human behavior, in which the principles emerging from the experimental analysis have been tested and put to work in the interpretation of empirical facts. The formal disciplines of government, education, economics, religion, and psychotherapy, among others, together with our everyday social experience, overwhelm us with a flood of facts. To interpret these facts with the formulation which emerges from an experimental analysis has proved to be strenuous but healthful exercise. In particular, the nature and function of *verbal* behavior have taken on surprisingly fresh and promising aspects when reformulated under the strictures of such a framework.

In the long run, of course, mere interpretation is not enough. If we have achieved a true scientific understanding of human behavior, we should be able to prove this in prediction and control. The experimental practices and the concepts emerging from our research on lower organisms have already been extended in this direction, not only in the experiments on psychotic subjects already mentioned, but in other promising areas. The details would take us too far afield, but perhaps I can indicate my faith in the possibilities in a single instance by hazarding the prediction that we are on the threshold of a revolutionary change in methods of education, based not only upon a better understanding of learning processes, but upon a workable conception of knowledge itself.

Whether or not this brief personal history seems to you to qualify me to discuss the question before us, there is no doubt that it has created a high probability that I will do so, as shown by the fact that I am here. What I have to say is admittedly methodological. I can understand a certain impatience with such discussion, particularly when, as in the field of psychiatry, many pressing problems call for action. The scientist who takes time out to consider human nature when so many practical things need to be done for human welfare is likely to be cast in the role of a Nero, fiddling while Rome burns. (It is quite possible that the fiddling referred to in this archetypal myth was a later invention of the historians, and that in actual fact Nero had called in his philosophers and scientists and was discussing "the fundamental nature of combustion" or "the epidemiology of conflagration.") But I should not be here if I believed that what I have to say is remote from practical consequences. If we are now entering an era of research in psychiatry which is to be as extensive and as productive as other types of medical research, then a certain detachment from immediate problems, a fresh look at human behavior in general, a survey of applicable formulations, and a consideration of relevant methods may prove to be effective practical steps with surprisingly immediate consequences.

The study of human behavior is, of course, still in its infancy, and it would be rash to suppose that anyone can foresee the structure of a well-developed and successful science. Certainly no current formulation will seem right 50 years hence. But although we cannot foresee the future clearly, it is not impossible to discover in what direction we are likely to change. There are obviously great deficiencies in our present ways of thinking about people; otherwise we should be more successful. What are they, and how are they to be remedied? What I have to say rests upon the assumption that the behavior of the psychotic is simply part and parcel of human behavior, and that certain considerations which have been emphasized by the experimental and theoretical analysis of behavior in general are worth discussing in this special application.

It is important to remember that I am speaking as an experimental scientist. A conception of human behavior based primarily on clinical information and practice will undoubtedly differ from a conception emanating from the laboratory. This does not mean that either is superior to the other, or that eventually a common formulation will not prove useful to both. It is possible that questions which have been suggested by the exigencies of an experimental analysis may not seem of first importance to those of you who are primarily concerned with human behavior under therapy. But as psychiatry moves more rapidly into experimental research and as laboratory results take on a greater clinical significance, certain problems in the analysis of behavior should become common to researcher and therapist alike, and should eventually be given common and co-operative solutions.

•   •   •

The study of behavior, psychotic or otherwise, remains securely in the company of the natural sciences so long as we take as our subject matter the observable activity of the organism, as it moves about, stands still, seizes objects, pushes and pulls, makes sounds, gestures, and so on. Suitable instruments will permit us to amplify small-scale activities as part of the same subject matter. Watching a person behave in this way is like watching any physical or biological system. We also remain within the framework of the natural sciences in explaining these observations in terms of external forces and events which act upon the organism. Some of these are to be found in the hereditary history of the individual, including membership in a given species as well as personal endowment. Others arise from the physical environment, past or present. We may represent the situation as in Figure 1. Our organism emits the behavior we are to account for, as our dependent variable, at the right. To explain this, we appeal to certain external, generally observable, and possibly controllable hereditary and environmental conditions, as indicated at the left. These are the independent variables of which behavior is to be expressed as a function. Both input and output of such a system may be treated with the accepted dimensional systems of physics and biology. A complete set of such relations would permit us to predict and, insofar as the independent variables are under our control, to modify or generate behavior at will. It would also permit us to *interpret* given instances of behavior by inferring plausible variables of which we lack direct information. Admittedly the data are subtle and complex, and many relevant conditions are hard to get at, but the program as such is an acceptable one from the point of view of scientific method. We have no reason to suppose in advance that a complete account cannot be so given. We have only to try and see.

It is not, however, the subtlety or complexity of this subject matter which is responsible for the relatively undeveloped state of such a science. Behavior has seldom been analyzed in this manner. Instead, attention has been diverted to activities which are said to take place within the organism. All sciences tend to fill in causal relationships, especially when the related events are separated by time and space. If a magnet affects a compass needle some distance away, the scientist attributes this to a "field" set up by the magnet and reaching to the compass needle. If a brick falls from a chimney, releasing energy which was stored there, say, 100 years ago when the chimney was built, the result is explained by saying that the brick has all this time possessed a certain amount of "potential energy." In order to fill such spatial and temporal gaps between cause and effect, nature has from time to time been endowed with many weird properties, spirits, and essences. Some

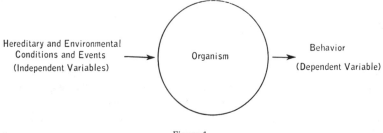

Figure 1

have proved helpful and have become part of the subject matter of science, especially when identified with events observed in other ways. Others have proved dangerous and damaging to scientific progress. Sophisticated scientists have usually been aware of the practice and alert to its dangers. Such inner forces were, indeed, the hypotheses which Newton refused to make.

Among the conditions which affect behavior, hereditary factors occupy a primary position, at least chronologically. Differences between members of different species are seldom, if ever, disputed, but differences between members of the same species, possibly due to similar hereditary factors, are so closely tied up with social and ethical problems that they have been the subject of seemingly endless debate. In any event, the newly conceived organism begins at once to be influenced by its environment; and when it comes into full contact with the external world, environmental forces assume a major role. They are the only conditions which can be changed so far as the individual is concerned. Among these are the events we call "stimuli," the various interchanges between organism and environment such as occur in breathing or eating, the events which generate the changes in behavior we call emotional, and the coincidences between stimuli or between stimuli and behavior responsible for the changes we call learning. The effects may be felt immediately or only after the passage of time— perhaps of many years. Such are the "causes"—the independent variables— in terms of which we may hope to explain behavior within the framework of a natural science.

In many discussions of human behavior, however, these variables are seldom explicitly mentioned. Their place is taken by events or conditions within the organism for which they are said to be responsible (see Figure 2). Thus, the species status of the individual is dealt with as a set of instincts, not simply as patterns of behavior characteristic of the species, but as biological drives. As one text puts it, "instincts are innate biological forces, urges, or impulsions driving the organism to a certain end." The individual genetic

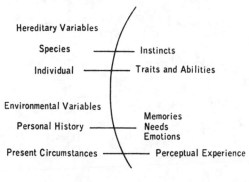

Figure 2

endowment, if not carried by body type or other observable physical characteristics, is represented in the form of inherited traits or abilities, such as temperament or intelligence. As to the environmental variables, episodes in the past history of the individual are dealt with as memories and habits, while certain conditions of interchange between organism and environment are represented as needs or wants. Certain inciting episodes are dealt with as emotions, again in the sense not of patterns but of active causes of behavior. Even the present environment as it affects the organism is transmuted into "experience," as we turn from what is the case to what "seems to be" the case to the individual.

The same centripetal movement may be observed on the other side of the diagram (see Figure 3). It is rare to find behavior dealt with as a subject matter in its own right. Instead it is regarded as evidence for a mental life, which is then taken as the primary object of inquiry. What the individual does—the topography of the behavior—is treated as the functioning of one or more personalities. It is clear, especially when personalities are multiple, that they cannot be identified with the biological organism as such, but are conceived of, rather, as inner behavers of doubtful status and dimensions. The act of behaving in a given instance is neglected in favor of an impulse or wish, while the probability of such an act is represented as an excitatory tendency or in terms of psychic energy. Most important of all, the changes in behavior which represent the fundamental behavioral processes are characterized as mental activities—such as thinking, learning, discriminating, reasoning, symbolizing, projecting, identifying, and repressing.

The relatively simple scheme shown in the first figure does not, therefore, represent the conception of human behavior characteristic of most current theory. The great majority of students of human behavior assume that they are concerned with a series of events indicated in the

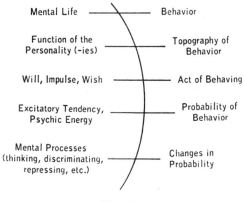

Figure 3

expanded diagram of Figure 4. Here the hereditary and environmental conditions are assumed to generate instincts, needs, emotions, memories, habits, and so on, which in turn lead the personality to engage in various activities characteristic of the mental apparatus, and these in turn generate the observable behavior of the organism. All four stages in the diagram are accepted as proper objects of inquiry. Indeed, far from leaving the inner events to other specialists while confining themselves to the end terms, many psychologists and psychiatrists take the mental apparatus as their primary subject matter.

Perhaps the point of my title is now becoming clearer. Is the scientific study of behavior—whether normal or psychotic—concerned with the behavior of the observable organism under the control of hereditary and environmental factors, or with the functioning of one or more personalities engaged in a variety of mental processes under the promptings of instincts, needs, emotions, memories, and habits? I do not want to raise the question of the supposed *nature* of these inner entities. A certain kinship between such an explanatory system and primitive animism can scarcely be missed, but whatever the historical sources of these concepts, we may assume that they have been purged of dualistic connotations. If this is not the case, if there are those who feel that psychiatry is concerned with a world beyond that of the psychobiological or biophysical organism, that conscious or unconscious mind lacks physical extent, and that mental processes do not affect the world according to the laws of physics, then the following arguments should be all the more cogent. But the issue is not one of the nature of these events, but of their usefulness and expedience in a scientific description.

It can scarcely be denied that the expansion of subject matter represented by Figure 4 has the unfortunate effect of a loss of physical status. This is more than a question of prestige or "face." A subject matter which is unquestionably part of the field of physics and biology has been relinquished

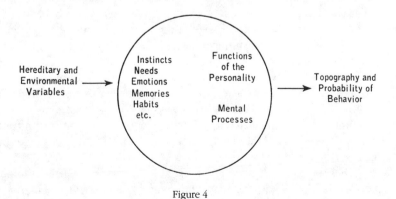

Figure 4

for one of doubtful characteristics. This cannot be corrected merely by asserting our faith in the ultimately physical nature of inner processes. To protest that the activities of the conscious and unconscious mind are only in some sense an aspect of the biological functioning of the organism will not answer the practical question. In abandoning the dimensional systems of physics and biology, we abandon the techniques of measurement which would otherwise be a natural heritage from earlier achievements in other sciences. This is possibly an irreparable loss. If we come out flatly for the existence of instincts, needs, memories, and so on, on the one hand, and the mental processes and functions of the personality on the other, then we must accept the responsibility of devising methods of observing these inner events and of discovering dimensional systems according to which they can be measured. The loss of the opportunity to measure and manipulate in the manner characteristic of the physical sciences would be offset only by some extraordinary advantage gained by turning to inner states or conditions.

It is possible, however, to argue that these inner events are merely ways of representing the outer. Many theorists will contend that a habit is only a sort of notation useful in reporting a bit of the history of the individual, just as so-called "mental processes" are ways of talking about changes in behavior. This is a tempting position, for we may then insist that the only dimensional systems required are those appropriate to the terminal events. But if we are to take that line, a great deal still needs to be done to put our house in scientific order. The concepts which one encounters in current behavior theory represent the observable events in an extremely confusing way. Most of them have arisen from theoretical or practical considerations which have little reference to their validity or usefulness as scientific constructs, and they bear the scars of such a history. For example, Freud pointed to important relationships between the behavior of an adult and certain episodes in early childhood, but he chose to bridge the very considerable gap between cause and effect with activities or states of the mental apparatus. Conscious or unconscious wishes or emotions in the adult represent the earlier episodes and are said to be directly responsible for their effect upon behavior. The adult is said, for example, to be suffering from conscious or unconscious anxiety generated by punishment received as a child for aggressive behavior toward a sibling. But many details of the early episode are glossed over (and may, as a result, be neglected) in attributing the current behavioral disturbances to a current anxiety rather than to the earlier punishment. The number of references to anxiety in treatises on behavior must greatly exceed the number of references to punishing episodes, yet we must turn to the latter for full details. If the details are not available, nothing can take their place.

Other kinds of independent variables provide similar examples. Everyone is familiar with the fact that, in general, organisms eat or do not eat depending upon a recent history of deprivation or ingestion. If we can establish that a boy does not eat his dinner because he has recently eaten other food, there may seem to be no harm in expressing this by saying that "he is not hungry," provided we explain this in turn by pointing to the history of ingestion. But the concept of hunger represents quite inadequately the many features of schedules of deprivation and other conditions and events which alter the behavior of eating. In the same way the inner surrogates of hereditary variables function beyond the line of duty. We often have no other explanation of a given bit of behavior than that, like other features of anatomy and physiology, it is characteristic of a species; but when we choose instead to attribute this behavior to a set of instincts, we obscure the negative nature of our knowledge and suggest more active causes than mere species status warrants. Similarly, we accept the fact that individuals differ in their behavior, and we may, in some instances, show a relation between aspects of the behavior of successive generations, but these differences and relationships are optimistically misrepresented when we speak of hereditary traits and abilities. Again, the term *experience* incorrectly represents our information about a stimulating field. It has often been observed, for example, that some trivial incident generates a reaction altogether out of proportion to its magnitude. A person seems to be reacting, not to the physical world as such, but to what the world "means." Eventually, of course, the effect must be explained—for example, by pointing to some earlier connection with more important events. But whatever the explanation, it is almost certainly not adequately expressed by the notion of a momentary experience. There are obvious difficulties involved in representing a physical environment *plus a personal history* as a current psychological environment alone.

So far as our independent variables are concerned, then, the practice we are examining tends to gloss over many important details and complexities. The conceptual structure conceals from us the inadequacy of our present knowledge. Much the same difficulty is encountered with respect to the dependent variable, when observable behavior takes second place to mental functionings of a personality. Just as the physical environment is transmuted into experience, so physical behavior comes to be described in terms of its purpose or meaning. We may walk down the street in precisely the same way upon two occasions, although in one instance we are out for exercise and in another we are going to mail a letter. And so it is thought necessary to consider, not the behavior itself, but "what it means" to us. But the additional information to be conveyed is not a property of behavior but of an independent variable. The behavior observed in the two cases *is* the same. In reading meaning or intention into it, we are speculating about some of its causes. To take another example, it is commonly said that we can "see" aggression. But we "see" it in two steps: (1) We observe the behavior of an organism, and (2) we relate it to observed or inferred variables having to do with injurious consequences and with the kinds of circumstances which make such behavior probable. No behavior is itself aggressive by nature, although some forms of behavior are so often a function of variables which make them aggressive that we are inclined to overlook the inferences involved. Similarly, when we observe two or more behavioral systems in the same individual and attribute them to different personalities, we gain a considerable advantage for certain descriptive purposes. For example, we can then describe oppositions between such systems as we would between different persons. But we have almost certainly suggested a unity which is not justified by the observed systems of behavior, and we have probably made it more difficult to represent the actual extent of any conflicts as well as to explain their origins. And when we observe that the behavior of a person is characterized by a certain responsiveness or probability of responding and speak instead of a given amount of psychic energy, we neglect many details of the actual facts and dodge the responsibility of finding a dimensional system. Lastly, mental processes are almost always conceived of as simpler and more orderly than the rather chaotic material from which they are inferred and which they are used to explain. The "learning process" in experimental psychology, for example, does not give us an accurate account of measured changes in behavior.

We look inside the organism for a *simpler* system, in which the causes of behavior are less complex than the actual hereditary and environmental events and in which the behavior of a personality is more meaningful and orderly than the day-to-day activity of the organism. All the variety and complexity of the input in our diagram seem to be reduced to a few relatively amorphous states, which in turn generate relatively amorphous functions of the personality, which then suddenly explode into the extraordinary variety and complexity of behavior. But the simplification achieved by such a practice is, of course, illusory, for it follows only from the fact that a one-to-one correspondence between inner and outer events has not been demanded. It is just this lack of correspondence which makes such an inner system unsuitable in the experimental analysis of behavior. If "hunger" is something which is produced by certain schedules of deprivation, certain drugs, certain states of health, and so on, and if in turn it produces changes in the probability of a great variety of responses, then it must have very complex properties. It cannot be any simpler than its causes or its effects. If the behavior we observe simply expresses the functioning of a personality, the personality cannot be any simpler than the behavior. If some common learning process is responsible for the changes observed in a number of different situations, then it cannot be any simpler than these changes. The apparent simplicity of the inner system explains the eagerness with which we turn to it, but from the point of view of scientific method it must be regarded as a spurious simplicity, which foreshadows ultimate failure of such an explanatory scheme.

There is another objection. Although speculation about what goes on within the organism seems to show a concern for completing a causal chain, in practice it tends to have the opposite effect. Chains are left incomplete. People commonly feel that they have explained behavior when they have attributed it to something inside themselves—as in saying "I went *because* I wanted to go" or "I could not work *because* I was worried about my health." Such statements may have value in suggesting the relevance of one set of causes as against another, but they do not give a full explanation until it is explained *why* you wanted to go, or why you were worried. Frequently this additional step is taken, but perhaps just as often these incomplete explanations bring inquiry to a dead stop.

No matter how we may wish to represent such a sequence of causal events, we cannot satisfy the requirements of interpretation, prediction, or control unless we go back to events acting upon the organism from without— events, moreover, which are observed as any event is observed in the physical and biological sciences. It is only common sense, therefore, as well as good scientific practice, to make sure that the concepts which enter into a theory of behavior are explicitly and carefully related to such events. What is needed is an operational definition of terms. This means more than simple translation. The operational method is commonly misused to patch up and preserve concepts which are cherished for extraneous and irrelevant reasons. Thus it might be possible to set up acceptable definitions of instincts, needs, emotions, memories, psychic energy, and so on in which each term would be carefully related to certain behavioral and environmental facts. But we have no guarantee that these concepts will be the most useful when the actual functional relationships are better understood. A more reasonable program at this stage is to attempt to account for behavior without appeal to inner explanatory entities. We can do this within the accepted framework of biology, gaining thereby not only a certain personal reassurance from the prestige of a well-developed science but an extensive set of experimental practices and dimensional systems. We shall be prevented from oversimplifying and misrepresenting the available facts because we shall not transmute our descriptions into other terms. The practical criteria of prediction and control will force us to take into account the complete causal chain in every instance. Such a program is not concerned with establishing the existence of inferred events, but with assessing the state of our knowledge.

This does not mean, of course, that the organism is conceived of as actually empty, or that continuity between input and output will not eventually be established. The genetic development of the organism and the complex interchanges between organism and environment are the subject matters of appropriate disciplines. Some day we shall know, for example, what happens when a stimulus impinges upon the surface of an organism, and what happens inside the organism after that, in a series of stages the last of which is the point at which the organism acts upon the environment and possibly changes it. At that point we lose interest in this causal chain. Some day, too, we shall know how the ingestion of food sets up a series of events, the last of which to engage our attention is a reduction in the probability of all behavior previously reinforced with similar food. Some day we may even know how to bridge the gap between the behavioral characteristics common to parents and offspring. But all these inner events will be accounted for with techniques of observation and measurement appropriate to the physiology of the various parts of the organism, and the account will be expressed in terms appropriate to that subject matter. It would be a remarkable coincidence if the concepts now used to refer inferentially to inner events were to find a place in that account. The task of physiology is not to find hungers, fears, habits, instincts, personalities, psychic energy, or acts of willing, attending, repressing, and so on. Nor is that task to find entities or processes of which all these could be said to be other aspects. Its task is to account for the causal relations between input and output which are the special concern of a science of behavior. Physiology should be left free to do this in its own way. Just to the extent that current conceptual systems fail to represent the relationships between terminal events correctly, they misrepresent the task of these other disciplines. A comprehensive set of causal relations stated with the greatest possible precision is the best contribution which we, as students of behavior, can make in the co-operative venture of giving a full account of the organism as a biological system.

But are we not overlooking one important source of knowledge? What about the direct observation of mental activity? The belief that the mental apparatus is available to direct inspection anticipated the scientific analysis of human behavior by many hundreds of years. It was refined by the introspective psychologists at the end of the 19th century into a special theory of knowledge which seemed to place the newly created science of consciousness on a par with natural science by arguing that all scientists necessarily begin and end with their own sensations and that the psychologist merely deals with these in a different way for different purposes. The notion has been revived in recent theories of perception, in which it has been suggested that the study of what used to be called "optical illusions," for example, will supply principles which help in understanding the limits of scientific knowledge. It has also been argued that the especially intimate empathic understanding which frequently occurs in psychotherapy supplies a kind of direct knowledge of the mental processes of other people. Franz Alexander and Lawrence Kubie have argued in this manner in defense of psychoanalytic practices. Among clinical psychologists Carl Rogers has actively defended a similar view. Something of the same notion may underlie the belief that the psychiatrist may better understand the psychotic if, through the use of lysergic acid, for example, he may temporarily experience similar mental conditions.

Whether the approach to human behavior which I have just outlined ignores some basic fact, whether it is unable to take into account the "stubborn fact of consciousness," is part of a venerable dispute which will not be settled here. Two points may be made, however, in evaluating the evidence from direct "introspection" of the mental apparatus. Knowledge is not to be identified with how things look to us, but rather with what we do about them. Knowledge is power because it is action. How the surrounding world soaks into the surface of our body is merely the first chapter of the story and would be meaningless were it not for the parts which follow. These are concerned with behavior. Astronomy is not how the heavens look to an astronomer. Atomic physics is not the physicist's perception of events within the atom, or even of the macroscopic events from which the atomic world is inferred. Scientific knowledge is what people *do* in predicting and controlling nature.

The second point is that knowledge depends upon a personal history. Philosophers have often insisted that we are not aware of a difference until it makes a difference, and experimental evidence is beginning to accumulate in support of the view that we should probably not know anything at all if we were not forced to do so. The discriminative behavior called knowledge arises only in the presence of certain reinforcing contingencies among the things known. Thus, we should probably remain blind if visual stimuli were never of any importance to us, just as we do not hear all the separate instruments in a symphony or see all the colors in a painting until it is worthwhile for us to do so.

Some interesting consequences follow when these two points are made with respect to our knowledge of events within ourselves. That a small part of the universe is enclosed within the skin of each of us, and that this constitutes a private world to which each of us has a special kind of access can scarcely be denied. But the world with which we are in contact does not for that reason have any special physical or metaphysical status. Now, it is presumably necessary to learn to observe or "know" events within this private world just as we learn to observe or "know" external events, and our knowledge will consist of doing something about them. But the society from which we acquire such behavior is at a special disadvantage. It is easy to teach children to distinguish between colors by presenting different colors and reinforcing their responses as right or wrong accordingly, but it is much more difficult to teach them to distinguish between different aches or pains, since the information as to whether their responses are right or wrong is much less reliable. It is this limited accessibility of the world within the skin, rather than its nature, which has been reponsible for so much metaphysical speculation.

Terms which refer to private events tend to be used inexactly. Most of them are borrowed in the first place from descriptions of external events. (Almost all the vocabulary of emotion, for example, has been shown to be metaphorical in origin.) The consequences are well known. The testimony of the individual regarding mental processes, feelings, needs, and so on is, as the psychiatrist above all others has insisted, unreliable. Technical systems of terms referring to private events seldom resemble each other. Different schools of introspective psychology have emphasized different features of experience, and the vocabulary of one may occasionally be unintelligible to another. This is also true of different dynamic theories of mental life. Exponents of a "system" may show extraordinary conviction in their use of terms and in their defense of a given set of explanatory entities, but it is usually easy to find others showing the same conviction and defending a different and possibly incompatible system. Just as introspective psychology once found it expedient to train observers in the use of terms referring to mental events, so the education of experimental psychologists, educators, applied psychologists, psychotherapists, and many others concerned with human behavior is not always free from a certain element of indoctrination. Only in this way has it been possible to make sure that mental processes will be described by two or more people with any consistency.

Psychiatry itself is responsible for the notion that one need not be aware of the feelings, thoughts, and so on which are said to affect behavior. People often behave *as if* they were thinking or feeling in a given way although they cannot themselves say that they are doing so. Mental processes which do not have the support of the testimony supplied by introspection are necessarily defined in terms of, and measured as, the behavioral facts from which they are inferred. Unfortunately, the notion of mental activity was preserved in the face of such evidence with the help of the notion of an unconscious mind. It might have been better to dismiss the concept of mind altogether as an explanatory fiction which had not survived a crucial test. The modes of inference with which we arrive at knowledge of the unconscious need to be examined with respect to the conscious mind as well. Both are conceptual entities, the relations of which to observed data need to be carefully reexamined.

In the long run the point will not be established by argument, but by the effectiveness of a given formulation in the design of productive research. An example of research on psychotic subjects which emphasizes the end terms in our diagram is the project already mentioned. This is not the place for technical details, but the rationale of this research may be relevant. In these experiments patients spend 1 or more hours daily, alone, in a small pleasant room. They are never coerced into going there and are free to leave at any time. The room is furnished with a chair, and contains a device similar to a vending machine, which can be operated by pushing a button or pulling a plunger. The machine delivers candies, cigarettes, or substantial food, or projects colored pictures on a translucent screen. Most patients eventually operate the machine and then continue to operate it daily for long periods of time—possibly a year or more. During this time the behavior is "reinforced" on various "schedules"—for example, once every minute or once for every 30 responses—in relation to various stimuli. The behavior is recorded in another room in a continuous curve which is read somewhat in the manner of an electrocardiogram and which permits a ready inspection and measurement of the rate of responding.

The isolation of this small living space is, of course, not complete. The patients do not leave their personal histories behind as they enter the room, and to some extent what they do there resembles what they do or have done elsewhere. Nevertheless, as time goes on, the conditions arranged by the experiment begin to compose, so to speak, special personal histories, the important details of which are known. Within this small and admittedly artificial life space, we can watch the patients' behavior change as we change conditions of reinforcement, motivation, and to some extent emotion. With respect to these variables their behavior becomes more and more predictable and controllable or—as characteristic of the psychotic subject—fails to do so in specific ways.

The behavior of the patient may resemble that of a normal human or infrahuman subject in response to similar experimental conditions, or it may differ in a simple quantitative way—for example, the record may be normal except for a lower overall rate. On the other hand, a performance may be broken by brief psychotic episodes. The experimental control is interrupted momentarily by the intrusion of extraneous behavior. In some cases it has been possible to reduce or increase the time taken by these interruptions, and to determine where during the session they will occur. As in similar work with other organisms, this quantitative and continuous account of the behavior of the individual under experimental control provides a highly sensitive baseline for the observation of the effects of drugs and of various forms of therapy. For our present purposes, however, the important thing is that it permits us to apply to the psychotic a fairly rigorous formulation of behavior based upon much more extensive work under the much more propitious control of conditions obtained with other species. This formulation is expressed in terms of input and output without reference to inner states.

The objection is sometimes raised that research of this sort reduces the human subject to the status of a research animal. Increasing evidence of the lawfulness of human behavior only seems to make the objection all the more cogent. Medical research has met this problem before, and has found an answer which is available here. Thanks to parallel work on animals, it has been possible, in some cases at least, to generate healthier behavior in human beings, even though at this stage we may not be directly concerned with such a result.

Another common objection is that we obtain our results only through an oversimplification of conditions, and that they are therefore not applicable to daily life. But one always simplifies at the start of an experiment. We have already begun to make our conditions more complex and will proceed to do so as rapidly as the uniformity of results permits. It is possible to complicate the task of the patient without limit, and to construct not only complex intellectual tasks but such interactions between systems of behavior as are seen in the Freudian dynamisms.

One simplification sometimes complained of is the absence of other human beings in this small life space. This was, of course, a deliberate preliminary measure, for it is much more difficult to control social than mechanical stimulation and reinforcement. But we are now moving on to situations in which one patient observes the behavior of another working on a similar device, or observes another patient receiving a reinforcement at the same time, and so on. In another case a patient's behavior is reinforced only when it corresponds in some way to the behavior of another. Techniques for achieving extraordinarily precise competition and co-operation between two or more individuals have already been worked out with lower organisms, and are applicable to the present circumstances.

This project has, of course, barely scratched the surface of the subject of psychotic behavior. But so far as it has gone, it seems to us to have demonstrated the value of holding to the observable data. Whether or not you will all find them significant, the data we report have a special kind of simple objectivity. At least we can say that this is what psychotic subjects did under these circumstances, and that this is what they failed to do under circumstances which would have had a different effect had they not been psychotic.

Although we have been able to describe and interpret the behavior observed in these experiments without reference to inner events, such references are, of course, not interdicted. Others may prefer to say that what we are actually doing is manipulating habits, needs, and so on, and observing changes in the structure of the personality, in the strength of the ego, in the amount of psychic energy available, and so on. But the advantage of this over a more parsimonious description becomes more difficult to demonstrate as evidence of the effectiveness of an objective formulation accumulates. In that bright future to which research in psychiatry is now pointing, we must be prepared for the possibility that increasing emphasis will be placed on immediately observable data and that theories of human behavior will have to adjust themselves accordingly. It is not inconceivable that the mental apparatus and all that it implies will be forgotten. It will then be more than a mere working hypothesis to say—to return at long last to my title—that psychotic behavior, like all behavior, is part of the world of observable events to which the powerful methods of natural science apply and to the understanding of which they will prove adequate.

POSTSCRIPT

Although this paper was written for an audience composed almost entirely of psychiatrists, it is scarcely more than an elementary lecture on behaviorism. I had seen the need for it in the reaction of psychiatrists in the Boston area to the research described near the end of the paper. The research was carried out at the Metropolitan State Hospital in Waltham, Massachusetts. Dr. Harry Solomon, then of the Boston Psychopathic Hospital, collaborated with me in setting up the laboratory, and Dr. Ogden R. Lindsley took immediate charge and was responsible for most of the overall experimental design and the day-to-day conduct of the experiments.

Although the behavioristic argument is, I think, presented in much greater detail than was usually the case at the time, further details are to be found in "Why I Am Not a Cognitive Psychologist" (Chapter 8), published about 20 years later.

C H A P T E R 12

Pigeons in a Pelican

EDITOR'S NOTE

The article first appeared in the *American Psychologist* (1960, *15*, 28–37)
and has been reprinted in the second and third editions of *Cumulative
Record.* It recounts Skinner's well-known attempt to train pigeons to
guide missiles in World War II. During the years 1940 to 1944, with
funding from General Mills and the U.S. Office of Scientific Research and
Development, Skinner and his associates constructed a series of
laboratory devices which pigeons guided to simulated targets with great
precision. In the final version, a series of lenses and mirrors projected an
image of the target area onto three translucent plates in the nose cone.
Three pigeons, held in harnesses, faced the plates. Their pecks at the
target jarred the plates and opened valves at the edges. Pecks at the center
opened all valves equally and kept the device on target, while off-center
pecks opened valves unequally and changed the direction of the device.
If pigeons disagreed, the majority ruled.

In spite of the project's laboratory success, it never actually got off the
ground, primarily, Skinner writes, because the very concept seemed so
absurd to many scientists and military men. A presentation before
scientists in 1944 was greeted with "[restrained] merriment." "It was
obvious," writes Skinner, "that our case was lost."

The project left several technological and scientific advances in its
wake: a precursor to the "Pick-off Display Converter" (touching the tip of
a pen to some location on a screen transmits the location to another
device), further "organic control" ("ORCON") research by the Navy, the
training technique commonly known as "shaping" (see "Reinforcement
Today," 1958), and techniques for bringing the behavior of the pigeon
under an extraordinarily high degree of control.

The project strengthened Skinner's conviction that a technology of
human behavior was possible. He notes that he wrote his utopian novel,
Walden Two, shortly after the project was terminated and that he

developed his first teaching machine only a few years later. A science of behavior, he concludes, may be the key to a future "in which, among other things, there will be no need for guided missiles."

This is the history of a crackpot idea, born on the wrong side of the tracks intellectually speaking, but eventually vindicated in a sort of middle-class respectability. It is the story of a proposal to use living organisms to guide missiles—of a research program during World War II called "Project Pigeon" and a peacetime continuation at the Naval Research Laboratory called "ORCON" from the words "organic control." Both of these programs have now been declassified.

We have always made use of the sensory capacities of animals, either because they are more acute than our own or more convenient. The watchdog probably hears better than its master and, in any case, listens while its master sleeps. As a detecting system the dog's ear comes supplied with an alarm (the dog need not be taught to announce the presence of an intruder), but special forms of reporting are sometimes set up. The tracking behavior of the bloodhound and the pointing of the hunting dog are usually modified to make them more useful. Training is sometimes quite explicit. It is said that sea gulls were used to detect submarines in the English Channel during World War I. The British sent their own submarines through the Channel releasing food to the surface. Gulls could see the submarines from the air and learned to follow them, whether they were British or German. A flock of gulls, spotted from the shore, took on special significance. In the seeing-eye dog the repertoire of artificial signaling responses is so elaborate that it has the conventional character of the verbal interchange between people.

The detecting and signaling systems of lower organisms have a special advantage when used with explosive devices which can be guided toward the objects they are to destroy, whether by land, sea, or air. Homing systems for guided missiles have now been developed which sense and signal the position of a target by responding to visible or invisible radiation, noise, radar reflections, and so on. These have not always been available, and in any case a living organism has certain advantages. It is almost certainly cheaper and more compact and, in particular, is especially good at responding to patterns and those classes of patterns called "concepts." Lower organisms are not used because they are more sensitive than people—after all, the kamikaze did very well—but because they are readily expendable.

PROJECT PELICAN

The ethical question of our right to convert a lower creature into an unwitting hero is a peacetime luxury. There were bigger questions to be answered in the late thirties. A group of men had come into power who promised, and eventually accomplished, the greatest mass murder in history. In 1939 the city of Warsaw was laid waste in an unprovoked bombing, and the airplane emerged as a new and horrible instrument of war against which only the feeblest defenses were available. Project Pigeon was conceived against that background. It began as a search for a homing device to be used in a surface-to-air guided missile as a defense against aircraft. As the balance between offensive and defensive weapons shifted, the direction was reversed, and the system was to be tested first in an air-to-ground missile called the "Pelican." Its name is a useful reminder of the state of the missile art in America at that time. Its detecting and servomechanisms took up so much space that there was no room for explosives: hence the resemblance to the pelican "whose beak can hold more than its belly can." My title is perhaps now clear. Figure 1 shows the pigeons, jacketed for duty. Figure 2 shows the beak of the Pelican.

At the University of Minnesota in the spring of 1940 the capacity of the pigeon to steer toward a target was tested with a moving hoist. The pigeon, held in a jacket and harnessed to a block, was immobilized except for its neck and head. It could eat grain from a dish and operate a control system by moving its head in appropriate directions. Movement of the head operated the motors of the hoist. The bird could ascend by lifting its head, descend by lowering it, and travel from side to side by moving appropriately. The whole system, mounted on wheels, was pushed across a room toward a bull's-eye

Figure 1   Thirty-two pigeons, jacketed for testing.

Figure 2   Nose of the Pelican, showing lenses.

on the far wall. During the approach the pigeon raised or lowered itself and moved from side to side in such a way as to reach the wall in position to eat grain from the center of the bull's-eye. The pigeon learned to reach any target within reach of the hoist, no matter what the starting position and during fairly rapid approaches.

The experiment was shown to John T. Tate, a physicist, then dean of the Graduate School at the University of Minnesota, who brought it to the attention of R.C. Tolman, one of a group of scientists engaged in early defense activities. The result was the first of a long series of rejections. The proposal "did not warrant further development at the time." The project was accordingly allowed to lapse. On December 7, 1941, the situation was suddenly restructured; and, on the following day, with the help of Keller Breland, then a graduate student at Minnesota, further work was planned. A simpler harnessing system could be used if the bomb were to rotate slowly during its descent, when the pigeon would need to steer in only one dimension: from side to side. We built an apparatus in which a harnessed pigeon was lowered toward a large revolving turntable across which a target was driven according to contacts made by the bird during its descent. It was not difficult to train a pigeon to "hit" small ship models during fairly rapid descents. We made a demonstration film showing hits on various kinds of targets, and two psychologists then engaged in the war effort in Washington, Charles Bray and Leonard Carmichael, undertook to look for government support. Tolman, then at the Office of Scientific Research and Development, again felt that the project did not warrant support, in part because the United States had at that time no missile capable of being guided toward a target. Commander (now Admiral) Luis de Florez, then in the Special Devices Section of the Navy, took a sympathetic view. He dismissed the objection that there was no available vehicle by suggesting that the pigeon be connected with an automatic pilot mounted in a small plane loaded with explosives. But he was unable to take on the project because of other commitments and because, as he explained, he had recently bet on one or two other equally long shots which had not come in.

The project lapsed again and would probably have been abandoned if it had not been for a young man whose last name I have ungratefully forgotten, but whose first name—Victor—we hailed as a propitious sign. His subsequent history led us to refer to him as Vanquished; and this, as it turned out, was a more reliable omen. Victor walked into the Department of Psychology at Minnesota one day in the summer of 1942 looking for an animal psychologist. He had a scheme for installing dogs in antisubmarine torpedoes. The dogs were to respond to faint acoustic signals from the submarine and to steer the torpedo toward its goal. He wanted a statement from an animal psychologist as to its feasibility. He was understandably surprised to learn of our work with pigeons but seized upon it eagerly; citing it in support of his contention that dogs could be trained to steer torpedoes, he went to a number of companies in Minneapolis. His project was rejected by everyone he approached; but one company, General Mills, Inc., asked for more information about our work with pigeons. We described the project and presented the available data to Arthur D. Hyde, Vice-President in Charge of Research. The company was not looking for new products, but Hyde thought that it might, as a public service, develop the pigeon system to the point at which a governmental agency could be persuaded to take over.

Breland and I moved into the top floor of a flour mill in Minneapolis and with the help of Norman Guttman, who had joined the project, set to work on further improvements. It had been difficult to induce the pigeon to respond to the small angular displacement of a distant target. It would start working dangerously late in the descent. Its natural pursuit behavior was not appropriate to the characteristics of a likely missile. A new system was therefore designed. An image of the target was projected on a translucent screen as in a camera obscura. The pigeon was held near the screen, and pecking at the image on the screen was reinforced. The guiding signal was to be picked up from the point of contact of screen and beak.

In an early arrangement the screen was a translucent plastic plate forming the larger end of a truncated cone bearing a lens at the smaller end. The cone was mounted, lens down, in a gimbal bearing. An object within range threw its image on the translucent screen; and the pigeon, held vertically just above the plate, pecked the image. When a target was moved about within range of the lens, the cone continued to point to it. In another apparatus a translucent disk, free to tilt slightly on gimbal bearings, closed contacts operating motors which altered the position of a large field beneath the apparatus. Small cutouts of ships and other objects were placed on the field. The field was constantly in motion, and a target would go out of range unless the pigeon continued to control it. With this apparatus we began to study the pigeon's reactions to various patterns and to develop sustained steady rates of responding through the use of appropriate schedules of reinforcement, the reinforcement being a few grains occasionally released onto the plate. By building up large extinction curves a target could be tracked continuously for a matter of minutes without reinforcement. We trained pigeons to follow a variety of land and sea targets, to neglect large patches intended to represent clouds or flak, to concentrate on one target while another was in view, and so on. We found that a pigeon could hold the missile on a particular street intersection in an aerial map of a city. The map which came most easily to hand was of a city which, in the interests of international relations, need not be identified. Through appropriate schedules of reinforcement it was possible to maintain longer uninterrupted runs than could conceivably be required by a missile.

We also undertook a more serious study of the pigeon's behavior, with the help of W.K. Estes and Marion Breland, who joined the project at this time. We ascertained optimal conditions of deprivation, investigated other kinds of deprivations, studied the effect of special reinforcements (for example, pigeons were said to find hemp seed particularly delectable), tested the effects of energizing drugs and increased oxygen pressures, and so on. We differentially reinforced the force of the pecking response and found that pigeons could be induced to peck so energetically that the base of the beak became inflamed. We investigated the effects of extremes of temperature, of changes in atmospheric pressure, of accelerations produced by an improvised centrifuge, of increased carbon dioxide pressure, of increased and prolonged vibration, and of noises such as pistol shots. (The birds could, of course, have been deafened to eliminate auditory distractions, but we found it easy to maintain steady behavior in spite of intense noises and many other distracting conditions using the simple process of adaptation.) We investigated optimal conditions for the quick development of discriminations and began to study the pigeon's reactions to patterns, testing for induction from a test figure to the same figure inverted, to figures of different sizes and colors, and to figures against different grounds. A simple device using carbon paper to record the points at which a pigeon pecks a figure showed a promise which has never been properly exploited.

We made another demonstration film and renewed our contact with the Office of Scientific Research and Development. An observer was sent to

Minneapolis, and on the strength of his report we were given an opportunity to present our case in Washington in February, 1943. At that time we were offering a homing device capable of reporting with an on-off signal the orientation of a missile toward various visual patterns. The capacity to respond to pattern was, we felt, our strongest argument, but the fact that the device used only visible radiation (the same form of information available to the human bombardier) made it superior to the radio-controlled missiles then under development because it was resistant to jamming. Our film had some effect. Other observers were sent to Minneapolis to see the demonstration itself. The pigeons, as usual, behaved beautifully. One of them held the supposed missile on a particular intersection of streets in the aerial map for 5 minutes although the target would have been lost if the pigeon had paused for a second or two. The observers returned to Washington, and 2 weeks later we were asked to supply data on (a) the population of pigeons in the United States (fortunately, the census bureau had some figures) and (b) the accuracy with which pigeons struck a point on a plate. There were many arbitrary conditions to be taken into account in measuring the latter, but we supplied possibly relevant data. At long last, in June, 1943, the Office of Scientific Research and Development awarded a modest contract to General Mills, Inc., to "develop a homing device."

At that time we were given some information about the missile the pigeons were to steer. The Pelican was a wing-steered glider, still under development and not yet successfully steered by any homing device. It was being tested on a target in New Jersey consisting of a stirrup-shaped pattern bulldozed out of the sandy soil near the coast. The white lines of the target stood out clearly against brown and green cover. Colored photographs were taken from various distances and at various angles, and the verisimilitude of the reproduction was checked by flying over the target and looking at its image in a portable camera obscura.

Because of security restrictions we were given only very rough specifications of the signal to be supplied to the controlling system in the Pelican. It was no longer to be simply on-off; if the missile was badly off-target, an especially strong correcting signal was needed. This meant that the quadrant-contact system would no longer suffice. But further requirements were left mainly to our imagination. The General Mills engineers were equal to this difficult assignment. With what now seems like unbelievable speed, they designed and constructed a pneumatic pickup system giving a graded signal. A lens in the nose of the missile threw an image on a translucent plate within reach of the pigeon in a pressure-sealed chamber. Four air valves resting against the edges of the plate were jarred open momentarily as the pigeon pecked. The valves at the right and left admitted air to chambers on opposite sides of one tambour, while the valves at the top and bottom admitted air to opposite sides of another. Air on all sides was exhausted by a Venturi cone on the side of the missile. When the missile was on target, the pigeon pecked the center of the plate, all valves admitted equal amounts of air, and the tambours remained in neutral positions. But if the image moved as little as a quarter of an inch off-center, corresponding to a very small angular displacement of the target, more air was admitted by the valves on one side, and the resulting displacement of the tambours sent appropriate correcting orders directly to the servosystem.

The device required no materials in short supply, was relatively foolproof, and delivered a graded signal. It had another advantage. By this time we had begun to realize that a pigeon was more easily controlled than a physical scientist serving on a committee. It was very difficult to convince the latter that the former was an orderly system. We therefore multiplied the probability of success by designing a multiple-bird unit. There was adequate space in the nose of the Pelican for three pigeons, each with its own lens and plate. A net signal could easily be generated. The majority vote of three pigeons offered an excellent guarantee against momentary pauses and aberrations. (We later worked out a system in which the majority took on a more characteristically democratic function. When a missile is falling toward *two* ships at sea, for example, there is no guarantee that all three pigeons will steer toward the same ship. But at least two must agree, and the third can then be punished for its minority opinion. Under proper contingencies of reinforcement a punished bird will shift immediately to the majority view When all three are working on one ship, any defection is immediately punished and corrected.)

The arrangement in the nose of the Pelican is shown in Figure 3. Three systems of lenses and mirrors, shown at the left, throw images of the target area on the three translucent plates shown in the center. The ballistic valves resting against the edges of these plates and the tubes connecting them with the manifolds leading to the controlling tambours may be seen. A pigeon is being placed in the pressurized chamber at the right.

The General Mills engineers also built a simulator (Figure 4)—a sort of Link trainer for pigeons—designed to have the steering characteristics of the Pelican, insofar as these had been communicated to us. Like the wing-steered Pelican, the simulator tilted and turned from side to side. When the three-bird nose was attached to it, the pigeons could be put in full control—the "loop could be closed"—and the adequacy of the signal tested under pursuit conditions. Targets were moved back and forth across the far wall of a room at prescribed speeds and in given patterns of oscillation, and the tracking response of the whole unit was studied quantitatively.

Meanwhile we continued our intensive study of the behavior of the pigeon. Looking ahead to combat use we designed methods for the mass production of trained birds and for handling large groups of trained subjects. We were proposing to train certain birds for certain *classes* of targets, such as ships at sea, while special squads were to be trained on special targets,

Figure 3   Demonstration model of the three-pigeon guidance system.

photographs of which were to be obtained through reconnaissance. A large crew of pigeons would then be waiting for assignment, but we developed harnessing and training techniques which should have solved such problems quite easily.

A multiple-unit trainer is shown in Figure 5. Each box contained a jacketed pigeon held at an angle of 45° to the horizontal and perpendicular to an 8-inch by 8-inch translucent screen. A target area is projected on each screen. Two beams of light intersect at the point to be struck. All on-target responses of the pigeon are reported by the interruption of the crossed beams and by contact with the translucent screen. Only a 4-inch, disk-shaped portion of the field is visible to the pigeon at any time, but the boxes move slowly about the field, giving the pigeon an opportunity to respond to the target in all positions. The positions of all reinforcements are recorded to reveal any weak areas. A variable-ratio schedule is used to build sustained, rapid responding.

By December, 1943, less than 6 months after the contract was awarded, we were ready to report to the Office of Scientific Research and Development. Observers visited the laboratory and watched the simulator follow a target about a room under the control of a team of three birds. They also

Figure 4   Simulator for testing the adequacy of the pigeon signal

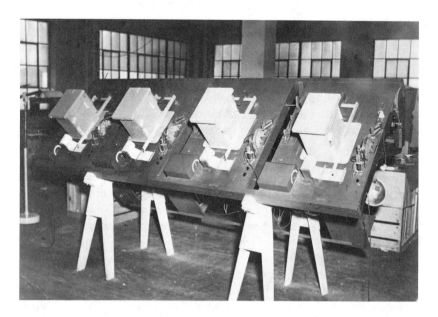

Figure 5   A trainer for four pigeons.

reviewed our tracking data. The only questions which arose were the inevitable consequence of our lack of information about the signal required to steer the Pelican. For example, we had had to make certain arbitrary decisions in compromising between sensitivity of signal and its integration or smoothness. A high vacuum produced quick, rather erratic movements of the tambours, while a lower vacuum gave a sluggish but smooth signal. As it turned out, we had not chosen the best values in collecting our data, and in January, 1944, the Office of Scientific Research and Development refused to extend the General Mills contract. The reasons given seemed to be due to misunderstandings or, rather, to lack of communication. We had already collected further data with new settings of the instruments, and these were submitted in a request for reconsideration.

We were given one more chance. We took our new data to the radiation lab at the Massachusetts Institute of Techology where they were examined by the servospecialists working on the Pelican controls. To our surprise the scientist whose task it was to predict the usefulness of the pigeon signal argued that our data were inconsistent with respect to phase lag and certain other characteristics of the signal. According to his equations, our device could not possibly yield the signals we reported. We knew, of course, that it had done so. We examined the supposed inconsistency and traced it, or so we thought, to a certain nonlinearity in our system. In pecking an image near the edge of the plate, the pigeon strikes a more glancing blow; hence the air admitted at the valves is not linearly proportional to the displacement of the target. This could be corrected in several ways: for example, by using a lens to distort radial distances. It was our understanding that in any case the signal was adequate to control the Pelican. Indeed, one servo authority, upon looking at graphs of the performance of the simulator, exclaimed: "This is better than radar!"

Two days later, encouraged by our meeting at MIT, we reached the summit. We were to present our case briefly to a committee of the country's top scientists. The hearing began with a brief report by the scientist who had discovered the "inconsistency" in our data, and to our surprise he still regarded it as unresolved. He predicted that the signal we reported would cause the missile to "hunt" wildly and lose the target. But his prediction should have applied as well to the closed loop simulator. Fortunately another scientist was present who had seen the simulator performing under excellent control and who could confirm our report of the facts. But reality was no match for mathematics.

The basic difficulty, of course, lay in convincing a dozen distinguishd physical scientists that the behavior of a pigeon could be adequately controlled. We had hoped to score on this point by bringing with us a demonstration. A small black box had a round translucent window in one end. A slide projector placed some distance away threw on the window an image of the New Jersey target. In the box, of course, was a pigeon—which, incidentally, had at that time been harnessed for 35 hours. Our intention was to let each member of the committee observe the reponse to the target by looking down a small tube; but time was not available for individual observation, and we were asked to take the top off the box. The translucent screen was flooded with so much light that the target was barely visible, and the peering scientists offered conditions much more unfamiliar and threatening than those likely to be encountered in a missile. In spite of this the pigeon behaved perfectly, pecking steadily and energetically at the image of the target as it moved about on the plate. One scientist with an experimental turn of mind intercepted the beam from the projector. The pigeon stopped instantly. When the image again appeared, pecking began within a fraction of a second and continued at a steady rate.

It was a perfect performance, but it had just the wrong effect. One can talk about phase lag in pursuit behavior and discuss mathematical predictions of hunting without reflecting too closely upon what is inside the black box. But the spectacle of a living pigeon carrying out its assignment, no matter how beautifully, simply reminded the committee of how utterly fantastic our proposal was. I will not say that the meeting was marked by unrestrained merriment, for the merriment was restrained. But it was there, and it was obvious that our case was lost.

Hyde closed our presentation with a brief summary: We were offering a homing device, unusually resistant to jamming, capable of reacting to a wide variety of target patterns, requiring no materials in short supply, and so simple to build that production could be started in 30 days. He thanked the committee, and we left. As the door closed behind us, he said to me: "Why don't you go out and get drunk!"

Official word soon came: "Further prosecution of this project would seriously delay others which in the minds of the Division would have more immediate promise of combat application." Possibly the reference was to a particular combat application at Hiroshima a year and a half later, when it looked for a while as if the need for accurate bombing had been eliminated for all time. In any case we had to show, for all our trouble, only a loftful of curiously useless equipment and a few dozen pigeons with a strange interest in a feature of the New Jersey coast. The equipment was scrapped, but 30 of the pigeons were kept to see how long they would retain the appropriate behavior.

In the years which followed there were faint signs of life. Winston Churchill's personal scientific advisor, Lord Cherwell, learned of the project and "regretted its demise." A scientist who had had some contact with the project during the war, and who evidently assumed that its classified status was not to be taken seriously, made a good story out of it for the *Atlantic Monthly,* names being changed to protect the innocent. Other uses of animals began to be described. The author of the *Atlantic Monthly* story also published an account of the "incendiary bats." Thousands of bats were to be released over an enemy city, each carrying a small incendiary time bomb. The bats would take refuge, as is their custom, under eaves and in other out-of-the-way places; and shortly afterwards thousands of small fires would break out practically simultaneously. The scheme was never used because it was feared that it would be mistaken for germ warfare and might lead to retaliation in kind.

Another story circulating at the time told how the Russians trained dogs to blow up tanks. I have described the technique elsewhere.[1] A Swedish proposal to use seals to achieve the same end with submarines was not successful. The seals were to be trained to approach submarines to obtain fish attached to the sides. They were then to be released carrying magnetic mines in the vicinity of hostile submarines. The required training was apparently never achieved. I cannot vouch for the authenticity of probably the most fantastic story of this sort, but it ought to be recorded. The Russians were said to have trained sea lions to cut mine cables. A complicated device attached to the sea lion included a motor-driven cable cutter, a tank full of small fish, and a device which released a few fish into a muzzle covering the sea lion's head. In order to eat, the sea lion had to find a mine cable and swim alongside it so that the cutter was automatically triggered, at which point a few fish were released from the tank into the muzzle. When a given number of cables had been cut, both the energy of the cutting mechanism and the supply of fish were exhausted, and the sea lion received a special stimulus upon which it returned to its home base for special reinforcement and reloading.

ORCON

The story of our own venture has a happy ending. With the discovery of German accomplishments in the field of guided missiles, feasible homing systems suddenly became very important. Franklin V. Taylor of the Naval Research Laboratory in Washington, D.C. heard about our project and asked for further details. As a psychologist Taylor appreciated the special capacity of living organisms to respond to visual patterns and was aware of recent advances in the control of behavior. More important, he was a skillful practitioner in a kind of control which our project had conspicuously lacked: He knew how to approach the people who determine the direction of research. He showed our demonstration film so often that it was completely worn out—but to good effect, for support was eventually found for a thorough investigation of "organic control" under the general title ORCON. Taylor also enlisted the support of engineers in obtaining a more effective report of the pigeon's behavior. The translucent plate upon which the image of the target was thrown had a semiconducting surface, and the tip of the bird's beak was covered with a gold electrode. A single contact with the plate sent an immediate report of the location of the target to the controlling mechanism. The work which went into this system contributed to the so-called Pick-off Display Converter developed as part of the Naval Data Handling System for human observers. It is no longer necessary for radar operators to give a verbal report of the location of a pip on the screen. Like the pigeons, they have only to touch the pip with a special contact. (The contact is held in the hand.)

At the Naval Research Laboratory in Washington the responses of pigeons were studied in detail. Average peck rate, average error rate, average hit rate, and so on were recorded under various conditions. The tracking behavior of the pigeon was analyzed with methods similar to those employed with human operators. Pattern perception was studied, including generalizaton from one pattern to another. A simulator was constructed in which the pigeon controlled an image projected by a moving-picture film of an actual target: for example, a ship at sea as seen from a plane approaching at 600 miles per hour.

The publications from the Naval Research Laboratory which report this work[2] provide a serious evaluation of the possibilities of organic control. Although in simulated tests a single pigeon occasionally loses a target, its tracking characteristics are surprisingly good. A three- or seven-bird unit with the same individual consistency should yield a signal with a reliability which is at least of the order of magnitude shown by other kinds of guided missiles in their present stage of development. Moreover, in the 7 years which have followed the last of these reports, a great deal of relevant information has been acquired. The color vision of the pigeon is now thoroughly understood; its generalization along single properties of a stimulus has been recorded and analyzed; and the maintenance of behavior through scheduling of reinforcement has been drastically improved, particularly in the development of techniques for pacing responses for less erratic and steadier signals.[3] Tests made with the birds salvaged from the old Project Pigeon showed that even after 6 years of inactivity a pigeon will immediately and correctly strike a target to which it has been conditioned and will continue to respond for some time without reinforcement.

The use of living organisms in guiding missiles is, it seems fair to say, no longer a crackpot idea. A pigeon is an extraordinarily subtle and complex mechanism capable of performances which at the moment can be equalled by electronic equipment only of vastly greater weight and size, and it can be put to reliable use through the principles which have emerged from an experimental analysis of its behavior. But this vindication of our original proposal is perhaps the least important result. Something happened during the brief life of Project Pigeon which it has taken a long time to appreciate.

The practical task before us created a new attitude toward the behavior of organisms. We had to maximize the probability that a given form of behavior would occur at a given time. We could not enjoy the luxury of observing one variable while allowing others to change in what we hoped was a random fashion. We had to discover all relevant variables and submit them to experimental control whenever possible. We were no doubt under exceptional pressure, but vigorous scientific research usually makes comparable demands. Psychologists have too often yielded to the temptation to be content with hypothetical processes and intervening variables rather than press for rigorous experimental control. It is often intellectual laziness rather than necessity which recommends the a posteriori statistical treatment of variation. Our task forced us to emphasize prior experimental control, and its success in revealing orderly processes gave us an exciting glimpse of the superiority of laboratory practice over verbal (including some kinds of mathematical) explanation.

THE CRACKPOT IDEA

If I were to conclude that crackpot ideas are to be encouraged, I should probably be told that psychology has already had more than its share of them. If it has, they have been entertained by the wrong people. Reacting against the excesses of psychological quackery, psychologists have developed an enormous concern for scientific respectability. They constantly warn their students against questionable facts and unsupported theories. As a result the usual Ph.D. thesis is a model of compulsive cautiousness, advancing only the most timid conclusions thoroughly hedged about with qualifications. But it is just the person capable of displaying such admirable caution who needs a touch of uncontrolled speculation. Possibly a generous exposure to psychological science fiction would help. Project Pigeon might be said to support that view. Except with respect to its avowed goal, it was, as I see it, highly productive; and this was in large measure because my colleagues and I knew that, in the eyes of the world, we were crazy.

One virtue in crackpot ideas is that they breed rapidly and their progeny show extraordinary mutations. Everyone is talking about teaching machines nowadays, but Sidney Pressey can tell you what it was like to have a crackpot idea in that field 40 years ago. His self-testing devices and self-scoring test forms now need no defense, and psychomotor training devices have also achieved a substantial respectability. This did not, however, prepare the way for devices to be used in verbal instruction—that is, in the kinds of teaching which are the principal concern of our schools and colleges. Even 5 short years ago that kind of instruction by machine was still in the crackpot category. (I can quote official opinion to that effect from high places.) Now, there is a direct genetic connection between teaching machines and Project

Pigeon. We had been forced to consider the mass education of pigeons. True, the scrap of wisdom we imparted to each was indeed small, but the required changes in behavior were similar to those which must be brought about in vaster quantities in human students. The techniques of shaping behavior and of bringing it under stimulus control which can be traced, as I have suggested elsewhere,[4] to a memorable episode on the top floor of that flour mill in Minneapolis needed only a detailed reformulation of verbal behavior to be directly applicable to education.

I am sure there is more to come. In the year which followed the termination of Project Pigeon I wrote *Walden Two,* a utopian picture of a properly engineered society. Some psychotherapists might argue that I was suffering from personal rejection and simply retreated to a fantasied world where everything went according to plan, where there never was heard a discouraging word. But another explanation is, I think, equally plausible. That piece of science fiction was a declaration of confidence in a technology of behavior. Call it a crackpot idea if you will; it is one in which I have never lost faith. I still believe that the same kind of wide-ranging speculation about human affairs, supported by studies of compensating rigor, will make a substantial contribution toward that world of the future in which, among other things, there will be no need for guided missiles.

REFERENCES AND NOTES

[1]See Chapter 2 in this volume.

[2]Taylor, F.V. ORCON. Part I. Outline of proposed research. *Naval Res. Lab. lett. Rep.,* 1949, No. S-3600-157/50 (June 17). Searle, L.V., & Stafford, B.H. ORCON. Part II. Report of phase I research and bandpass study. *Naval Res. Lab. lett. Rep.,* 1950, No. S-3600-157/50 (May 1). Chernikoff, R., & Newlin, E.P. ORCON. Part III. Investigations of target acquisition by the pigeon. *Naval Res. Lab. lett. Rep.,* 1951, No. S-3600-629a/51 (Sept. 10). Conklin, J.E., Newlin, E.P., Jr., Taylor, F.V., & Tipton, C.L. ORCON. Part IV. Simulated flight tests. *Naval Res. Lab Rep.,* 1953, No. 4105. White, C.F. Development of the NRL ORCON tactile missile simulator. *Naval Res. Lab. Rep.,* 1952, No. 3917.

[3]See, for example, "The Experimental Analysis of Behavior" (*American Scientist,* 1957, *45,* 343–371; reprinted in *Cumulative Record).*

[4]See "Reinforcement Today" (*American Psychologist,* 1958, *13,* 94–99; reprinted in *Cumulative Record,* especially page 94).

POSTSCRIPT

The original Project Pigeon remained classified for many years, in part because of subsequent research carried out along the same lines at the

Naval Research Laboratories in Washington. By 1959, however, it could be reported, and when I received an award from the American Psychological Association in return for which I was expected to give a lecture, I chose the pigeon guided missile story as the topic.

It was, of course, a crackpot idea—unless one knew what those of us in the field of the experimental analysis of behavior knew, that the behavior of a pigeon could be controlled with precision. Why was the idea never put into effect? It would be easy to say simply that it was because we could never convince those in high places that behavior could be precisely controlled. But there were other reasons. During the war the United States had no missile worth guiding, and by the late fifties when intercontinental missiles were beginning to be discussed, other ways of reaching a target were being actively investigated. (The problem of the final control of missiles is still not fully resolved, however.)

Other possible military uses of pigeons and other organisms have since been investigated. For example, pigeons have been trained to spot and report ambushes; other pigeons, carried under helicopters, spot life rafts and other objects at sea. Porpoises have been trained to seek out and blow up submarines.

A very natural question arises: Is it not a dirty trick to send a porpoise or even a pigeon on a mission which results in its death? Certainly by analogy with the use of a human subject it is. It is true that the method used to reduce pigeon populations in cities and the drownings of tens of thousands of porpoises each year by tuna fishermen are far more cruel than instantaneous death; nevertheless, you have asked the pigeon or the porpoise to do something for you, and you have concealed the price it must pay. An ethical question of that sort is perhaps to be decided by asking whether a culture seems to be more likely to survive if it taboos dirty tricks.

C H A P T E R 13

How to Teach Animals

EDITOR'S NOTE

The article first appeared in *Scientific American* (December 1951, *185*, 26–29) and has been reprinted in all editions of *Cumulative Record.* Conditioning techniques that have been developed in the laboratory, notes Skinner, may be used to train one's pets. The basic steps include: finding a "reinforcer" (for example, food works well for a hungry dog), establishing a "conditioned reinforcer" (loosely speaking, a signal for the reinforcer), and "shaping" the desired response (that is, reinforcing successive approximations). Procedures for training a dog, teaching a pigeon to "read," and conditioning a human baby are outlined, among others.

Teaching, it is often said, is an art, but we have increasing reason to hope that it may eventually become a science. We have already discovered enough about the nature of learning to devise training techniques which are much more rapid and give more reliable results than the rule-of-thumb methods of the past. Tested on animals, the new techniques have proved superior to traditional methods of professional animal trainers; they yield more remarkable results with much less effort.

It takes rather subtle laboratory conditions to test an animal's full learning capacity, but you may be surprised at how much you can accomplish even under informal circumstances at home. Since nearly everyone at some time or other has tried to train a dog, a cat, or some other animal, perhaps the most useful way to explain the learning process is to describe some simple experiments which you can perform yourself.

"Catch your rabbit" is the first item in a well-known recipe for rabbit stew. Your first move, of course, is to choose an experimental subject. Any available animal—a cat, a dog, a pigeon, a mouse, a parrot, a chicken, a pig—will do. (Children or other members of your family may also be available, but it is suggested that you save them until you have had practice with less valuable material.) Suppose you choose a dog.

The second thing you will need is something your subject wants, say food. This serves as a reward or—to use a term which is less likely to be misunderstood—a "reinforcer" for the desired behavior. Many things besides food are reinforcing—for example, simply letting the dog out for a run—but food is usually the easiest to administer in the kind of experiment to be described here. If you use food, you must of course perform the experiment when the dog is hungry, perhaps just before its dinnertime.

Reinforcement (the delivery of a reinforcer) gives you a means of controlling the behavior of the animal. It rests on the simple principle that when the kind of thing we call a reinforcer follows behavior, it increases the chances that the animal will repeat that behavior. This makes it possible to shape an animal's behavior almost as a sculptor shapes a lump of clay. There is, of course, nothing new in this principle. What is new is a better understanding of the conditions under which reinforcement works best.

To be effective a reinforcer must be presented almost simultaneously with the desired behavior; a delay of even 1 second destroys much of the effect. This means that offering food in the usual way is likely to be ineffective; it is not fast enough. The best way to reinforce the behavior with the necessary speed is to use a "conditioned" reinforcer. This is a signal which the animal has observed in association with food. The animal is always given food immediately after the signal, and the signal itself then becomes a reinforcer. The better the association between the two events, the better the result.

For a conditioned reinforcer you need a clear signal which can be given instantly and to which the subject is sure to respond. It may be a noise or a flash of light. A whistle is not recommended because of the time it takes to draw a breath before blowing it. A visual signal like a wave of the arm may not always be seen by the animal. A convenient signal is a rap on a table with a small hard object or the noise of a high-pitched device such as a "cricket."

You are now ready to start the experiment with your dog. Work in a convenient place as free as possible from distraction. Let us say that you have chosen a "cricket" as your conditioned reinforcer. To build up its reinforcing power begin by tossing a few pieces of food, one at a time and not oftener than once or twice a minute, where the dog may eat them. Use pieces so small that 30 or 40 will not appreciably reduce the animal's hunger. As soon as the dog eats pieces readily and without delay, begin to pair the cricket with the food. Sound the cricket and then toss a piece of food. Wait half a minute or so and repeat. Sound the cricket suddenly, without any preparatory movement such as reaching for food.

At this stage your subject will probably show well-marked begging behavior. It may watch you intently, perhaps jump on you, and so on. You must break up this behavior, because it will interfere with other parts of the experiment. Never sound the cricket or give food when the dog is close to you or facing you. Wait until it turns away, then reinforce. Your conditioned reinforcer will be working properly when the dog turns immediately and approaches the spot where it receives food. Test this several times. Wait until the dog is in a fairly unusual position, then sound the signal. Time spent in making sure the dog immediately approaches the food will later be saved manyfold.

Now, having established the noise as a reinforcer, you may begin teaching the dog. To get the feel of the technique start with some simple task, such as getting the dog to approach the handle on a low cupboard door and touch it with its nose. At first you reinforce any activity which will be part of the final completed act of approaching and touching the handle of the cupboard. The only permissible contact between you and the dog is via the cricket and the food. Do not touch the dog, talk to it, coax it, "draw its attention," or interfere in any other way with the experiment. If your subject just sits, you may have to begin by reinforcing any movement, however slight. As soon as the dog moves, sound the cricket and give food. Remember that your reaction time is important. Try to reinforce as nearly simultaneously with the movement as possible.

After your subject has begun to move about, reinforce when it turns to the cupboard. Almost immediately you will notice a change in its behavior. It will begin to face toward the cupboard most of the time. Then begin to reinforce only when the dog moves nearer the cupboard. (If you withhold reinforcement too long at this stage, you may lose the facing response. If so, go back and pick it up.) In a very short time—perhaps a minute or two—you should have the dog standing close to the cupboard. Now begin to pay attention to its head. Reinforce any movement which brings the nose close to the handle. You will have to make special efforts now to reduce the time between the movement and the reinforcement to the very minimum. Presently the dog will touch the handle with its nose, and after reinforcement it will repeat this behavior so long as it remains hungry.

Usually it takes no more than 5 minutes, even for a beginner, to teach a dog this behavior. Moreover, the dog does not have to be particularly "smart" to learn it; contrary to the usual view, all normal dogs learn with about equal facility with this conditioning technique.

Before going on with other experiments test the effect of your conditioned reinforcer again two or three times. If the dog responds quickly and eats without delay you may safely continue. You should "extinguish" the response the dog has already learned, however, before teaching it another. Stop reinforcing the act of touching the cupboard handle until the dog abandons this activity.

As a second test, let us say, you want to teach the dog to lift its head in the air and turn around to the right. The general procedure is the same, but you may need some help in sharpening your observation of the behavior to be reinforced. As a guide to the height to which the dog's head is to be raised, sight some horizontal line on the wall across the room. Whenever the dog, in its random movements, lifts its head above this line, reinforce immediately. You will soon see the head rising above the line more and more frequently. Now raise your sights slightly and reinforce only when the head rises above the new level. By a series of gradual steps you can get the dog to hold its head much higher than usual. After this you can begin to emphasize any turning movement in a clockwise direction while the head is high. Eventually the dog should execute a kind of dance step. If you use available food carefully, a single session should suffice for setting up this behavior.

Having tested your ability to produce these simple responses, you may feel confident enough to approach a more complex assignment. This time suppose you try working with a pigeon. Pigeons do not tame easily. You will probably want a cage to help control the bird, and for this you can rig up a large cardboard carton with a screen or lattice top and windows cut in the side for observing the bird. It is much less disturbing to the bird if you watch it from below its line of vision than if you peer at it from above. In general keep yourself out of the experimental situation as much as possible. You may still use a cricket as a conditioned reinforcer, and feed the bird by dropping a few grains of pigeon food into a small dish through a hole in the wall. It may take several daily feedings to get the bird to eat readily and to respond quickly to the cricket.

Your assignment is to teach the pigeon to identify the visual patterns on playing cards. To begin with, hang a single card on a nail on the wall of the cage a few inches above the floor so that the pigeon can easily peck it. After you have trained the bird to peck the card by reinforcing the movements which lead to that end, change the card and again reinforce the peck. If you shuffle the cards and present them at random, the pigeon will learn to peck any card offered.

Now begin to teach it to discriminate among the cards. Let us say you are using diamonds and clubs (excluding face cards and aces) and want the bird to select diamonds. Reinforce only when the card presented is a diamond, never when it is a club. Almost immediately the bird will begin to show a preference for diamonds. You can speed up its progress toward complete rejection of clubs by discontinuing the experiment for a moment (a mild form of punishment) whenever it pecks a club. A good conditioned punishment is simply to turn off the light ["blacking out"] or cover or remove the card. After half a minute replace the card or turn on the light and continue the experiment. Under these conditions the response which is positively reinforced with food remains part of the repertoire of the bird, while the response which leads to a blackout quickly disappears.

There is an amusing variation of this experiment by which you can make it appear that a pigeon can be taught to read. You simply use two printed cards bearing the words PECK and DON'T PECK, respectively. By reinforcing responses to PECK and blacking out when the bird pecks DON'T PECK, it is quite easy to train the bird to obey the commands on the cards.

The pigeon can also be taught the somewhat more "intellectual" performance of matching a sample object. Let us say the sample to be matched is a certain card. Fasten three cards to a board, with one above and the two others side by side just below it. The board is placed so that the bird can reach all the cards through windows cut in the side of the cage. After training the bird to peck a card of any kind impartially in all three positions, present the three chosen cards. The sample to be matched, say the three of diamonds, is at the top, and below it put a three of diamonds and a three of clubs. If the bird pecks the sample three of diamonds at the top, do nothing. If it pecks the matching three of diamonds below, reinforce; if it pecks the three of clubs, black out. After each correct response and reinforcement, switch the positions of the two lower cards. The pigeon should soon match the sample each time. Conversely, it can also be taught to select the card which does not match the sample. It is important to reinforce correct choices immediately. Your own behavior must be letter-perfect if you are to expect perfection from your subject. The task can be made easier if the pigeon is conditioned to peck the sample card before you begin to train it to match the sample.

In a more elaborate variation of this experiment we have found it possible to make a pigeon choose among four words so that it appears to "name the suit" of the sample card. You prepare four cards about the size of small calling cards, each bearing in block letters the name of a suit: SPADES, HEARTS, DIAMONDS, and CLUBS. Fasten these side by side in a row and teach the pigeon to peck them by reinforcing in the usual way. Now arrange a sample playing card just above them. Cover the name cards and reinforce a few pecks to the sample. Now present, say, the three of diamonds as the sample. When the pigeon pecks it, immediately uncover the name cards. If the pigeon pecks DIAMONDS, reinforce instantly. If it pecks a wrong name instead, black out for half a minute and then resume the experiment with the three of diamonds still in place and the name cards covered. After a correct choice, change the sample card to a different suit while the pigeon is eating. Always keep the names covered until the sample card has been pecked. Within a short time you should have the bird following the full sequence of pecking the sample and then the appropriate name card. As time passes the correct name will be pecked more and more frequently and, if you do not too often reinforce wrong responses or neglect to reinforce right ones, the pigeon should soon become letter-perfect.

A toy piano offers interesting possibilities for performances of a more artistic nature. Reinforce any movement of the pigeon that leads toward its pressing a key. Then, by using reinforcements and blackouts appropriately, narrow the response to a given key. Then build up a two-note sequence by reinforcing only when the sequence has been completed and by blacking out when any other combination of keys is struck. The two-note sequence will quickly emerge. Other notes may then be added. Pigeons, chickens, small dogs, and cats have been taught in this way to play tunes of four or five notes. The situation soon becomes too complicated, however, for the casual experimenter. You will find it difficult to control the tempo, and the reinforcing contingencies become very complex. The limit of such an experiment is determined as much by the experimenter's skill as by that of the animal. In the laboratory we have been able to provide assistance to the experimenter by setting up complicated devices which always reinforce consistently and avoid exhaustion of the experimenter's patience.

The increased precision of the laboratory also makes it possible to guarantee performance up to the point of almost complete certainty. When relevant conditions have been controlled, the behavior of the organism is fully determined. Behavior may be sustained in full strength for many hours by utilizing different schedules of reinforcement. Some of these correspond to the contingencies established in industry in daily wages or in piecework pay; others resemble the subtle but powerful contingencies of gambling devices, which are notorious for their ability to command sustained behavior.

The human baby is an excellent subject in experiments of the kind described here. You will not need to interfere with feeding schedules or create any other state of deprivation, because the human infant can be affected by very trivial environmental events; it does not need such a reward as food. Almost any "feedback" from the environment is reinforcing if it is not too intense. A crumpled newspaper, a pan and a spoon, or any convenient noisemaker quickly generates appropriate behavior, often amusing in its violence. The baby's rattle is based upon this principle.

One reinforcer to which babies often respond is the flashing on and off of a table lamp. Select some arbitrary response—for example, lifting the hand. Whenever the baby lifts its hand, flash the light. In a short time a well-defined response will be generated. (Human babies are just as "smart" as dogs or pigeons in this respect.) Incidentally, the baby will enjoy the experiment.

The same principle is at work in the behavior of older children and adults. Important among human reinforcers are those aspects of the behavior of others, often very subtle, which we call "attention," "approval," and "affection." Behavior which is successful in achieving these reinforcers may come to dominate the repertoire of the individual.

All this may be easily used—and just as easily misused—in our relations with other people. To the reader who is anxious to advance to the human subject a word of caution is in order. Reinforcement is only one of the procedures through which we alter behavior. To use it, we must build up some degree of deprivation or at least permit a deprivation to prevail which it is within our power to reduce. We must embark upon a program in which we sometimes apply relevant reinforcement and sometimes withhold it. In doing this, we are quite likely to generate emotional effects. Unfortunately the science of behavior is not yet as successful in controlling emotion as it is in shaping practical behavior.

A scientific analysis can, however, bring about a better understanding of personal relations. We are almost always reinforcing the behavior of others, whether we mean to be or not. A familiar problem is that of the child who seems to take an almost pathological delight in annoying its parents. In many cases this is the result of conditioning which is very similar to the animal training we have discussed. The attention, approval, and affection which a mother gives a child are all extremely powerful reinforcers. Any behavior of the child which produces these consequences is likely to be strengthened. The mother may unwittingly promote the very behavior she does not want. For example, when she is busy she is likely not to respond to a call or request made in a quiet tone of voice. She may answer the child only when it raises its voice. The average intensity of the child's vocal behavior therefore moves up to another level—precisely as the head of the dog in our experiment was raised to a new height. Eventually the mother gets used to this level and again reinforces only louder instances. This vicious circle brings about louder and louder behavior. The child's voice may also vary in intonation, and any change in the direction of unpleasantness is more likely to get the attention of the mother and is therefore strengthened. One might even say that "annoying" behavior is just that behavior which is especially effective in arousing another person to action. The mother behaves, in fact, as if she had been given the assignment of teaching the child to be annoying! The remedy in such a case is simply for the mother to make sure that she responds with attention and affection to most if not all the responses of the child which are of acceptable intensity and tone of voice and that she never reinforces the annoying forms of behavior.

POSTSCRIPT

Shortly after the paper was published, a writer for *Look* magazine called on me. He wanted me to prove that behavior could be shaped as easily as I had said it could. He bought a beautiful dalmatian dog, and I explained how the photographer's flash was to be converted into a conditioned reinforcer. I saw the dog for the first time one evening. We agreed that I was to teach it to stand on its hind legs. Within half an hour, by reinforcing higher and higher positions of the dog's head, I was able to get the dog to leap straight up in the air, its hind feet a foot off the floor. Pictures were taken at every stage in the process.

CHAPTER 14

Baby in a Box

EDITOR'S NOTE

The article first appeared in the *Ladies' Home Journal* (October 1945, *62,* 30-31; 135-136; 138) and has been reprinted in *Cumulative Record.* In 1944 the Skinners had their second child, Deborah. The article describes one of several of Skinner's inventions that Deborah inspired: an air-conditioned crib, designed to ease and improve child care. Called the "baby-tender" in the article, later models became known as "Aircribs." The original article included five black-and-white photographs, including one, like one shown in this chapter, of a cheerful Deborah looking out at the world through the large safety-glass window at the front of the box.

Advantages of the box are described. It allowed accurate control of the temperature so the baby could be kept comfortable and warm without being encumbered with bulky clothing or blankets. Without such encumbrances, Deborah was free to move about and exercise, which she did frequently. It was laborsaving for the mother: The box was at a convenient height so that it could double as a changing table, and, instead of having to clean bedding, one pulled in a new section of the long canvas sheet that served as the floor.

Deborah spent most of her time in the box in early months and less as she grew, just as in a conventional crib. Deborah, wrote Skinner, was unusually cheerful and healthy and probably received even more affection than she would have were her mother burdened with the usual problems of child care. The subsequent history of the baby-tender and its occupant—who, in spite of rumors to the contrary, had a normal childhood and became a normal adult—is outlined in *The Shaping of a Behaviorist,* as well as in an expanded excerpt from the book, "My Experience with the Baby-Tender" (*Psychology Today,* 1979).

In that brave new world which science is preparing for the housewife of the future, the young mother has apparently been forgotten. Almost nothing has been done to ease her lot by simplifying and improving the care of babies.

When we decided to have another child, my wife and I felt that it was time to apply a little laborsaving invention and design to the problems of the nursery. We began by going over the disheartening schedule of the young mother, step by step. We asked only one question: Is this practice important for the physical and psychological health of the baby? When it was not, we marked it for elimination. Then the "gadgeteering" began.

The result was an inexpensive apparatus in which our baby daughter has now been living for 11 months. Her remarkable good health and happiness and my wife's welcome leisure have exceeded our most optimistic predictions, and we are convinced that a new deal for both mother and baby is at hand.

We tackled first the problem of warmth. The usual solution is to wrap the baby in half-a-dozen layers of cloth—shirt, nightdress, sheet, blankets. This is never completely successful. The baby is likely to be found steaming in its own fluids or lying cold and uncovered. Schemes to prevent uncovering may be dangerous, and in fact they have sometimes even proved fatal. Clothing and bedding also interfere with normal exercise and growth and keep the baby from taking comfortable postures or changing posture during sleep. They also encourage rashes and sores. Nothing can be said for the system on the score of convenience, because frequent changes and launderings are necessary.

Why not, we thought, dispense with clothing altogether—except for the diaper, which serves another purpose—and warm the space in which the baby lives? This should be a simple technical problem in the modern home. Our solution is a closed compartment about as spacious as a standard crib (Figure 1). The walls are well insulated, and one side, which can be raised like a window, is a large pane of safety glass. The heating is electrical, and special precautions have been taken to insure accurate control.

After a little experimentation we found that our baby, when first home from the hospital, was completely comfortable and relaxed without benefit of clothing at about 86° F. As she grew older, it was possible to lower the temperature by easy stages. Now, at 11 months, we are operating at about 78°, with a relative humidity of 50 percent.

Raising or lowering the temperature by more than a degree or two produces a surprising change in the baby's condition and behavior. This response is so sensitive that we wonder how a comfortable temperature is ever reached with clothing and blankets.

The discovery which pleased us most was that crying and fussing could always be stopped by slightly lowering the temperature. During the first 3 months, it is true, the baby would also cry when wet or hungry, but in that

Figure 1

case she would stop when changed or fed. During the past 6 months she has not cried at all except for a moment or two when injured or sharply distressed—for example, when inoculated. The "lung exercise" which so often is appealed to to reassure the mother of a baby who cries a good deal takes the much pleasanter form of shouts and gurgles.

How much of this sustained cheerfulness is due to the temperature is hard to say, because the baby enjoys many other kinds of comfort. She sleeps in curious postures, not half of which would be possible under securely fastened blankets.

When awake, she exercises almost constantly and often with surprising violence. Her leg, stomach, and back muscles are especially active and have become strong and hard. It is necessary to watch this performance for only a few minutes to realize how severely restrained the average baby is, and how much energy must be diverted into the only remaining channel—crying.

A wider range and variety of behavior are also encouraged by the freedom from clothing. For example, our baby acquired an amusing, almost apelike skill in the use of her feet. We have devised a number of toys which are occasionally suspended from the ceiling of the compartment. She often plays with these with her feet alone and with her hands and feet in close co-operation.

One toy is a ring suspended from a modified music box. A note can be played by pulling the ring downward, and a series of rapid jerks will produce "Three Blind Mice." At 7 months our baby would grasp the ring in her toes, stretch out her leg and play the tune with a rhythmic movement of her foot.

We are not especially interested in developing skills of this sort, but they are valuable for the baby because they arouse and hold her interest. Many babies seem to cry from sheer boredom—their behavior is restrained and they have nothing else to do. In our compartment, the waking hours are invariably active and happy ones.

Freedom from clothes and bedding is especially important for the older baby who plays and falls asleep off and on during the day. Unless the mother is constantly on the alert, it is hard to cover the baby promptly when it falls asleep and to remove and arrange sheets and blankets as soon as it is ready to play. All this is now unnecessary.

Remember that these advantages for the baby do not mean additional labor or attention on the part of the mother. On the contrary, there is an almost unbelievable saving in time and effort. For one thing, there is no bed to be made or changed. The "mattress" is a tightly stretched canvas, which is kept dry by warm air. A single bottom sheet operates like a roller towel.[1] It is stored on a spool outside the compartment at one end and passes into a wire hamper at the other. It is 10 yards long and lasts a week. A clean section can be locked into place in a few seconds. The time which is usually spent in changing clothes is also saved. This is especially important in the early months. When we take the baby up for feeding or play, she is wrapped in a small blanket or a simple nightdress. Occasionally she is dressed up "for fun" or for her play period. But that is all. The wrapping blanket, roller sheet, and the usual diapers are the only laundry actually required.

Time and labor are also saved because the air which passes through the compartment is thoroughly filtered. The baby's eyes, ears, and nostrils remain fresh and clean. A weekly bath is enough, provided the face and diaper region are frequently washed. These little attentions are easy because the compartment is at waist level (Figure 2).

It takes about 1½ hours each day to feed, change, and otherwise care for the baby. This includes everything except washing diapers and preparing formula. We are not interested in reducing the time any further. As a baby grows older, it needs a certain amount of social stimulation. And after all, when unnecessary chores have been eliminated, taking care of a baby is fun.

Figure 2

An unforeseen dividend has been the contribution to the baby's good health. Our pediatrician readily approved the plan before the baby was born, and he has followed the results enthusiastically from month to month. Here are some points on the health score: When the baby was only 10 days old, we could place her in the preferred face-down position without danger of smothering, and she has slept that way ever since, with the usual advantages. She has always enjoyed deep and extended sleep, and her feeding and eliminative habits have been extraordinarily regular. She has never had a stomach upset, and she has never missed a daily bowel movement.

The compartment is relatively free of spray and airborne infection, as well as dust and allergic substances. Although there have been colds in the family, it has been easy to avoid contagion, and the baby has completely escaped. The neighborhood children troop in to see her, but they see her through glass and keep their school-age diseases to themselves. She has never had a diaper rash.

We have also enjoyed the advantages of a fixed daily routine. Child specialists are still not agreed as to whether the mother should watch the baby or the clock, but no one denies that a strict schedule saves time, for the mother can plan her day in advance and find time for relaxation or freedom for other activities. The trouble is that a routine acceptable to the baby often conflicts with the schedule of the household. Our compartment helps out here in two ways. Even in crowded living quarters it can be kept free of unwanted lights and sounds. The insulated walls muffle all ordinary noises, and a curtain can be drawn down over the window. The result is that, in the space taken by a standard crib, the baby has in effect a separate room. We are never concerned lest the doorbell, telephone, piano, or children at play wake the baby, and we can therefore let her set up any routine she likes.

But a more interesting possibility is that her routine may be changed to suit our convenience. A good example of this occurred when we dropped her schedule from four to three meals per day. The baby began to wake up in the morning about an hour before we wanted to feed her. This annoying habit, once established, may persist for months. However, by slightly raising the temperature during the night we were able to postpone her demand for breakfast. The explanation is simple. The evening meal is used by the baby mainly to keep herself warm during the night. How long it lasts will depend in part upon how fast heat is absorbed by the surrounding air.

One advantage not to be overlooked is that the soundproofing also protects the family from the baby! Our intentions in this direction were misunderstood by some of our friends. We were never put to the test, because there was no crying to contend with, but it was never our policy to use the compartment in order to let the baby "cry it out."

Every effort should be made to discover just why a baby cries. But if the condition cannot be remedied, there is no reason why the family, and perhaps the neighborhood as well, must suffer. (Such a compartment, by the way, might persuade many a landlord to drop a "no babies" rule, since other tenants can be completely protected.)

Before the baby was born, when we were still building the apparatus, some of the friends and acquaintances who had heard about what we proposed to do were rather shocked. Mechanical dishwashers, garbage disposers, air cleaners, and other laborsaving devices were all very fine, but a mechanical baby tender—that was carrying science too far! However, all the specific objections which were raised against the plan have faded away in the bright light of our results. A very brief acquaintance with the scheme in operation is enough to resolve all doubts. Some of the toughest skeptics have become our most enthusiastic supporters.

One of the commonest objections was that we were going to raise a "softie" who would be unprepared for the real world. But instead of becoming hypersensitive, our baby has acquired a surprisingly serene tolerance for annoyances. She is not bothered by the clothes she wears at playtime, she is not frightened by loud or sudden noises, she is not frustrated by toys out of reach, and she takes a lot of pommeling from her older sister like a good sport. It is possible that she will have to learn to sleep in a noisy room, but adjustments of that sort are always necessary. A tolerance for any annoyance can be built up by administering it in controlled dosages, rather than in the usual accidental way. Certainly there is no reason to annoy the child throughout the whole of its infancy, merely to prepare it for later childhood.

It is not, of course, the favorable conditions to which people object, but the fact that in our compartment they are "artificial." All of them occur naturally in one favorable environment or another, where the same objection should apply but is never raised. It is quite in the spirit of the "world of the future" to make favorable conditions available everywhere through simple mechanical means.

A few critics have objected that they would not like to live in such a compartment themselves—they feel that it would stifle them or give them claustrophobia. The baby obviously does not share in this opinion. The compartment is well ventilated and much more spacious than a Pullman berth, considering the size of the occupant. The baby cannot get out, of course, but that is true of a crib as well. There is less actual restraint in the compartment because the baby is freer to move about. The plain fact is that she is perfectly happy. She has never tried to get out nor resisted being put back in, and that seems to be the final test.

Another early objection was that the baby would be socially starved and robbed of the affection and mother love which she needs. This has simply not been true. The compartment does not ostracize the baby. The large window is no more of a social barrier than the bars of a crib. The baby follows what is going on in the room, smiles at passers-by, plays "peek-a-boo" games, and obviously delights in company. And she is handled, talked to, and played with whenever she is changed or fed, and each afternoon during a play period which is becoming longer as she grows older.

The fact is that a baby will probably get more love and affection when it is easily cared for, because the mother is not so likely to feel overworked and resentful of the demands made upon her. She will express her love in a practical way and give the baby genuinely affectionate care.

It is common practice to advise the troubled mother to be patient and tender and to enjoy her baby. And, of course, that is what any baby needs. But it is the exceptional mother who can fill this prescription upon demand, especially if there are other children in the family and she has no help. We need to go one step further and treat the mother with affection also. Simplified child care will give mother love a chance.

A similar complaint was that such an apparatus would encourage neglect. But easier care is sure to be better care. The mother will resist the temptation to put the baby back into a damp bed if she can conjure up a dry one in 5 seconds. She may very well spend less time with her baby, but babies do not suffer from being left alone but only from the discomforts which arise from being left alone in the ordinary crib.

How long do we intend to keep the baby in the compartment? The baby will answer that in time, but almost certainly until she is 2 years old, or perhaps 3. After the first year, of course, she will spend a fair part of each day in a play-pen or out-of-doors. The compartment takes the place of a crib and will get about the same use. Eventually it will serve as sleeping quarters only.

We cannot, of course, guarantee that every baby raised in this way will thrive so successfully. But there is a plausible connection between health and happiness and the surroundings we have provided, and I am quite sure that our success is not an accident. The experiment should, of course, be repeated again and again with different babies and different parents. One case is enough, however, to disprove the flat assertion that it can't be done. At least we have shown that a moderate and inexpensive mechanization of baby care will yield a tremendous saving in time and trouble, without harm to the child and probably to its lasting advantage.

REFERENCES AND NOTES

[1]The canvas and "endless" sheet arrangement was soon replaced with a single layer of woven plastic, which could be cleaned and instantly wiped dry. More recently, strong, soft synthetics have been used.

POSTSCRIPT

It remains only to add that Deborah is now Mrs. Barry Buzan. Her husband teaches International Studies at Warrick University, and they live in a garden flat in London. Deborah is a successful artist, specializing in colored etchings.

Many hundreds of babies have been raised in similar devices, most of them made by their fathers. My daughter, Professor Julie Vargas, used a commercial model for my two granddaughters.

BIBLIOGRAPHY OF
SKINNER'S WORKS

This list includes all of Skinner's published books and papers as of December, 1981. Coauthors' names appear following the full bibliographic entry, and the bracketed number beside each name indicates the position in which that name appeared.

Omitted are prefaces, forewords, book reviews, and abstracts, of which there are more than a hundred. Many are substantive; some notable ones include:

A new method for the experimental analysis of the behavior of psychotic patients (Abstract and discussion). *Journal of Nervous and Mental Disease*, 1954, *120*, 403-406. (with H.C. Solomon [2] and O.R. Lindsley [3])

Review of Bush and Mosteller's *Stochastic models for learning. Contemporary Psychology*, 1956, *1*, 101-103.

Review of Hull's *Principles of behavior. The American Journal of Psychology*, 1944, *57*, 276-281.

Walden Two revisited (Preface to the 1976 edition of *Walden Two*). New York: Macmillan, 1976, pp. v-xvi.

Initials sometimes appear at the end of an entry. These indicate that the work has been reprinted in one or more of four books of collected writings:

TT — *The Technology of Teaching* (1968)
COR — *Contingencies of Reinforcement* (1969)
CR — *Cumulative Record* (3rd ed.) (1972)
RBS — *Reflections on Behaviorism and Society* (1978)

The progressive increase in the geotropic response of the ant *Aphaenogaster. Journal of General Psychology*, 1930, *4*, 102-112. (with T.C. Barnes [1])

On the inheritance of maze behavior. *Journal of General Psychology*, 1930, *4*, 342-346.

On the conditions of elicitation of certain eating reflexes. *Proceedings of the National Academy of Sciences*, 1930, *16*, 433-438.

The concept of the reflex in the description of behavior. *Journal of General Psychology*, 1931, *5*, 427-458. **CR**

Drive and reflex strength. *Journal of General Psychology*, 1932, *6*, 22-37.

Drive and reflex strength: II. *Journal of General Psychology*, 1932, *6*, 38-48.

On the rate of formation of a conditioned reflex. *Journal of General Psychology*, 1932, *7*, 274-286.

A paradoxical color effect. *Journal of General Psychology*, 1932, *7*, 481-482. **CR**

On the rate of extinction of a conditioned reflex. *Journal of General Psychology*, 1933, *8*, 114-129.

The measurement of "spontaneous activity." *Journal of General Psychology*, 1933, *9*, 3-23.

The rate of establishment of a discrimination. *Journal of General Psychology*, 1933, *9*, 302-350.

"Resistance to extinction" in the process of conditioning. *Journal of General Psychology*, 1933, *9*, 420-429.

The abolishment of a discrimination. *Proceedings of the National Academy of Sciences*, 1933, *19*, 825-828.

Some conditions affecting intensity and duration thresholds in motor nerve, with reference to chronaxie of subordination. *American Journal of Physiology*, 1933, *106*, 721-737. (with E.F. Lambert [1] and A. Forbes [3])

Has Gertrude Stein a secret? *Atlantic Monthly*, January 1934, pp. 50-57. **CR**

The extinction of chained reflexes. *Proceedings of the National Academy of Sciences*, 1934, *20*, 234-237.

A discrimination without previous conditioning. *Proceedings of the National Academy of Sciences*, 1934, *20*, 532-536.

The generic nature of the concepts of stimulus and response. *Journal of General Psychology*, 1935, *12*, 40-65. **CR**

Two types of conditioned reflex and a pseudo type. *Journal of General Psychology*, 1935, *12*, 66-77. **CR**

A discrimination based upon a change in the properties of a stimulus. *Journal of General Psychology*, 1935, *12*, 313-336.

A failure to obtain "disinhibition." *Journal of General Psychology*, 1936, *14*, 127-135.

The reinforcing effect of a differentiating stimulus. *Journal of General Psychology*, 1936, *14*, 263-278.

The effect on the amount of conditioning of an interval of time before reinforcement. *Journal of General Psychology*, 1936, *14*, 279-295.

Conditioning and extinction and their relation to drive. *Journal of General Psychology*, 1936, *14*, 296-317.

Thirst as an arbitrary drive. *Journal of General Psychology*, 1936, *15*, 205-210.

The verbal summator and a method for the study of latent speech. *Journal of Psychology*, 1936, *2*, 71-107.

Two types of conditioned reflex: A reply to Konorski and Miller. *Journal of General Psychology*, 1937, *16*, 272-279. **CR**

Changes in hunger during starvation. *Psychological Record*, 1937, *1*, 51-60. (With W.T. Heron [1])

The distribution of associated words. *Psychological Record*, 1937, *1*, 71-76.

Effects of caffeine and benzedrine upon conditioning and extinction. *Psychological Record*, 1937, *1*, 340-346. (with W.T. Heron [2])

The behavior of organisms: An experimental analysis. New York: Appleton-Century-Crofts, 1938.

An apparatus for the study of animal behavior. *Psychological Record*, 1939, *3*, 166-176. (with W.T. Heron [1])

Some factors influencing the distribution of associated words. *Psychological Record*, 1939, *3*, 178-184. (with S.W. Cook [1])

The alliteration in Shakespeare's sonnets: A study in literary behavior. *Psychological Record*, 1939, *3*, 186-192. **CR**

The rate of extinction in maze-bright and maze-dull rats. *Psychological Record*, 1940, *4*, 11-18. (with W.T. Heron [1])

A method of maintaining an arbitrary degree of hunger. *Journal of Comparative Psychology*, 1940, *30*, 139-145.

The psychology of design. In *Art education today.* New York: Bureau Publications, Teachers College, Columbia University, 1941, pp. 1-6.

A quantitative estimate of certain types of sound-patterning in poetry. *American Journal of Psychology*, 1941, *54*, 64-79. **CR**

Some quantitative properties of anxiety. *Journal of Experimental Psychology*, 1941, *29*, 390-400. (with W.K. Estes [1]) **CR**

The processes involved in the repeated guessing of alternatives. *Journal of Experimental Psychology*, 1942, *30*, 495-503. **CR**

Reply to Dr. Yacorzynski. *Journal of Experimental Psychology*, 1943, *32*, 93-94.

The operational analysis of psychological terms. *Psychological Review*, 1945, *52*, 270-277; 291-294. **CR**

Baby in a box. *Ladies' Home Journal*, October 1945, pp. 30-31; 135-136; 138. **CR**

An automatic shocking-grid apparatus for continuous use. *Journal of Comparative and Physiological Psychology*, 1947, *40*, 305-307. (with S.L. Campbell [2])

Experimental psychology. In W. Dennis et al., *Current trends in psychology.* Pittsburgh: University of Pittsburgh Press, 1947, pp. 16-49. **CR**

'Superstitition' in the pigeon. *Journal of Experimental Psychology*, 1948, *38*, 168-172. **CR**

Card-guessing experiments. *American Scientist*, 1948, *36*, 456; 458.

Walden Two. New York: Macmillan, 1948.

Are theories of learning necessary? *Psychological Review*, 1950, *57*, 193-216. **CR**

How to teach animals. *Scientific American*, *185* (12), 26-29. **CR**

Some contributions of an experimental analysis of behavior to psychology as a whole. *American Psychologist*, 1953, *8*, 69-78.

Science and human behavior. New York: Macmillan, 1953.

The science of learning and the art of teaching. *Harvard Educational Review*, 1954, *24*, 86-97. **TT**

A critique of psychoanalytic concepts and theories. *Scientific Monthly*, 1954, *79*, 300-305. **CR**

The control of human behavior. *Transactions of the New York Academy of Sciences*, 1955, *17*, 547-551. **CR**

Freedom and the control of men. *American Scholar*, Winter 1955-56, *25*, 47-65. **CR**

A case history in scientific method. *American Psychologist,* 1956, *11,* 221-233. **CR**

What is psychotic behavior? In *Theory and treatment of the psychoses: Some newer aspects.* St. Louis: Committee on Publications, Washington University, 1956, pp. 77-99. **CR**

Some issues concerning the control of human behavior: A symposium. *Science,* 1956, *124,* 1057-1066. (with C.R. Rogers [1]) **Portions in CR**

The psychological point of view. In H.D. Kruse (Ed.), *Integrating the approaches to mental disease.* New York: Hoeber-Harper, 1957, pp. 130-133. **Retitled version in CR**

The experimental analysis of behavior. *American Scientist,* 1957, *45,* 343-371. **CR**

A second type of superstition in the pigeon. *American Journal of Psychology,* 1957, *70,* 308-311. (with W.H. Morse [1]) **CR**

Concurrent activity under fixed-interval reinforcement. *Journal of Comparative and Physiological Psychology,* 1957, *50,* 279-281. (with W.H. Morse [2] **CR**

Verbal behavior. New York: Appleton-Century-Crofts, 1957.

Schedules of reinforcement. New York: Appleton-Century-Crofts, 1957. (with C.B. Ferster [1])

Diagramming schedules of reinforcement. *Journal of the Experimental Analysis of Behavior,* 1958, *1,* 67-68.

Some factors involved in the stimulus control of operant behavior. *Journal of the Experimental Analysis of Behavior,* 1958, *1,* 103-107. (with W.H. Morse [1])

Reinforcement today. *American Psychologist,* 1958, *13,* 94-99. **CR**

Teaching machines. *Science,* 1958, *128,* 969-977, **TT**

Sustained performance during very long experimental sessions. *Journal of the Experimental Analysis of Behavior,* 1958, *1,* 235-244. (with W.H. Morse [2]) **CR**

Fixed-interval reinforcement of running in a wheel. *Journal of the Experimental Analysis of Behavior,* 1958, *1,* 371-379. (with W.H. Morse [2])

John Broadus Watson, behaviorist. *Science,* 1959, *129,* 197-198. **CR**

The programming of verbal knowledge. In E. Galanter (Ed.), *Automatic teaching: The state of the art.* New York: John Wiley, 1959, pp. 63-68.

Animal research in the pharmacotherapy of mental disease. In J. Cole & R. Gerard (Eds.), *Psychopharmacology: Problems in evaluation.* Washington, D.C.: National Academy of Sciences—National Research Council, 1959, pp. 224-228.

The flight from the laboratory. In B.F. Skinner, *Cumulative record.* New York: Appleton-Century-Crofts, 1959, pp. 242-257. **CR**

Cumulative record. New York: Appleton-Century-Crofts, 1959. Enlarged edition, 1961. Third edition, 1972.

Special problems in programming language instruction for teaching machines. In F.J. Oinas (Ed.), *Language teaching today.* Bloomington, Ind.: Indiana University Research Center in Anthropology, Folklore, and Linguistics, 1960, pp. 167-174.

Concept formation in philosophy and psychology. In S. Hook (Ed.), *Dimensions of mind: A symposium.* New York: New York University Press, 1960, pp. 226-230.

The use of teaching machines in college instruction (Parts II-IV). In A.A. Lumsdaine & R. Glaser (Eds.), *Teaching machines and programmed learning: A source book.* Washington, D.C.: Department of Audio-Visual Instruction, National Education Association, 1960, pp. 159-172. (with J.G. Holland [2])

Pigeons in a pelican. *American Psychologist,* 1960, *15,* 28-37. **CR**

Teaching machines. *The Review of Economics and Statistics,* August 1960 (Supplement), *42,* 189-191.

Modern learning theory and some new approaches to teaching. In J.W. Gustad (Ed.), *Faculty utilization and retention.* Winchester, Mass.: New England Board of Higher Education, 1960, pp. 64-72.

The theory behind teaching machines. *Journal of the American Society of Training Directors,* July 1961, *15,* 27-29.

The design of cultures. *Daedalus,* 1961, *90,* 534-546. **CR**

Why we need teaching machines. *Harvard Educational Review,* 1961, *31,* 377-398. **CR, portions in TT**

Learning theory and future research. In J. Lysaught (Ed.), *Programmed learning: Evolving principles and industrial applications.* Ann Arbor: Foundation for Research on Human Behaviors, 1961, pp. 59-66.

Teaching machines. *Scientific American,* 1961, *205* (11), 90-102.

The analysis of behavior: A program for self-instruction. New York: McGraw-Hill, 1961. (with J.G. Holland [1])

Technique for reinforcing either of two organisms with a single food magazine. *Journal of the Experimental Analysis of Behavior,* 1962, *5,* 58. (with G.S. Reynolds [1])

Operandum. *Journal of the Experimental Analysis of Behavior,* 1962, *5,* 224.

Squirrel in the yard: Certain sciurine experiences of B.F. Skinner. *Harvard Alumni Bulletin,* 1962, *64,* 642-645. **CR**

Two "synthetic social relations." *Journal of the Experimental Analysis of Behavior,* 1962, *5,* 531-533. **CR**

Verbal behaviour. *Encounter,* November 1962, pp. 42-44. (with I.A. Richards [1]) **Portions in CR**

Conditioned and unconditioned aggression in pigeons. *Journal of the Experimental Analysis of Behavior,* 1963, *6,* 73-74. (with G.S. Reynolds [1] and A.C. Catania [2])

Behaviorism at fifty. *Science,* 1963, *140,* 951-958. **COR**

Operant behavior. *American Psychologist,* 1963, *18,* 503-515. **COR**

Reply to Thouless. *Australian Journal of Psychology,* 1963, *15,* 92-93.

Reflections on a decade of teaching machines. *Teachers College Record,* 1963, *65,* 168-177. **CR, portions in TT**

L'avenir des machines à enseigner. *Psychologie Française,* 1963, *8,* 170-180.

A Christmas caramel, or, a plum from the hasty pudding. *The Worm Runner's Digest,* 1963, *5* (2), 42-46.

On the relation between mathematical and statistical competence and significant scientific productivity. *The Worm Runner's Digest,* 1964, *6* (1), 15-17. (published under the pseudonym F. Galton Pennywhistle)

New methods and new aims in teaching. *New Scientist,* 1964, *122,* 483-484.

"Man." *Proceedings of the American Philosophical Society,* 1964, *108,* 482-485. **CR**

The technology of teaching. *Proceedings of the Royal Society of London,* Series B, 1965, *162,* 427-443, **TT**

Stimulus generalization in an operant: A historical note. In D.I. Mostofsky (Ed.), *Stimulus generalization.* Stanford: Stanford University Press, 1965, pp. 193-209.

Why teachers fail. *Saturday Review,* October 16, 1965, pp. 80-81; 98-102. **TT**

The phylogeny and ontogeny of behavior. *Science,* 1966, *153,* 1205-1213. **COR**

An operant analysis of problem solving. In B. Kleinmuntz (Ed.), *Problem solving: Research, method, and theory.* New York: John Wiley, 1966, pp. 225-257. **COR**

Conditioning responses by reward and punishment. *Proceedings of the Royal Institution of Great Britain,* 1966, *41,* 48-51.

Contingencies of reinforcement in the design of a culture. *Behavioral Science,* 1966, *11,* 159-166. **COR**

What is the experimental analysis of behavior? *Journal of the Experimental Analysis of Behavior,* 1966, *9,* 213-218. **COR**

Some responses to the stimulus "Pavlov." *Conditional Reflex,* 1966, *1,* 74-78. **CR**

B.F. Skinner...An autobiography. In E.G. Boring & G. Lindzey (Eds.), *A history of psychology in autobiography* (Vol. 5). New York: Appleton-Century-Crofts, 1967, pp. 387-413.

Visions of utopia. *The Listener,* January 5, 1967, pp. 22-23. **COR**

Utopia through the control of human behavior. *The Listener,* January 12, 1967, pp. 55-56. **COR**

The problem of consciousness—a debate. *Philosophy and Phenomenological Research,* 1967, *27,* 317-337. (with B. Blanshard [1]) **Portions in COR**

The science of human behavior. In *Twenty-five years at RCA laboratories 1942-1967.* Princeton, N.J.: RCA Laboratories, 1968, pp. 92-102.

Teaching science in high school—What is wrong? *Science,* 1968, *159,* 704-710. **CR**

The design of experimental communities. In *International encyclopedia of the social sciences* (Vol. 16). New York: Macmillan, 1968, pp. 271-275. **CR**

Development of methods of preparing materials for teaching machines. Alexandria, Va.: Human Resources Research Office, George Washington University, 1968. (edited by L.M. Zook)

The technology of teaching. New York: Appleton-Century-Crofts, 1968.

Edwin Garrigues Boring. In *The American Philosophical Society: Year book 1968.* Philadelphia: The American Philosophical Society, 1969, pp. 111-115.

Contingency management in the classroom. *Education,* 1969, *90,* 93-100. **CR**

The machine that is man. *Psychology Today,* April 1969, pp. 20-25; 60-63. **COR**

Contingencies of reinforcement: A theoretical analysis. New York: Appleton-Century-Crofts, 1969.

Creating the creative artist. In A.J. Toynbee et al., *On the future of art.* New York: Viking Press, 1970, pp. 61-75. **CR**

Humanistic behaviorism. *The Humanist,* May/June 1971, *31,* 35.

Autoshaping. *Science,* 1971, *173,* 752.

A behavioral analysis of value judgments. In E. Tobach, L.R. Aronson, & E.Shaw (Eds.), *The biopsychology of development.* New York: Academic Press, 1971, pp. 543-551.

B.F. Skinner says what's wrong with the social sciences. *The Listener,* September 30, 1971, pp. 429-431. **Retitled version in CR**

Beyond freedom and dignity. New York: Alfred A. Knopf, 1971.

Some relations between behavior modification and basic research. In B.F. Skinner, *Cumulative record* (3rd ed.). New York: Appleton-Century-Crofts, 1972, pp. 276-282. **CR**

Compassion and ethics in the care of the retardate. In B.F. Skinner, *Cumulative record* (3rd ed.). New York: Appleton-Century-Crofts, 1972, pp. 283-291. **CR**

A lecture on "having a poem." In B.F. Skinner, *Cumulative record* (3rd ed.). New York: Appleton-Century-Crofts, 1972, pp. 345-355. **CR**

Humanism and behaviorism. *The Humanist,* July/August 1972, *32,* 18-20. **RBS**

Freedom and dignity revisited. *New York Times,* August 11, 1972, p. 29. **RBS**

Reflections on meaning and structure. In R. Brower, H. Vendler, & J. Hollander (Eds.), *I.A. Richards: Essays in his honor.* New York: Oxford University Press, 1973, pp. 199-209. **RBS**

Answers for my critics. In H. Wheeler (Ed.), *Beyond the punitive society.* San Francisco: W.H. Freeman, 1973, pp. 256-266.

Some implications of making education more efficient. In C.E. Thoresen (Ed.), *Behavior modification in education.* Chicago: National Society for the Study of Education, 1973, pp. 446-456. **RBS**

Are we free to have a future? *Impact,* 1973, *3*(1), 5-12. **RBS**

Walden (One) and *Walden Two. The Thoreau Society Bulletin,* Winter 1973, pp. 1-3. **RBS**

The free and happy student. *New York University Education Quarterly,* 1973, *4* (2), 2-6. **RBS**

Designing higher education. *Daedalus,* 1974, *103,* 196-202. **RBS**

About behaviorism. New York: Alfred A. Knopf, 1974.

Comments on Watt's "B.F. Skinner and the technological control of social behavior." *The American Political Science Review,* 1975, *69,* 228-229.

The shaping of phylogenic behavior. *Acta Neurobiologiae Experimentalis,* 1975, *35,* 409-415. **RBS**

The steep and thorny way to a science of behaviour. In R. Harré (Ed.), *Problems of scientific revolution: Progress and obstacles to progress in the sciences.* Oxford: Clarendon Press, 1975, pp. 58-71. **RBS**

The ethics of helping people. *Criminal Law Bulletin,* 1975, *11,* 623-636. **RBS**

Farewell, my LOVELY! *Journal of the Experimental Analysis of Behavior,* 1976, *25,* 218.

Particulars of my life. New York: Alfred A. Knopf, 1976.

The force of coincidence. In B.C. Etzel, J.M. LeBlanc, & D.M. Baer (Eds.), *New developments in behavioral psychology: Theory, method, and application.* Hillsdale, N.J.: Lawrence Erlbaum Associates, 1977, pp. 3-6. **RBS**

The experimental analysis of operant behavior. In R.W. Rieber & K. Sal Zinger (Eds.), *The roots of American psychology: Historical influences and implications for the future* (Annals of the New York Academy of Sciences, Vol. 291). New York: New York Academy of Sciences, 1977, pp. 374-385. **Retitled version in RBS**

Freedom, at last, from the burden of taxation. *New York Times,* July 26, 1977, p. 29. **RBS**

Why I am not a cognitive psychologist. *Behaviorism,* 1977, *5,* 1-10. **RBS**

Between freedom and despotism. *Psychology Today,* September 1977, pp. 80-82; 84; 86; 90-91. **Retitled version in RBS**

Herrnstein and the evolution of behaviorism. *American Psychologist,* 1977, *32,* 1006-1012.

Reflections on behaviorism and society. Englewood Cliffs, N.J.: Prentice-Hall, 1978.

Why don't we use the behavioral sciences? *Human Nature,* March 1978, *1,* 86-92.
Retitled version in RBS

The shaping of a behaviorist: Part two of an autobiography. New York: Alfred A. Knopf, 1979.

A happening at the annual dinner of the Association for Behavioral Analysis, Chicago, May 15, 1978. *The Behavior Analyst,* 1979, *2* (1), 30-33. (published anonymously)

My experience with the baby-tender. *Psychology Today,* March 1979, pp. 28-31; 34; 37-38; 40. (an expanded excerpt from *The Shaping of a Behaviorist* [1979])

Le renforçateur arrangé. *Revue de modification du comportement,* 1979, *9,* 59-69. (translated into French by Raymond Beausoleil)

Symbolic communication between two pigeons *(Columba livia domestica). Science,* 1980, *207,* 543-545. (with R. Epstein [1] and R.P. Lanza [2])

Resurgence of responding after the cessation of response-independent reinforcement. *Proceedings of the National Academy of Sciences,* 1980, *77,* 6251-6253. (with R. Epstein [1])

Notebooks. Englewood Cliffs, N.J.: Prentice-Hall, 1980. (edited by R. Epstein)

The species-specific behavior of ethologists. *The Behavior Analyst,* 1980, *3* (1), 51.

Pavlov's influence on psychology in America. *Journal of the History of the Behavioral Sciences,* 1981, *17,* 242-245.

"Self-awareness" in the pigeon. *Science,* 1981, *212,* 695-696. (with R. Epstein [1] and R.P. Lanza [2])

Charles B. Ferster—A personal memoir. *Journal of the Experimental Analysis of Behavior,* 1981, *35,* 259-261.

How to discover what you have to say—A talk to students. *The Behavior Analyst,* 1981, *4* (1), 1-7.

Selection by consequences. *Science,* 1981, *213,* 501-504.

The spontaneous use of memoranda by pigeons. *Behaviour Analysis Letters,* 1981, *1,* 241-246. (with R. Epstein [1])

Index

Scientific method, 74-75, 78, 79, 81, 83, 84, 85, 89, 90, 92, 94, 96-97, 257
Scranton, 17
Scriven, Michael, 31
Sebeok, Thomas, 172
Seeing, 123
Selected Letters of Robert Frost, 17
"Selection by Consequences," 153
Self-analysis, 29
Self-awareness, 105
Sensation(s), 120, 122, 125, 126, 130
Seton, Ernest T., 18
Sexual identity, development of, 179-180
Sexual modesty, 166, 171
Shakespeare, William, 12, 19, 24, 199
Shame, 166
Shaping, 38, 110, 157, 171, 186, 209, 212, 243, 258, 261, 263, 266
Shaping of a Behaviorist, The, 9, 37, 74, 207, 269
"Shaping of Phylogenic Behavior, The," 153
Sherrington, Charles S., 22, 32, 77, 78, 167
Sidman, Murray, 89
Silent release box, 73, 77, 79
Simmelhag, Virginia L., 99
Single-subject research, 86
Skinner, Deborah (Mrs. Barry Buzan), 25, 34, 35 n. 17, 269, 276
Skinner, Eve (née Yvonne Blue), 24
Skinner, Julie (Mrs. Ernest Vargas), 25, 35 n. 17, 276
Skinner, William, 10, 17
Skinner box, 73, 83
Skinner Primer, The: Behind Freedom and Dignity, 9
Social sciences, 131
Society of Fellows, Harvard, 22, 23
Sociobiology, 174
Solomon, Harry, 28, 224, 241
"Some Implications of Making Education More Efficient," 207
"Some Issues Concerning the Control of Human Behavior," 135

"Some Relations Between Behavior Modification and Basic Research," 223
Something to Think About, 28
"Special Problems in Programming Language Instruction for Teaching Machines," 207
Spender, Steven, 195
Spontaneous recovery, 51, 56
"Spontaneous Use of Memoranda by Pigeons, The," 105
Staddon, J.E.R., 99
Statistics, 20, 74-75, 86, 88, 92, 93, 94, 209
Stein, Gertrude, 23
Stevens, S. Smith, 120
Storage, 184-187
Strength of bond, 45, 48
Structuralism, 192
Structure, cognitive, 185
Superstitious behavior, 99-104, 153, 158, 160
Supplement to the Voyage of Bougainville, 166
Susquehanna, 10
Swinburne, Algernon, 24

Tate, John T., 246
Taylor, Franklin V., 255
Teaching animals. *See* Animals, training of
Teaching machine, 28-29, 207-208, 217-222, 244, 257
"Teaching Machines," 207
"Teaching Science in High School— What is Wrong?" 207
Technology, behavioral, 87, 92, 137
"Technology of Teaching, The," 207
Technology of Teaching, The, 207, 208
Terrace, Herbert S., 28
Territoriality, 184, 212, 214
Thackeray, William M., 17
Theory, 41, 42-44, 45, 48, 54, 62, 63, 70, 71-72, 85, 91, 121
"Theory Behind Teaching Machines, The," 207
Thompson, Lawrence, 17

Thorndike, Edward L., 32, 115, 117-
    118, 199
Thorpe, W.H., 162
Thought processes. *See* Mental
    processes; Cognitive processes
Thurber, James, 71
Time, sense of, 180
Time, 36
Tinbergen, Niko, 162 n. 16, 181
Tolman, Edward C., 32-33, 41
Tolman, Richard C., 246
Trainer, pigeon, 252
Traits, 115, 154, 162, 230, 233
Translation, 190
Troland, Leonard, 20
Trueblood, Charles K., 20

Unconscious, 118, 129, 200, 231, 238
Uniformity, 145
Unit of responding, 156
"Use of Teaching Machines in College
    Instruction, The," 207
Utopia, 135-136, 137
Utopia, 165
"Utopia Through the Control of
    Human Behavior," 135

Value judgments, 139
Values, 132
Van Sommers, Peter, 125
Vargas, Julie. *See* Skinner, Julie
Variable-interval reinforcement, 42,
    185. *See also* Aperiodic
    reinforcement
Variable-ratio reinforcement, 252
Verbal behavior, 23, 121, 128, 139,
    172-173, 182, 185, 187, 188,

    190, 221, 226, 258
Verbal Behavior, 23, 24, 26, 29, 31,
    111, 116, 191, 192, 193, 194,
    197
Verbal slip, 118
Verbal summator, 23
Victor (originator of plan to use dogs
    to guide torpedoes), 247
"Visions of Utopia," 135
Vocal responses, 172

Waddington, Charles H., 181
Walden Two, 25-26, 30, 33, 34, 74, 95,
    135, 146, 150, 151, 243, 258
"Walden Two Revisited," 135
Walpole, Horace, 85
Wann, T.W., 115
Watson, John B., 20, 22, 32, 76, 115,
    118, 155, 174
Weber, Max, 30
Weigel, John A., 9
Weisner, Jerome, 197
What is B.F. Skinner Really Saying? 9
White, E.B., 71
Whitehead, Alfred N., 21, 23
"Why I Am Not a Cognitive
    Psychologist," 116, 241
"Why Teachers Fail," 207
"Why We Need Teaching Machines,"
    207
Wilder, Thornton, 24
Will, 117, 180, 182, 187, 200
William James Lectures, 24, 27
Wundt, Wilhelm, 19
Wyckoff, L. Benjamin, Jr., 211

Yule, G. Udney, 20

Robert Epstein received his Ph.D. from Harvard University, where he worked closely with Professor Skinner for 5 years. He is currently the Executive Director of the Cambridge Center for Behavioral Studies, Inc., and an adjunct assistant professor at the University of Massachusetts. Dr. Epstein has published numerous articles on operant conditioning, the history of psychology, and other topics, and is the editor of Skinner's *Notebooks* (Prentice-Hall, 1980).